Flats and Durders Offload

Flats and Durders Offload

RUGBY LAID BARE

David Flatman and
Mark Durden-Smith

SIMON &
SCHUSTER

London · New York · Sydney · Toronto · New Delhi

First published in Great Britain by Simon & Schuster UK Ltd, 2021

1 3 5 7 9 10 8 6 4 2

Simon & Schuster UK Ltd
1st Floor
222 Gray's Inn Road
London WC1X 8HB

www.simonandschuster.co.uk
www.simonandschuster.com.au
www.simonandschuster.co.in

Simon & Schuster Australia, Sydney
Simon & Schuster India, New Delhi

A CIP catalogue record for this book is available from the British Library

Hardback ISBN: 978-1-3985-0710-4
eBook ISBN: 978-1-3985-0711-1

Typeset in Bembo by M Rules
Printed in the UK by CPI Group (UK) Ltd, Croydon, CR0 4YY

—*For Freya, Peanut, Buddha and Hetty*

—*No it's not – it's for Tatty, Freddie, Rosie, Archie and Flossie the Tibetan Terrier*

—*Can't it be for everyone?*

—*Agreed*

Contents

Introduction	1
The Six Nations	5
Referees	22
Tours	34
Best and Worst Days	48
Friendship	71
Retirement	78
Perks of the Job	90
Nutrition	111
Front Row	123
Injuries	139
Characters	164
Health, Safety and Bad Behaviour	192
Grassroots and Academies	213

Unlikely Heroes and Villains   230

Our Ultimate Fifteen   239

Hero Fifteen   262

World Cup   276

The Gallagher Premiership and the Future
of the Game   298

Acknowledgements   311

Introduction

DURDERS – For those of you browsing in a bookshop or digitally dipping your literary toes into this tome to see if it's your kind of thing, or could possibly be the kind of thing of someone you like and you've got the urge to express that feeling in book form, I believe you are owed an explanation.

The first question you may well be asking is – who are they – this Flats and Durders? That's a toughie. We're niche. (That's not a typo FYI, but I'd like to think we're nice too.) We've been described by *The Guardian*'s Robert Kitson as rugby's answer to Ant and Dec. Now, Robert is a first-rate journalist, and bloke as it happens, but he must have had some mind-altering substance sprinkled on his granola that morning. Multi-million-pound earning, universally loved, fêted national treasures Ant and Dec we are not. We're more the Kermit and Miss Piggy of rugby. Who's who we should leave to you, the reader, to decide, although I concede it's not one of the most fundamental questions of the age, so don't dedicate too much time to it. (Here's a clue if you need it – I'm the green one.)

FLATS – It's not even Page One and you've begun the

weight-based gags. I was tiring of these hefty snipes about three hours after meeting you for the first time in Manchester circa 2010, yet they live on. Could be a long read, this.

DURDERS – That wasn't a weight-based reference. It's Kermit and Miss Piggy's character traits I was alluding to. I think they mirror ours. Anyway, since teaming up to present the *Gallagher Premiership Rugby Highlights* show, originally on ITV before moving to Channel 5 eight years ago, we've become the oddest of odd couples. Tinder or Grinder or match.com would never have put us together in a million galaxies. Rugby Lovers United might have though.

FLATS – Actually I think they might. You're posh, you drive a crumbling old car, and you wear threadbare old dinner jackets. I'm from Maidstone, I drive a luxury 4x4 and wear designer clothes. You're all class and I'm a bit of rough. You're old money, I'm so *nouveau* it aches. We've actually got a good few markets covered there. Is the last one a real dating app or are you just waffling as per?

DURDERS – Just rambling. But it's an idea. My idea, so back off. Anyway, we've become an item. Which can be annoying. Such is the unfathomable but annoyingly undeniable appeal of Flats that I can't turn up to a ground or a rugby-themed gathering without being greeted with 'Where's Flats?' It's humiliating. I often feel like the Prince Albert to his Queen Victoria – a reference to the monarchs, not the body piercing for the more infantile among our, presumably, cosy book club. If I had a pound for every time I'd been asked where the bipedal aubergine was, I'd be able to clear the national debt of Greece.

FLATS – Robert Kitson also called us 'Posh and Pecs' by the way, which would make me David Beckham. Or David Peckham. And you, Victoria.

DURDERS – I'm more than happy with that. She's all about the style and the pout. That's me all over. The point we're trying to make is that, despite the pandemic and the cost of asparagus being at an all-time high, I think we both feel very lucky to have done the job we've done, with each other for company, and in the bigger picture – isn't it a good time to be a rugby fan?

FLATS – Indeed it is. Which brings us nicely on to our book. Books on rugby union are basically everywhere yet, if we're being honest, they're often quite serious and a bit gloomy with the odd stunning declaration slotted in to help with sales. But why have just one former rugby player writing a supposedly humorous and entertaining book about one of the most technical and celebrated field sports on the planet, when you can have one former rugby player and the son of Judith Chalmers? That's what's on offer here. David Luke Flatman – 109 appearances for Saracens, 161 for Bath, and not as many as he should have had for England (some may debate this), and a posh bloke from Highgate with thick-but-malleable hair who played for Durham University a few times and has a very well-travelled mum, waffling on about the sport we both love. That's what's on the table. Imagine there's a large bucket in the sky labelled 'rugby books'. Well this is one, and it goes in that bucket.

DURDERS – Our mission was to produce an objective, at times dramatic and very, very occasionally – think wafer-thin needles in a mountainous haystack – humorous celebration of rugby union by pound for pound, the hardest presenter in British broadcasting and one of its hungriest and lesser-capped former players. It's something the world has been crying out for.

But what will you find inside this instant classic of ours? Well, we'll be covering all the intellectual stuff such as rugby's hardest players and tours, not to mention our ultimate XV and our hero XV, which has required a bit of juxtaposing. (I don't even know what that means but I've thrown it in there so you high-brow types might be tempted by the promise of bigger words to come.) Then you have player safety, which is a hot and controversial topic these days, the Five then Six Nations, the World Cup, life in the front row, best days, worst days, referees, and retirement. We even have a chapter on the perks of doing what we do and how I once got into trouble for taking an unhealthy interest in a pair of celebrity Y-fronts. That's our big sell – Jackie Collins, eat your heart out.

FLATS – She's no longer with us, actually, so well done.

The Six Nations

DURDERS – I feel I have to kick this chapter off with a potentially awkward question to my esteemed(ish) colleague-slash-loosely termed friend here. Did you ever play in a Six Nations game or were all of your eight England caps won on tours to North America that the top-end players couldn't be arsed to go on?

FLATS – I actually did play in a Six Nations match. It was against France and, would you believe it, it has rather an interesting story attached to it.

DURDERS – Bitter experience suggests that's very unlikely but we have a few pages to fill so let's give you the benefit of the doubt. Bet I'm proved right, though.

FLATS – You wait. And you are going to have to wait as I think we should start with what the Six Nations means to us as rugby fans. People may assume that players who take part in the Six Nations will experience something different to the warm, fuzzy feeling that you get as a spectator, but the truth is it's exactly the same.

One of my earliest rugby viewing experiences was

watching England versus Ireland at Twickenham in what would then have been the Five Nations. I could be imagining this but I'm pretty sure we sat on wooden seats that day. Then again, that could be nostalgia playing a trick on me. Something I'm a lot surer of seeing happen is Rory Underwood score on the left wing just beneath us and me and my dad going wild. I could evoke that memory a hundred times a day and it would still make the hairs on my palms stand on end. That's what the Six Nations means to me and, regardless of how many times you play in the tournament (a potentially dangerous statement given my one cap, but I'm standing by it), it's your experiences as a spectator that make it special. You build your own legend of the Six Nations and if you don't have that as a platform it can't possibly have the same significance. Again, I'm being slightly presumptuous, but that's who I am. I presume things.

DURDERS – It's refreshing to hear you say that and it makes perfect sense. Not the presumptuous bit, that's just you being pretentious, but that the tournament means the same to its protagonists as it does to us mere fans. I was lucky because my dad used to have four debentures at Twickenham so from about the age of eight, he, my mum and a mystery guest would go there each year to watch England's home fixtures. And no, you weren't imagining the wooden seats. I remember them clearly. They were green fold-down jobs. I was a proper obsessive about the Five/Six Nations and I remember vividly presenting my first game in the tournament: England against France at the Stade de France in Paris, when Sky Sports had the rights to the England games across the Channel. I handed over to the lead commentator, the

6

brilliant Miles Harrison, who said 'Welcome to your annual tingle down the spine.' That's exactly how I feel about the Six Nations. Almost nothing beats a Six Nations tingle.

Unlike, I should think, the vast majority of the population, when I was young I used to long for January and February to arrive. The Six Nations was what I lived for – that and M&S Toffee and Almond ice cream – a pioneering tub of gorgeousness from the 1970s and 80s.

FLATS – Going to Twickenham for one of the two England fixtures with my dad was obviously incredible, but if it hadn't been for *Rugby Special*, which from memory was on at about 4.45 p.m. on a Sunday and used to cover the tournament in its entirety, I think I might have exploded from frustration. That was the other half of the fix.

DURDERS – Me and Neil the Deal (my father) were there at 4.45 p.m. too. I loved that programme – *do do do do dadoo, do do do dadoo* – that title music was the sweetest sound of my childhood, that and Supertramp live in Paris. Oh, and the sound of my mum's garlic chicken drumsticks sizzling in the oven.

FLATS – What?

DURDERS – Garlic chicken drumsticks are another essential factor in my deep love for the Six Nations. My mum, Jude the Dude, would get up at the crack of dawn on match days to stick vast numbers of garlic-slathered chicken drumsticks in the oven, later to be hoovered up out of the boot of my parents' car in the west car park at Twickenham. Wrapped in tin foil, pre-match they were still warm. I loved them! Consumed them like a tree surgeon's shredder consumes recently chopped branches. I must have resembled a kind of miniature Henry VIII. Although not that miniature. I think my record for one sitting was 11 drumsticks, which isn't bad going. Although my breath can't have been Alpine-fresh when I come to think about it. That might explain the social distancing around me before it was even a thing. Such fond memories.

FLATS – The breath's still a bit of an issue, by the way. But what about on the pitch, then? What was your first Rory Underwood moment?

DURDERS – He's also on my quite extensive England hero list, actually – you can't claim Rory all for yourself. I have so many good memories of watching the tournament and they're all so vivid. Watching Jonathan Webb kicking goals, for instance. Sounds a bit dull, but for some reason I worshipped that man. I remember watching Ben Clarke, who played in the back row for Bath, Richmond and the British and Irish Lions, as well as England, catching a ball from a restart way above his head. A forward showing that skill level probably happens thirty times a match these days but back then it seemed exceptional. A forward catching the ball way above their head from a restart? Wow! Twickenham rose as one and cheered like mad. That is an odd moment to be etched in the memory, but who am I to argue with my memory?

Funnily enough, if I had to pick just one player who really captured my imagination, and my heart, I'd probably go for Ollie Campbell, the great Irish fly-half. He was quite quirky and a bit of a maverick, which I liked, but the reason I became such a fan of his, apart from him being such a great player, was because he had this weird superstition where he would never stand on the white lines before a game. Whenever England were playing Ireland I'd become completely obsessed by watching him. After he'd stepped over the white line as the teams took to the field I'd then watch him closely for the entire 80 minutes to see if he'd do it during the match. As I'm hearing myself recall these things, I'm beginning to think I might have been quite a peculiar child.

FLATS — No shit . . .

DURDERS — I'm going to ignore that . . . I also had room in my heart to obsess about Peter Winterbottom. I'd 'be' the England No. 7 when I was mucking about with my mates, but can there be a more heroic sporting warrior than France's Jean-Pierre Rives? Has any player, in the history of the sport, ever spilled more blood for his country? He was a one-man episode of *Casualty*. That's a proper hero.

FLATS — So as a child you were obsessed by superstitious Irishmen, garlic drumsticks that made you sick and a man covered in blood called Jean-Pierre?

One of the things that has allowed the Six Nations to become so special to so many people is its continuity. Because it happens every year and in a similar format it has become part our own cultural fabric, and that familiarity is as reassuring as it is exhilarating. We're back to what I said about the tournament developing its own legend. I'm hypothesising here, but you might remember that moment from a previous year when Liam Williams did some damage, or when Paul O'Connell nicked England's line-outs at Twickenham. That recall will help you set the scene for the next tournament. That's rare in international sport. It's obviously not as exotic as a World Cup but it's far more intimate and far more familiar.

DURDERS – You've hit the nail on the head. That's twice in four pages. You're very wise for one so young. That familiarity we have with the players of all the competing nations is essential to the tournament's appeal. One factor we haven't touched on yet, however, which I believe is key to the success of the Six Nations tournament, is tribalism. In fact, if you had to choose one adjective to describe the Six Nations you could do a lot worse than go for 'tribal'. When you marry a Welsh woman, as I have, this fact becomes all too apparent. My Welsh in-laws are actually very mild-mannered, amazingly lovely people, but a few hours after our first two children, twin boys, were born they were there at the hospital brandishing two Welsh dragon-emblazoned Babygros. Archie and Freddie had barely mastered the art of breathing and Rachel's family were trying to indoctrinate my boys, who I hoped and dreamed would grow up to share my passion for English rugby, into the cult of Wales. They were like a gaggle of demented witch hunters. The spell worked. My two sons, it pains me to my core, support Wales. I'm weeping as I write. But I have convinced my daughter, Rosie, that the red rose is a better way forward. So she's with me. (Essentially because she went through a phase of fancying Owen Farrell. It was too good an opportunity to miss so I signed her up at the height of her crush.)

FLATS – Quick joke for you. How do you know if somebody is from Wales? Don't worry, they'll tell you. I believe the same joke is used to mock vegans and CrossFitters these days. And they all seem to have this Welsh dragon sticker on the back of their cars. What's that all about? If I put a St George's cross sticker on the back of my car I'm either Nigel Farage or somebody who wants their sovereignty back despite not being able to spell it. The Welsh can't even cross the border into England without having a dragon on display. Just get over it! It's like being proud of being ridiculously tall. You were born that way! Also, if dogs are anything to go by, you probably won't live as long as a normal-sized person. Welsh people haven't achieved Welshness. They were simply born Welsh.

DURDERS – Are you going into partnership with Austin Healey or something? You know that he has Welsh fatwas on his head, don't you? I'm now beginning to feel uncomfortable, for the sake of my half-Welsh offspring, with your unenlightened attitude. I will not tolerate you being in league with Healey – who I like very much by the way – but he takes his Welsh-baiting to a level that no fully sane person should take it to. It's reckless.

FLATS – What gives me the right to sound off about the Welsh, but to a far lesser degree than Austin Healey, is that I could have played for them. I should have done. I'd have won a lot more caps if I had.

DURDERS – That's a lie ... and patronising ... and fanciful ... but go on, explain this delusion of yours.

FLATS – What I usually say when people ask me why I could have played for Wales is that my mum was conceived in Pontypool (it usually gets a laugh), whereas she was actually conceived in Durham but was born in Pontypool. My grandfather's also Scottish so I could have played for them, too. The reason I say I could have won more caps playing for Wales is because they have fewer players. I still wouldn't have been first choice, though, because Gethin Jenkins was there. He also sounds a lot more Welsh than I do and that's important. Gethin Jenkins? Could there be anything more Welsh?

DURDERS – So, you've just debunked your own 'I could have been a Welsh legend' delusion. What about Scotland?

FLATS – Tom Smith would have been first choice for the first half of my career, but after that I'd have walked in. I'd be a centurion. A Scottish legend like Christopher Lambert in *Highlander*. In all seriousness, I didn't want to simply choose the country where I knew I'd win the most caps.

Anyway, back to what you were saying about tribalism. I think the tribal atmosphere associated with Six Nations matches has lessened slightly over the years. Not to the extent that it no longer exists, but enough for you to notice that it's not quite as omnipresent as it once was.

DURDERS – Omnipresent? Have you been lunching with Stephen Fry again? Your words don't usually have so many syllables in them. But I agree. It'd be easy to blame it all on corporate hospitality or prawn bagels or something, but there's probably a bit more to it. Take Twickenham, for instance. Twickenham's sometimes accused of being quite sanitised, which is usually blamed on the fact that there are a lot of reserved middle-class people in attendance. I'll grant you that some of them might not be as vocal as many of their Welsh counterparts before the match (he says, blatantly sucking up to his wonderful and generous in-laws, whom he loves very much), but as soon as that whistle goes, to borrow phrase from old Frankie who went to Hollywood, two tribes go to war. It is tribal, whether you're a lawyer, a glass-blower or a labourer.

Anyway, shall we all find a comfy chair and let you share your 'interesting' Six Nations tale with us?

FLATS – Why not? If the rules about there being two props on the bench had come in a year earlier, I'd probably have had a few more to tell, but that's life. Then again, had I played for Scotland or Wales I might have had hundreds, so you could judge that as being quite a lucky escape.

The match in question was against France and I obviously played in the front row. Playing in the front row against France or Argentina used to be one of the challenges in world rugby, although not any more. They're just not as good as they were. That had always been my dream growing up, as France, in particular, always had the roughest and toughest front rows. They were almost like mythical creatures in their own country. Revered and feared in equal measure. We talk about the Six Nations crowds being tribal, but ultimately that's just an extension of what takes place on the pitch.

DURDERS – As far as the French front row were concerned, that used to be bloodlust! There's no other word for it. It was gruesome, it was violent and it was fraught with danger. It's obviously changed a great deal since then – primarily because of safety – and despite that being both a positive and sensible move, I do miss those battles. Brian Moore was a master of making the French lose their marbles. What's the French for 'marbles' . . . *J'ai perdu mon* . . . ?

FLATS – *Marblez.*

DURDERS – Ridiculous man. I just googled it. It's actually 'marbres', so your infantile response wasn't a million miles off. But I used to read those Brian Moore incendiary head-lines and think, *What the hell's he doing?* But of course he was getting under their skin. Very effectively.

One of my favourite Six Nations experiences of recent-ish times was watching England play in Dublin for the first time. I'd been working in rugby since my mid-twenties but I'd never done a Six Nations game, professionally or per-sonally, in Dublin. What an amazing city to watch rugby in. It was magical. After the match, we went to a fantastic bar/nightclub/fairy light-festooned nocturnal dreamworld and as we arrived a very famous Irish actor who I obviously can't name stumbled out, full of the joys of a Six Nations weekend in Dublin. I wondered if he was paid by the Irish tourist board to be out and about, adding to the authentic Dublin experience. It's wondrous.

FLATS – Hang on. So you believe the Six Nations tourna-ment, which was established in 1883 as the Home Nations tournament by lots of extremely distinguished people and is loved and revered the world over, is all about watching middle-aged actors falling out of bars and onto pavements, having drunk their own bodyweights in Guinness? I'm guessing it was Guinness, by the way, and appreciate that by doing so I'm probably reinforcing certain outdated stereo-types. Sorry.

DURDERS – And so you should be. I was talking about the experience as a whole – making the journey to Dublin, wallowing in the atmosphere, meeting all the different characters, watching a great and hard-fought game of rugby, soaking up more atmosphere, meeting yet more characters. And yes, getting just a little bit alcoholically bamboozled and taking a certain amount of delight in watching people I recognise from the telly doing the same.

FLATS – You are right on this occasion. The reasons that people adore the Six Nations are manifold, yet what sits astride them all is the experience it provides as a whole and the memories it leaves you with. That's why we love it so much and it's also why the players love it just as much as the fans. My dad loves the Six Nations for exactly the same reasons I do, and I love that.

DURDERS – We keep veering off course. What about your Six Nations story, then? You're several pages late.

FLATS – I got sidetracked. Right, it obviously involves my one appearance in our beloved Six Nations, which happened in the year 2000, and is a short yet agreeable tale of endeavour, triumph and brutally honest defence coaches from Oldham.

The squad would always get together on the Monday before a Test and then on the Tuesday afternoon or evening Clive Woodward would inform seven players that they were surplus to requirements and then send them off to join England A – or, as they're now known, the England Saxons, which I find a bit cringy.

On the Tuesday morning before the Test we were summoned to take part in a defence session. These days every pro rugby team in the world will have a defence coach, but in those days they were found at only the very richest clubs or within the international set-ups. England's defence coach was a Lancastrian gentleman called Phil Larder, who had once been head coach for the England and Great Britain rugby league teams. One of the first exercises we did in this session involved us standing in a line opposite players holding pads who were supposed to be a line of attackers. Somebody roaming around behind that line would then cut in and we'd have to try and stop them. Or just punch them very hard indeed, as is my wont. The guy roaming around at the back was Dan Luger and alongside me in the defence line were Julian White on one side, who was at Bristol, and Darren Garforth on the other, who played tighthead prop for Leicester Tigers. At one point early on, Luger came through one of the gaps next to Julian and went straight past him. 'Whitey, what the hell are you doing?' shouted Darren. If you shout at Julian White he'll give you one of his 'I'm going to fucking kill you' looks, and if you do it again he'll follow it through. Darren was on a warning.

A minute or two later, Luger came through again and this time he went straight past me. 'For fuck's sake, Flats,' shouted Darren. 'What the fuck are you doing?' Unlike Julian White, I have neither the menace nor the eyes to be able to inflict looks that threaten imminent death, so I decided to protest vocally. 'Daz,' I began. 'I've never done this before and I don't know what I'm supposed to be doing.' 'I gathered that,' he replied. 'Look,' he said. 'When he comes into the line, hit him!'

Just then, Lawrence Dallaglio walked over and elaborated. 'If he comes in there, you hit him, and if he comes in there, you move in. Okay?' 'That's all I needed to know,' I said indignantly. 'You've all done this before whereas I haven't.'

A couple of phases later Luger came through again and so I twatted him. I still didn't really know what I was doing, though. I was out of my comfort zone.

After the session Phil Larder held a debrief. There were about 30 players in attendance and he began by saying (assumes a Lancastrian accent), 'Every player in here is a top-class defender who I would trust to defend at Test match level.' There was then a pause of about five seconds. 'Apart from two of you. There are two men in here who I would not under any circumstances trust to defend at Test match level and they are Whitey and Flats. There's work to be done, lads. There's work to be done.'

Thanks, Phil.

I was indignant at the time and what I wanted to say in reply was something along the lines of, 'Why don't you explain it to us before you start, instead of chucking us in at the deep end, watching us fail and then humiliating us?' Clive was in the room, though, and I thought better of it.

DURDERS – I take it you were one of the 'not as magnificent as the rest' seven that week?

FLATS – Correct. Clive came over and said, 'You're on the list, Flats. You're not needed this week. You're going to be playing against France A.' 'Okay,' I said. 'Where are they playing?' 'Redruth,' said Clive. 'You have got to be fucking joking,' I said, very much under my breath.

Some of the lads at England A got wind of what had happened and just as I was setting off on the 15-hour drive an avalanche of texts began to arrive obviously wishing me well. 'Enjoy the drive, mate,' one said. 'We've got live scrums first thing in the morning.'

Our coach at England A was Ged Glynn, who was at Leicester Tigers until quite recently. I remember we were playing Scotland A once and before the match Ged said, 'I wouldn't swap any of you for any of the England team playing at Murrayfield tomorrow.' It was a very generous thing to say, but at the same time it was bollocks and I remember looking at Julian White and whispering, 'I fucking would. I'd swap about fourteen of us!' We ended up drawing 3-3. It was not a classic.

I arrived in Redruth at about 9 p.m. and, after accepting the anticipated barrage of abuse with as much good grace as I could muster, I went to bed. The following morning at breakfast Ged grabbed me mid-porridge. 'Pack your bags,' he said. 'You're wanted back with England. Trevor Woodman's twisted his ankle.' Twenty minutes later, I was back on the motorway and when I arrived at the training ground the first thing I was told was that I was going to be on the bench at Twickenham on Saturday for England versus France. I love Trev and would never wish him harm, but I was over the moon that he'd twisted his ankle.

Before the game Phil Larder came up to me and said (assumes a Lancastrian accent once again), 'You are a top-class defender and I know that you are capable of defending at Test match level. I have every confidence in you.' *No, you haven't*, I thought. *I haven't done any more training since you told me I was crap yesterday, so how could you?* Phil Vickery was standing next to me and he was pissing himself laughing, as my eyes were clearly betraying my thoughts. Most young players would have said, 'Thanks, Phil, that means a lot,' but I didn't because it would have been a lie.

DURDERS – What did Mr Larder say?

FLATS – 'Good man.'

DURDERS – What?

FLATS – 'Good man.' That's all he said before walking off. His line about me being a top-class defender who could deliver at Test match level was obviously something he rattled out to every single player and the replies he received, which were probably just variations of 'thank you', had obviously stopped registering.

DURDERS – How fortuitous! Okay, the question we're all asking now is, did you get a game?

FLATS – Of course I bloody did. Otherwise, what would be the point of the story? I came on after Jason Leonard was sinbinned, but couldn't take to the field until there was a try.

DURDERS – How long were you on the field of play, Flats?

FLATS – About 90 seconds. I didn't half put it about, though.

DURDERS – So your sole Six Nations appearance lasted a minute and a half? It takes longer to go to the loo. I'm talking about a number one for the avoidance of doubt.

FLATS – Try holding your breath for 90 seconds (actually, make it minutes).

DURDERS – I bet I could. There's a headline for you: 'Judith Chalmers' son can probably stay under water longer than David Flatman played Six Nations Rugby'.

FLATS — I didn't miss a single tackle in that game (or make any), and I also hit a scrum against a hero of mine called Peter de Villiers. Remember him? A South African prop who was renowned for his scrummaging ability. I thought it was going to be brutal in there, but actually it was okay. We won the scrum, I came off and England went on to win. After the match, Tom Shanklin called me up to see how I got on and when I told him what had happened he said, 'Oh well, you still get paid the same.' That lifted my pecker up a bit.

DURDERS — Well, that was definitely worth the wait. Does irony come across in print? Before we move on, any final words about the Six Nations?

FLATS — There is a conversation to be had around the continued presence of Italy. It's the tournament's very own elephant in the room but the issue has to be addressed. In my opinion another country should at least be given the chance to qualify.

DURDERS — So would you go down to five established nations and a sixth to qualify?

FLATS — No, that's not what I mean. You have to keep it honest. Nobody should be locked into the tournament and nobody should be safe. Whoever finishes sixth should have a play-off against the next best country and if that country wins they become the sixth nation. For me, Italy have been treading water for almost 20 years. They just haven't progressed. How much of that is down to the fact that they're guaranteed a place in the Six Nations, I'm not sure. What's much clearer is that by having a glass ceiling above the nations just behind Italy, such as Georgia, you're preventing them from investing enough to progress to the next level.

DURDERS — I see what you mean. They might get one big game every four years at a World Cup, but they won't have had much prep as they're not being tested in a decent regular tournament — like the Six Nations.

FLATS — Exactly. The idea that because it always was, it always should be, simply doesn't rub any more. Just as you have to qualify for the World Cup, I think you should have to qualify to be the sixth of the Six Nations. Not least because the games against Italy are often quite boring. Hard fought, but boring.

DURDERS — It's still the greatest rugby tournament in the world, is it not?

FLATS — Indeed it is. As Phil Larder might say (assumes a Lancastrian accent for the final time), the Six Nations is a top-class tournament and I have every faith that it will continue to deliver top-class rugby for a long time to come.

DURDERS — *Bellissimo!*

Referees

DURDERS – Having studied you closely in your playing days, as Chris Packham would study a water vole, I noted you were one of those players who tried to ingratiate themselves, smarm their way into the affections of the referee and make friends with them. 'All right, ref? What did you have for breakfast? How's the wife and kids? Love those socks, where did you get them? I'll be on your side, don't you worry.' But it was ultimately an insincere cynical ploy, was it not, as after sucking up you'd try to get away with as much as possible, you filthy, cheating baboon.

FLATS – Which proves absolutely nothing, least of all that my words were not sincere. Wily, perhaps, or even laced with an air of cunning. Nevertheless, I am an inquisitive soul by nature who also likes his food, so my having asked a referee what they had for breakfast would invariably have been a sincere enquiry and completely in character.

DURDERS – I can't argue with that. So you never cheated, then?

FLATS – Never. That said, I knew when I'd made mistakes that should have been penalised and went through phases of sucking up to refs and laughing about said mistakes, which made them less inclined to penalise me. I also went through phases of being very angry with referees and making that very clear indeed, but without swearing. It's a bit of a skill I developed, although sometimes I'd take it a bit far.

DURDERS – Any examples you'd like to share with us?

FLATS – I was playing for Bath against Leeds once and got penalised a few times. Wrongly, in my opinion. After the second or third time, I became very angry with the ref, to the point where my comments were making some of the players laugh and others feel uncomfortable. After the match I had a shower, went to see the ref and kicked his fucking head in and he went straight to A&E. Only joking. I sat down and actually apologised to him for being such an arsehole. I still thought he was wrong and I told him so, but I should never have spoken to him the way I did. The referee's name is Dave Pearson and we've got on very nicely since then.

DURDERS – We're not interested in happy-ever-afters. Not at this early point in the chapter. No, our readers will be disappointed if the pantomime villains of the sport don't get a bit of a verbal rucking – all within the laws of literary masterpieces of course. Come on, you are very, very disparaging about referees in a particular context and I'd like you to share these intolerant views of yours with the world. We've talked about this hundreds of times off camera while presenting our show on Channel 5.

FLATS – You mean the warm-ups, don't you?

DURDERS – I do indeed. Watching you watching the referees going through their pre-game plyometric high-intensity warm-up is one of life's great pleasures. Your attitude to people who take great pride in what they do does not reflect well on you, my favourite Obelix tribute act.

FLATS – I knew you'd bring this up. Why do I see referees warming up with more intensity than international rugby players? I'll tell you why, because they're obviously making up for the fact that they're a bunch of non-athletes who effectively jog for a living. Just stop it!

DURDERS – Don't hold back, will you? You've always had a slightly condescending attitude to these finely tuned athletes. Wayne Barnes, who we worked with on Channel 5, being one of them. Wayne's a lovely man – a barrister by profession – and he's supremely fit. The other day, Wayne did a bleep test and it was agreed by everyone present that he was probably 78 per cent fitter than David Luke Flatman in his prime.

FLATS – That's because Barnsey weighs less than my lunch! I could do better on the bleep test if you took away about 40 per cent of my bodyweight and forced me to practise running for about five years. If a car rolls into a ditch, Barnsey ain't getting it out. That's where I come in. I can pull a horse's legs off. He can't.

DURDERS – We're obviously being facetious for the sake of keeping things light-hearted, but can I assume that you do actually harbour a certain level of respect for referees?

FLATS – Of course I do, although I'd be lying if I said that the warming-up thing doesn't get on my nerves a bit. But what I was going to say before you mentioned the warm-ups was that referees can't be anywhere near perfect. There are just too many variables. The key to being a good referee is communication, which is why I think Barnsey is the best referee in the world today. The way he communicates, not just with the players but with assistants on the pitch, is a cut above anything I've ever seen before.

DURDERS – Surely you'd put Nigel Owens in the same bracket?

FLATS – Nigel Owens was widely regarded as being the best referee in the world for a long time, but in my opinion Barnsey's communication on the field gives him the edge now. Perhaps it has something to do with his pretend job as a barrister? I still think that's bullshit, by the way. Nobody I know has ever seen him in court. It sounds good, though, doesn't it? Wayne Barnstable Barnes QC, Premiership and international rugby referee and barrister. During the week he specialises in charging people tens of thousands of pounds just to send them a bloody email that he hasn't even written and at the weekend he's a top rugby referee with legs like twiglets who does a lovely line in plyometric warm-ups and who weighs less than a couple of roast chickens.

DURDERS – I'm hoping Wayne will find something in that last paragraph to give him good cause to sue you for defamation of character. Go on, Barnsey – show this upright protein shake your legal guns. Anyway, I think something Wayne's particularly good at is breaking down a decision in the moment. He'll say, 'This is what I saw, this is the law, and that is why I have made this decision.' It's very difficult to argue with somebody who makes eye contact – and those eyes of his are piercingly blue – and who calmly tells you why they've come to a decision. Not in an officious way. Not in the 'I am the law and you'll do what I say' kind of way. It actually reinforces his authority. And you know with Wayne Barnes that he's very happy to admit when he's made a mistake, which again is key to his success.

FLATS – I'm watching a series on Netflix at the moment about people who've been planted in prisons but who aren't really criminals. They're there to report back about the conditions inside the prisons and the number one problem they encounter is that people in positions of power, such as wardens, refuse to communicate with the inmates. They don't tell them why the hot water hasn't worked for 36 hours or why the visiting orders have been cancelled. They don't deem the inmates worthy of being a party to that kind of information, which in turn causes a great deal of resentment and consternation. But how on earth are you supposed to respect people who quite evidently believe that you're shit on their shoe?

When I was playing, there were two refs in particular who I thought fell right into that category. They were incredibly patronising and went out of their way to insult the players. I absolutely hated it and in turn I hated them. I used to think, *You are getting it so, so wrong, mate. You really are.* As a consequence, my fellow players and I had zero respect for these referees, which always made for a toxic atmosphere on the pitch. We hated it.

DURDERS – Hate is a strong word and emotion. I think

you're just showing off – you're no hater. Anyway, I was the same at my school.

FLATS – Here we go. You went to Radley, didn't you? Carried around a nice soft cushion I hope.

DURDERS – Said the hardened Maidstone gangster ... who went to Dulwich College in south London, where the motto is '*Detur Gloria Soli Deo*', which I think translates as 'We Glory in our Poshness'. All I was going to say was that teachers who used their elevated status, not the strength of their personalities, to get the attention of the class never won the hearts and minds of their pupils. Never got the best out of us. You'd learn despite, not because of, them.

FLATS – That's actually quite a good analogy. We had a couple of teachers on the other side of the coin, who went out of their way to get on with the pupils and, as well as creating a comfortable and positive atmosphere in the classroom, we all listened and were enthusiastic. I remember running out for a game once at The Rec, and Barnesy was refereeing. I said, 'Hello, Barnesy.' 'Hello, Flats,' he said. 'How're you doing, mate? Let me guess. Keep the tighthead straight today, is it?' I said, 'They say the same about you.' 'Ha,' said Barnesy. 'Good luck, Flats.' I remember thinking to myself, *That's how you do it*. My aim going into the game, apart from helping my team win, was not to let Barnesy down.

DURDERS – What you just said would probably sound ridiculous to some non-rugby fans, but it's the essence of the sport. Respecting the officials is one of the first things you're taught when you start to play rugby. It's a cultural cornerstone. The referee's word is final. It's a non-negotiable. Always has been.

Always will be. So get on with it. Having said that, a little bit of insubordination has started to creep into the sport with the introduction of the TMO, but the fact remains that I don't think, certainly at the professional level, a referee has ever felt genuinely intimidated by the players. They may well have been made to feel a little uncomfortable by frustrated fans – just ask Craig Joubert, the South African referee, after his controversial decision that ended Scotland's World Cup hopes at Twickenham in 2015 – but not by the players. Nor should they. The officials may well have had pressure heaped upon them by directors of rugby and coaches, as happened in the Lions series in South Africa in 2021. (The South African Rassie Erasmus taking it to the next level with his 62-minute video.) But I can't recall any officials ever having been made to feel intimidated by the players.

FLATS – Unlike in association football. I promise you this is not just a cheap win and I am conscious of the fact that rugby should never be superior in its attitude to other sports. However, the sports' cultures with regards to the treatment of referees are poles apart and that puzzles me to the point of distraction. They never used to be. What's frustrating is that the intimidation and bad language that is displayed towards referees and officials by pretty much everyone concerned could be stamped out in a matter of months if the powers that be wanted, but they don't.

Have you ever been to an Under-15s football match? The amount of abuse they give the referee is shocking and in some cases it's worse from the sidelines. The word respect doesn't exist in that environment and I wouldn't want to be anywhere near it. That isn't because I live in Bath and it's posh. (It is and I do.) There are plenty of football clubs down here in the West Country and sometimes I'll see it being played while I'm walking the dogs. Lots of it is very pleasant and lovely, but some of it is horrible. For some reason it brings out the very worst in people – parents and children alike – but what makes it especially distasteful is the fact that they're essentially given permission to act like that by the sport's governing bodies. They've basically rubber-stamped it. They're always talking about kicking out racism in football, which is vitally important, but what about instilling some basic respect? You'd stand more chance of kicking out racism if you did.

DURDERS – I remember that game when a referee in charge of a Man Utd game was chased by a pack of baying hounds. The names of those hounds were David Beckham, Nicky Butt, Jaap Stam, Ryan Giggs and of course Roy Keane, who was literally in the ref's face – their noses must have touched, and not in a nice Eskimo-kiss kind of way. Keane was the captain, which I guess makes it even worse. As you rightly said, Flats, rugby should not be superior in its attitude to other sports and the football authorities are trying to change attitudes. What rugby can and should do, though, is look at sports that no longer consider the respect of its officials to be an essential component and steer well clear.

As a professional rugby player, were you taught by your coaches to accept bad decisions on the field of play?

FLATS – Yes, all the time. You were taught to suck it up. As you just suggested, though, this kind of behaviour is starting to creep into rugby when decisions go against pro players. The thing is, football wasn't invented on a Monday and then on the Tuesday the players started abusing referees. It starts with, 'Aw, come on, ref!' or, 'Really, ref?' Also, if you watch football matches from two or three generations ago, nobody said a word to the ref.

The point I'm trying to make here, in addition to the fact that football is found lacking when it comes to protecting its officials, is that people wrongly assume that rugby is a perfect example of how to do it right, but it's not. Players are pleading with and baying at referees all the time. Owen Farrell spends a lot of time disagreeing with refs, but then again, I do believe that aggression is an important part of what makes Owen Farrell such a great player and although I think he can push it a bit sometimes, he's generally careful not to cross the line.

DURDERS – So if you could introduce one new rule to curb bad behaviour on the rugby field, what would it be?

FLATS – That's easy. If you try to tell a referee what to do, you'll get penalised. If you do it again, you'll get a yellow card and if you do it a third time you'll get a red. Simple as that. I got a red card when I was 15 years old. We were playing a team who'd been cheating and in my eyes the ref had turned a blind eye. During a break in play I said to the rest of the team, in earshot of the ref, 'Don't worry, boys. If the ref won't do anything, we'll sort it out.' It was industrial-strength petulance, really, especially from a kid. 'Excuse me,' said the ref. 'I heard that. Red card.' After the game, I still hadn't learned my lesson and when I went off the first thing I said to my dad was, 'What a tosser.' 'You're the one whose acting like a tosser,' said my dad. 'Now get back over there and apologise and don't you dare speak to a referee like that ever again.' I was one of the senior players of the Under-15s team and was supposed to be setting an example. 'Will Carling would never do that,' was my dad's usual riposte whenever I transgressed, which was often. I bet you Will Carling will have done something similar at some point – perceived injustices cut deep, even with those that have square jaws and an eye-catching mid-chin dimple.

DURDERS – That dimple is one of the great wonders of the world. I reckon you could eat a boiled egg from it. I'd love one of those. The dimple, not the boiled egg. I'm a poached man. Do plastic surgeons do mid-chin dimples these days?

FLATS – Are you being disrespectful to William David Charles Carling OBE?

DURDERS – Quite the opposite, I am being respectful to both him and his dimple.

FLATS – Let's drop this and get back to the refs.

DURDERS – Okay. Is there any benefit in comparing the referees from the amateur era with the refs of today?

FLATS – It's something I'm asked to do quite often in an interview environment and to be honest it's futile. Regardless of the sport turning professional, everything evolves, and everything has evolved. What turning professional has done, however, apart from forcing the referees into making fools of themselves before a match, is to bring the refereeing up to a standard that, hitherto, has never been seen before. The problem that has created is that some of the fans have become obsessed with achieving perfection and are now calling for scrum refs and more video refs. That, I'm afraid, is as a direct consequence of the game turning professional and should be stamped out. The nuances that each referee brings to a game of rugby are vital and add balance. We need those imperfections.

DURDERS — I take it that when the game turned professional the referees didn't suddenly turn into the world's fittest people and start making far fewer mistakes.

FLATS — Good God, no. As I just said, the game evolves no matter what. Referees of Wayne Barnes's calibre only started appearing about a decade ago, and when I was playing, the standard varied greatly. As did the amount of fun you could have. For instance, one of my absolute favourite referees was Tony Spreadbury. Spreaders is a great bloke and as well as being a superb referee I don't think he had an enemy anywhere in the game. He's from Bath originally and has a heavy West Country accent. I used to go into scrums and while Spreaders was standing there making the mark I'd grab him a bit to steady myself, so I could lean forward and gain an advantage. He'd say, 'Stop leaning on me, you bugger.' After letting go of him, I'd go back in for a second time and after putting my arm around him I'd tickle him around his midriff as though I was playing an accordion. 'Cor, good Christmas was it, Spreaders?' 'Bugger off, you!' He didn't like me touching his lovely tummy.

DURDERS — You couldn't do that with Barnsey.

FLATS — For the simple reason he has a BMI index of about 7.5. I've seen more fat on a chicken's lip. Spreaders did get his own back on me once. You know when you're in a scrum and you're bent at 90 degrees? In that situation you're always careful not to let your shirt ride up as your gut will stick out. One day in a scrum Spreaders came behind me, pulled my shirt right up and said, 'How was your Christmas, you fat bugger? Bloody hell, Flats, that's massive!' I used to try to pull him in when we were engaging. 'Get off me, you bugger!' He once penalised me for something and I said, 'Aww, come on, Spreaders.' 'Save your breath,' he said quickly. 'It sounds like you're running out.'

DURDERS – You must have missed him when he retired.

FLATS – We all did. I used to apologise to him when he penalised me. I genuinely felt guilty. He used to say, 'Well, you will keep on doing it, Dave, you old bugger.'

Halcyon days.

Tours

DURDERS – Although I believe this subject to be worthy of a chapter in our book, I am slightly embarrassed by the fact that despite having been on several rugby tours, I actually have very few stories. Or at least the kind of stories that our readers will take any delight in reading.

FLATS – You must have some, for heaven's sake.

DURDERS – Well, one or two. But my stories tend, on whatever subject actually, to be a little on the dull side. It's a bad combo – someone who likes the sound of his own voice and dull stories. I'm also concerned that these kind of stories tend to reinforce certain negative stereotypes about the game of rugby.

FLATS – Let the reader decide, Markie.

Look, rightly or wrongly, the narrative that I was fed since going on my first rugby tour, at the age of 12, wasn't that we'd go abroad and behave like arseholes. Not at all. We were always told to be polite and pleasant to people. The fact that we were also told that we'd be expected to get pissed and that rugby would sometimes be an afterthought was neither here nor there. I went on tour with the Kent county team when I was at school and there was one game we played that I could not recall a single solitary moment of when I got home.

DURDERS – Because you're dim-witted?

FLATS – Because I was pissed. Believe it or not, I don't actually enjoy getting trousered all that much. I love a night out and I love a few drinks, but not being able to remember what you did and feeling like utter shit the next morning doesn't sit well with me any more. The last time it happened was during the World Cup in Tokyo, believe it or not, so a while ago. I'll drink alcohol most nights but – and I can't believe I'm using these words – mainly in moderation.

DURDERS – How sensible/dull. Do you also power-hose the patio on a Sunday morning? Did you carry on getting bonkered on tour?

FLATS – Less and less as I got older. I really enjoyed the sneaking out after dark bit, though, and all the messing around. To me that was a bigger part of the fun.

DURDERS – My tour story locker is a little thin on the ground. I did kick a rugby ball over a plane we were about to get on in Zimbabwe, which didn't go down well with airport security. I also lost at Spoof and had to walk the entire length of a jumbo, at night, while everyone was trying to sleep, moving and clucking like a chicken. Actually I'd like to take this opportunity to apologise to all those on that flight from Harare to Heathrow in July 1992 – this tosser is full of regret and ashamed of his inconsiderate and juvenile actions. Still, not exactly jumping off a ferry in Auckland Harbour à la Manu Tuilagi. Told you my stories were dull.

FLATS – You've proved that point – thank you. That's all standard rugby tour fare, really. I think the general severity of behaviour can vary a lot. I went on a two-day 'tour' to the University of East Anglia when I was 20 or 21 to visit a mate of mine who was studying there and we ended up going out with his rugby team. I'd already been on a few big pro rugby tours by that time, but this was way more raucous than anything I'd experienced. It was all about getting naked and puking in pint glasses. Until then, I'd never done anything like that and to be honest I hated it. I'm all for having a laugh, but puking into a pint glass and then necking it back isn't my idea of fun. Regardless of the situation.

DURDERS – A few years ago the RFU tried to clamp down on things like initiation ceremonies at uni clubs. They really don't always fall into the category of harmless fun and I don't want to sound like a fun sponge but the more sinister, barbaric ones really do give rugby a bad name. I remember being on tour in Zimbabwe at a rugby club drinking cocktails called Puff Adders, which came in pint glasses. We found out afterwards that, as part of our 'warm' welcome, the opposition had been urinating into our Puff Adders. I'm all for trying local delicacies, but that's one I could happily have passed on. More bonhomie and less drinking wee. That's my motto. The essence of a rugby tour isn't about pushing boundaries or shocking people. It's about like-minded people having a laugh together in interesting places and all under the umbrella of rugby. If downing too many pints of something other than human urine and/or kicking rugby balls over aeroplanes becomes part of it – a bit of high jinks, you might say – then so be it. Just so long as nobody gets hurt and not too many people get offended.

FLATS – I concur entirely. I'm in danger of sounding even more puritanical than you, but when I joined Saracens at the end of the last century we went on a team-building trip and when we got back they asked each of us in turn what we liked about the trip and what we didn't like. I said that I really enjoyed the trip, but didn't enjoy having to neck pints of lager with raw eggs in them, which is what I'd had to do on the first night. The lads gave me so much stick for that. They were disgusted. Couldn't look at me.

On Silly Sunday, after the last match of the season, Brendan Reidy, a Samoan international prop who was at Saracens from 1997 to 1999, decided to punish me for having complained about drinking. 'Every time anyone has a pint,' he said, 'you have to down a pint of ice-cold Coca Cola.' First, this meant that I couldn't get drunk with the other lads, and second, it meant that I was the designated driver for the entire evening. There I was in my shitty little club car ferrying pissed-up rugby players to all the local nightclubs. Worse still, for the entire evening I felt as sick as a very badly bloated and sugar-drunk dog, having consumed about six or seven litres of Coca Cola. It was bloody horrible.

DURDERS – I feel your pain. Well, almost. I once watched my flatmate at Durham, Charlotte, nearly explode after she'd gone on a strict diet of Diet Coke and frankfurters. That diet never went mainstream for some reason. Just going back to your team-building trip, though, anyone who's in charge of a communal get-together should be conscious of the fact that within your group you'll have different characters and personalities. Forcing somebody to do something that you think is fun but they may find uncomfortable is not the way forward. I did everything I was asked to do on my rugby tours for the simple reason that I wanted to be part of the crew and the forfeits for not doing your bit could be pretty gruesome. And if you're going to have forfeits, I think they should be funny, not humiliating. Make them inclusive so you laugh with, not at, people.

FLATS – You mean have a list and let people choose?

DURDERS – I didn't mean anything of the sort but now you've suggested it I like it – and I've patented the idea. It's my IP so hands off. Be in charge of your own destiny. What should have happened on Silly Sunday when Brendan Reidy was dishing out the punishment was him handing you a list of three of four options. A) Set light to your chest hair. B) Sing Buck's Fizz's Eurovision Song Contest winner – with moves. C) Drink a pint of wee-wee.

FLATS – I'm a C) every time. It's a nice idea, but I can't see it catching on. The best times I ever had on tour were nothing to do with the level I played at, nor did they have anything to do with the amount of alcohol I consumed. Sorry, but that's the truth. My favourite tour was to Argentina with England in 2002. Legends like Phil Vickery were there and I roomed with Trevor Woodman. It was fantastic. I remember thinking that despite there being so many different characters and personalities on the tour, everyone was allowed to be themselves.

I went out for something to eat one night with Phil

Vickery and the first thing he did when we left the hotel was light up a rollie. I had no idea he smoked and, although I'm not a fan of it myself, there was something quite special about watching him roll it. I felt included. Part of a club. The following morning I was woken at about 5 a.m. by the sound of Alex Codling clearing his one lung of phlegm in the next room. That was a sound to behold. Beautiful! We definitely did go out and have a few beers on the tour, but that's not what I remember. What I remember is all of us being completely accepted for who we were. Mark Regan, the hooker, relentlessly harangued everybody throughout the entire trip. Nobody was safe, but because the abuse was inclusive and never crossed the line, we loved him for it. We literally laughed all day for three whole weeks.

DURDERS – As touching as that is, we are in danger of producing a rugby version of *Little House on the Prairie* here, or Mr Tumble on CBeebies. Big fan by the way. But look, I think we need to finish with some good old-fashioned high jinks. Nothing too OTT, but enough to make us sound less like twin Mother Theresas. Come on, let's give the people what they want. How about the dwarf-tossing story from 2011. Do you have inside intel? Did it actually happen?

FLATS – Talk about pissing on my woke parade. I am a reformed character. The story's absolute bollocks, by the way. The England rugby team walked into a bar where there were a number of vertically challenged people who had been paid – by the bar, not the players – to be thrown at a Velcro wall throughout the evening. The fact that some of the England players ended up dancing with these people of diminished stature and then encouraged them to punch them as hard as they could in the side of the head is neither here nor there, and would have made a pretty good story in its own right. Where it went wrong was when the (non-British) press started claiming that the dwarfs had been picked up by the ankles against their will and thrown at the Velcro wall. The press were trying to turn what had been just a bit of beery fun (albeit it a tad random, even for rugby players) into something untoward and potentially incriminating. It's a pretty shitty thing to do when you think about it. The trouble is it's almost expected, such is the reputation of a rugby tour, and if it isn't happening organically, the ladies and gentlemen of the press will try and engineer something. Or just make it up.

DURDERS – I think you're being slightly unfair on the press here. While I'm sure there are some who live by the rule of never letting a little thing like the truth get in the way of a good story, the vast majority are good eggs and want the game to flourish. In fact I can't think of a single rugby correspondent who isn't a lovely *œuf*. The trouble is that when you get a group of rugby players together in a beery environment, one person's high jinks will be another's high dudgeon, and when it comes to selling newspapers the latter will almost always prevail. It's unfortunate, but that's just the way it goes. One story that epitomises my hypothesis involves your good self, and is probably one of the most repeated and re-imagined rugby tour stories in the lengthy history of the rugby tour story. But you know the truth, the whole truth etc., etc.

FLATS – You're talking about Nelson Mandela. The reason I call the story Nelson Mandela is that over the years it's become quite apocryphal and the only name that hasn't been changed is his. People tailor it to suit their needs and, despite my having been at the very epicentre of the story, I'm fine with it.

DURDERS – Haven't you actually been in a situation where another person has told the story and replaced you with themselves?

FLATS – Several times. It's such a legendary tale, though, and people want to be part of it. As I said, that doesn't bother me. Sometimes my role in the story changes and sometimes I'm removed completely. I don't need to be a pedant about it, though. Anyway, do you want to know what actually happened?

DURDERS – I speak on behalf of the nation, i.e. the 12 discerning people who've bought our book, when I say *absolutely*.

FLATS – Okay. Before I start, I should point out that I was just 20 years of age when this took place and was basically a very quiet, polite and shy young man. Unfortunately, I was also quite impressionable, and so liable to be led from the primrose path.

DURDERS – Spare us the caveat. Nobody believes a word.

FLATS – Worth a try. The year was 2000 and we were over in South Africa playing the Springboks. I won't name all the players, but one night three of us went out and we ended up bringing some new friends back for a party. The next morning, I remember being woken up by a member of the team management.

The first thing I remember the person saying to me was, 'Where's the bloody handbag? Come on, where's the bloody handbag!?' 'What bloody handbag?' I asked. 'I don't know what you're talking about.' At that moment, I looked to my left and there in the next bed was a young lady who must have been one of our new friends. What first struck me about her, apart from the fact that she was snoring and was quite attractive, was that she appeared to be wearing the clothes I had on the previous evening. I then thought to myself, so if she's got my clothes on, who's got her ... Oh, Christ! After gingerly lifting up the sheets, my worst fears were confirmed. At some point during the evening, I had attempted to don our guest's clothes, but they'd obviously ripped a bit. I looked like a transvestite version of the Incredible Hulk shortly after he has gone through the big green change.

While all this was going on, the team management person was harping on about this handbag. 'Okay, okay, I'll find it,' I said, getting out of bed. The reason I was so cooperative, apart from being slightly alarmed by the presence of a female wearing my clothes, was because the person seeking the handbag had an air of genuine panic about them, and that unnerved me. After managing to locate the handbag, I was told to stay exactly where I was. 'Somebody's coming to collect you in about five minutes,' they said. 'Don't you dare move.'

About a minute later, two senior players walked into my room looking equally panicked. 'Flats, we need to get you out of here,' said one of them. 'They're coming to get you. Quick, come with us.' I felt like an overfed Jason Statham minus the martial arts qualifications and the weird cockney accent. Within a minute or so, I was safely ensconced in the bathroom of one of the aforementioned senior players and, although I felt quite comfortable – the bath was huge – I didn't know what on earth was going on.

DURDERS – And what *was* going on?

FLATS – Apparently we'd failed to invite a friend of this girl's to the party and the following morning she'd decided to tell the girl's father that we'd kidnapped her. What a reckless thing to do. We were limited on numbers – like Covid, I believe there was a rule of six in place – and we were trying to be responsible. She was also quite high up in the Fun Police and had advised the girl in question against swapping clothes with me, which apparently had taken place in the middle of a busy road at some point during the evening. Unfortunately, when reporting this episode back to the girl's father, she claimed that I'd ripped off all her clothes, which was entirely untrue.

DURDERS – As the English seventeenth-century playwright William Congreve wrote, Hell hath no fury like a suspected clothes-swapping kidnap victim's best friend.

FLATS – If you say so. Anyway, after being told that his daughter had been kidnapped, he understandably called the police, which brings us up to date. The people coming to collect me were the police, although when they arrived I'd obviously high-tailed it with two unnamed senior players. To cut a very long story slightly shorter, the powers that be eventually caught up with me in the bathroom and, although no actual charges were brought, my two accomplices and I were going to be investigated.

At the team meeting later that day, all eyes were on we three from the night before, who I won't name as they've moved on with their lives. The thing is, we assumed that the reason everyone was looking at us was because of the alleged kidnap, but it wasn't. Or, should I say, it wasn't *just* that.

'Okay, everyone,' said Clive (as in Woodward, England's World Cup-winning coach and national treasure), quietening everybody down. 'I've got something very serious to discuss, so I'd like you all to be quiet and pay attention. Last night three very serious incidents took place, all of which have brought embarrassment on the RFU and all of which I am determined to get to the bottom of.'

I remember turning around to my accomplices and whispering, 'Thank Christ we weren't the only ones!'

'I'll address the incidents in order of severity,' said Clive. 'Least serious is the alleged kidnapping involving Flats and . . .' *Jesus Christ*, I thought to myself. If my alleged kidnapping was the least serious of the three, then I could sit back and relax a bit. Saying that, all eyes were now firmly on me and, despite the allegation being untrue, I had to allow justice to take its course and so I sat there trying to look innocent and tried not to react to the goading.

'The second incident,' said Clive, 'involves a golf buggy being stolen and driven through a door. Unlike the kidnapping incident, however, the culprits have not owned up or been apprehended.' Once again all eyes, including Clive's, turned to me and my two accomplices. 'It bloody well wasn't us,' I said immediately. 'It wasn't!' The atmosphere then changed from being light-hearted, if that isn't too paradoxical, to severe and accusatory, and the Joburg Three, as we'd been christened, didn't like it. The goading had been replaced with calls from the other players to 'Just admit it, you three.' From then on, things started to become very tense, to the point where my accomplices and I felt convinced it was about to get confrontational.

'Anyway,' said Clive, realising that he wasn't going to get his confession and could well end up with a brawl on his hands if he didn't move quickly on. 'We'll come back to that. By far the most serious offence to have been committed last night involves the theft of a decanter of port from reception. A decanter of port that was given to the hotel by none other than Nelson Mandela.' There was actual a collective 'Ooooh' when he said Nelson Mandela. The kind Bruce Forsyth used to get when he unveiled a car on a quiz show.

Once again, the atmosphere changed. It was like that moment at school when you get a bollocking for something but then your mate next to you gets an even bigger one. You're left thinking that you kind of wish it wasn't happening, but you're really glad it's not you! Before the trip, my dad had said to me, 'Don't get pissed and don't say anything,' and I'd already gone against his wishes slightly. It was Nelson Mandela who made me feel better. He was like a felonious balm. As soon as I heard his name mentioned I knew that whoever had pinched the port would be public enemy number one and as soon as they'd been collared, me and my two accomplices would be like shoplifters in a room full of murderers. As if to confirm my premonition, the eyes in the room didn't land on us this time. It felt as though everyone suspected everyone else, which suited us just fine.

After going back to our room, the news came through that the charges of kidnap had been dropped, which meant we were in the clear. Everyone still thought that we were responsible for the golf buggy thing, but barring the hotel providing any footage of who'd actually nicked it and crashed it, we'd just carry on protesting our innocence. None of that really mattered, though, as all anybody was really bothered about was Nelson's decanter of port.

The first person to come and see us after the meeting was Lawrence Dallaglio. 'Well, boys,' he said. 'Whatever happened last night, at least you didn't nick the decanter.' 'Yes, indeed,' I concurred. 'Whoever nicked that is well and truly in the shit.' Just then, Lawrence looked at the television and, after looking back, he did a very quick double-take. 'Boys,' he said. 'What's that on top of the telly?' 'Where?' I said. 'Oh, bollocks!' There, on top of our television, was an ever-so-slightly damaged decanter that at some point in the recent past had been full to the brim with a lovely vintage port. 'What are we going to do?' asked one of my accomplices. A period of time passed, and another senior player collected the decanter and disposed of it, and as far as I know, at least for the duration of the tour, nobody was ever the wiser. The only thing that really pissed me off was that Clive still thought that the Joburg Three were responsible for the golf buggy, and we weren't.

DURDERS – How do you know you weren't?

FLATS – Because a member of our royal family did it, ably assisted, allegedly, by a lovely man from the Wirral.

DURDERS – The Queen Mum and one of Ken Dodd's Diddymen?

FLATS – Close but no cigar. I'm told it was indeed Mike

Tindall and a diminutive accomplice. I didn't find out until about 10 years ago and so until then the Joburg Three were widely thought to have been the perpetrators. I overheard somebody talking about it at a dinner in Bristol one night and couldn't believe my ears. They said that Mike Tindall had crashed a golf buggy during a tour to South Africa but had got away with it. Not any more! Ten fucking years we'd taken the blame for that.

Best and Worst Days

DURDERS – If we were in any way pretentious, we'd begin this chapter by plagiarising the great Charles Dickens' immortal opening to *A Tale of Two Cities*.

FLATS – You are pretentious.

DURDERS – No, I'm not. But I have just googled the opening to *A Tale of Two Cities* so it makes me come across a little more highbrow than you, the sweary, kidnapping type.

FLATS – Get on with it ... You're slipping into insufferable windbag mode.

DURDERS – Okay, okay. Charles Dickens, or 'Chazballs' to his heavy-drinking buddies at the tavern, wrote, according to Google, these fine words ...

It was the best of times, it was the worst of times. It was the age of wisdom, it was the age of foolishness. It was the epoch of belief, it was the epoch of incredulity. It was the season of light, it was the season of darkness. It was the spring of hope, it was the winter of despair.

FLATS – What? You've defo lost it now and that's far too many epochs for my liking. Although, I suppose, with a whopping stretch of the stretchiest imaginations it could just about, possibly, convey in a very odd way what we'll be trying to achieve in this chapter.

DURDERS – What, immortality within the pantheon of quality literature? You mean what we'll be trying to get across? Anyway, out of respect to C-Dog, I'm going to start off with an event that evokes a somewhat bittersweet memory with me, thus encompassing both sides of the coin. Picture this, if you will. The date is 19 September 2015; the venue, Falmer Stadium in Brighton, and Japan have just beaten the mighty South Africa in the opening match of Pool B in the 2015 Rugby World Cup. Although delighted to be involved in ITV's coverage, I confess I might have been a little disappointed that I'd been given a lot of the less high-profile games to cover – delusional egomaniac that I am. And like the majority of rugby fans, I'd been expecting the Springboks to swat Japan out of the way like a bullock's tail would do a fly on a hot day. The final score, in case you missed it, was South Africa 32, Japan 34, and to this day it's rightly considered one of the biggest upsets in the history of international rugby and one of the biggest shock results in sport full stop. And I was there, feeling incredibly fortunate to be covering it. It was jaw-dropping, awe inspiring, simply sensational.

Our pitch-side pundits that afternoon were Francois Pienaar and George Gregan. After the final whistle, Francois was in a state of shock – he couldn't believe what he'd just seen – whereas George and I were really quite chipper about having witnessed a fantastic game of rugby and a little bit of history. The moment we went off air, the old South African tighthead prop and former teammate of Francois', Cobus

Visagie – a mountain range of a man – strolled up to us, incandescent with rage. 'I just want to fucking hit some-body,' Cobus the Barbarian bellowed. I was about to reply with a quip such as, 'Well don't look at me, chum,' when all of a sudden I realised he was doing exactly that. As big as he is, there was no way Cobus the Barbarian was going to have a go at either Francois or George, which left me. His eyes, although glazed by tears of defeat, were ablaze like pools of fire, and with Francois and George just ignoring the giant and me having been rendered incapable of speech, he walked two steps in my direction and repeated his poten-tially painful missive. 'I JUST WANT TO FUCKING HIT SOMEBODY!'

FLATS – I take it you soiled yourself, as per?

DURDERS – Not quite. Fortunately, Cobus the Barbarian must have sensed what was about to take place in my Y-fronts and he decided to spare me. He just stomped into the corner, screamed for a while, and tore the legs off some pass-ing cows. It took the edge off the result a bit, to be honest. I'm not big on fear. Never have been. Okay, it's your turn.

FLATS – As your story ends with you being set upon by a giant South African flanker and almost pooing your pants, which could, by some, be construed as being a 'Worst Day' experience, I'm going to carry on in that vein, if you don't mind.

DURDERS – Worst days first?

FLATS – That's it. It'll give us something to look forward to at the end. One of my first worst days in rugby happened when

I was 10 years old and rendered me believing that my young life was coming to an end. I was playing for Maidstone down in Kent and the match in question was against New Ash Green. The pitch, such as it was, was carrying enough surface water to drown a Tyrannosaurus Rex and these days I doubt we'd have played on it. We did, though, and half-way through the first half I got caught at the bottom of a ruck. The fly-half, who I remember being called Scott, got tackled and he landed on my head. The first thing I thought was that he'd crushed my head and broken my nose, which fortunately he hadn't. I then realised that I couldn't get my head out of the puddle I was lying in – face down.

I'm not sure how long I was in there, but it was enough time for me to inhale at least a pint of pitch water. I remember thinking, *Oh my God, I'm actually going to die, and I'm only 10!* When I was finally extracted from the puddle, I was barely conscious. My mate, Tom Ratchford, got me up and gave me what I now realise was a version of the Heimlich manoeuvre. 'Come here,' he said while standing in front of me, and after picking me up and gripping me as hard as he could around the guts and chest, I spewed a load of dirty pitch water all over his neck and face. 'That's better,' he said. He saved my life that day, no doubt about it. Incidentally, Tom became a bouncer in Maidstone a few years later and one night someone bit his ear off.

DURDERS – Thank God for Saint Tom the Earless. I mean, where would the world be without David Flatman?

FLATS – Unfortunately, Kent Schools had no problem envisaging that particular dystopian scenario, which brings me on to my second worst day. They decided not to pick me one day for the Under-16s and I remember thinking it was the end of the world. The trouble is, so did my parents, so there wasn't a lot of joy to be had in our house that day. The same thing happened to me a few years later when I got dropped from the England Under-21s team. I was devastated. Afterwards, one of the coaches, whose name I forget, pulled me to one side and said, 'Mate, who cares? It's only the Under-21s. You'll be playing for Saracens first team next week in the Premiership.' I thought to myself, *My God, he's absolutely right. Wake up and smell the coffee, you arse.*

DURDERS – Any idea why you were dropped? Fitness issues? Nutritional discipline? General lack of skill and ability?

FLATS – Herein lies a tale. We were playing against Ireland away as we were awarded a penalty 10 yards out. Alex Sanderson, our captain, said to me, 'Can we push them over?' and I said, 'Not from this far out, mate!' Anyway, at half time I got subbed off and when I asked why, they claimed it was because I'd bottled it on that scrum. I said, 'I didn't bottle it. It was 10 yards out. Nobody's ever pushed anyone over from 10 yards out. And besides, you're only meant to push a metre and a half, aren't you?' 'Don't care,' they said. 'You bottled it, so you're out.' I did actually get picked again a game or two later, but at the time I was almost inconsolable.

DURDERS – Were you always the last kid to be picked for the school playground game of football? I've no doubt you were popular, but I can't imagine you were ever mistaken for Billy Elliot. You know the kind of thing, 'Oh go on then, we'll have Flatman.'

FLATS – Funny you should mention that. I was once on a

shortlist of 11 kids who'd been picked to play in a football tournament for our school, except only 10 could go – nine players and a substitute. I'd have been about 11 or 12 years old and the final place was going to go to either me or a mate of mine called Dean Martin.

DURDERS – Not *the* Dean Martin?

FLATS – Yes, my mate Dean was a septuagenarian crooner, a womaniser, a chronic alcoholic, a heavy smoker and a former member of the Rat Pack. Anyway, because there wasn't much between us talent-wise, the coach, who also happened to be Dean's dad, suggested we toss a coin for it and I ended up winning. Dean didn't seem to mind much, but his dad wasn't happy and when it came to the tournament he refused to bring me on for any of the games. Not even for a minute. I was the only kid in the entire tournament who didn't get to play and I remember thinking afterwards that if I ever got the chance I was going to mangle that prick.

DURDERS – So you're the notorious Prick Mangler of Maidstone?

FLATS – In the flesh. The opportunity to mangle this particular prick never arose during football practice, but halfway through a game of British Bulldog one day, which took place in the park and in which Dean's dad was taking part, I saw my chance. After he attempted to dodge me, I ended up spear-tackling him and then followed through with an elbow in the face. A friend of my dad's lost the plot with me and, after picking me up by the neck and shaking me, he threw me from the field of play. My neck hurt but I didn't care. The prick had been well and truly mangled and all was well with the world. I was thinking about this just the other day and remembered that Dean's dad was actually a gunsmith! Not only that, but a few months later he stuck up for us when an irate motorist tried to destroy a bike ramp that me and Dean were using. I remember feeling quite guilty at the time.

DURDERS – Is there something you'd like to say to Mr Martin, David?

FLATS – Sorry, Mr Martin.

DURDERS – My own playing days were obviously a lot more glittering than yours but as children we could well have been on the same path to greatness. My own first memorable 'worst day' was when my dad stopped a game once. I too would have been about 10 or 11 years old. Then, having been tackled round the head by a brutish member of the oppo, my dad and a friend of his charged onto the field of play and demanded that the referee stop the match. My God, it was embarrassing. 'It's okay, Dad,' I said, trying to reassure him while lying spreadeagled in the middle of the field. 'I'm fine!' 'You shut up, Markie,' he said. 'This has got nothing whatsoever to do with you. Referee, I DEMAND that you stop this game immediately so that my son can receive some attention!' I certainly received attention, but not of the medical variety.

Speaking of my lovely father, Neil the Deal, having been a sports producer and sports broadcaster, knew a few people in the industry, and I remember playing for Durham in my final year, against Cambridge. (I only made it into the team in my final year as I'd taken the captain and my mate on holiday in the previous summer, so I guess he felt that to pick me was the least he could do – decent sort, that Keeyman.) Anyway, I had the usual shocker being way out of my depth, as I was, and the next day there was a small report in *The Telegraph* in which the Durham full-back was painted as Mike Brown on steroids. I think the report might even have featured the words 'lightning fast' to describe my movement on the pitch. I was never anything but deceptively slow – that was my genius. I remember reading it thinking, *Bloody hell, father – did you dictate that to your mate the* Telegraph *journalist? What the hell have you done to me?* A couple of weeks later I was playing another game for Durham and at the end of the match, as we walked back to the Maiden Castle changing rooms, I overheard one of the oppo say to his mates, 'I thought that Durden-Smith bloke was meant to be brilliant. He was shit!' They'd obviously read the slightly embellished write-up. The short-lived myth was well and truly shattered that day. I've never recovered. The self-esteem has never been the same.

FLATS – I remember being in the tunnel at Kingsholm. I'd just played for Bath against Gloucester and as I was standing there I saw a woman I recognised. It was only from a social event or something, but she was definitely familiar. It ended up being Trevor Woodman's girlfriend, who I'd met at a couple of parties. Anyway, they were going to be announcing the England squad for the next Test the following day and just as Trevor was walking past us in the tunnel I said, 'Poor old Trev had a shocker today. There's no way they can pick him for England. What a joke!' He'd actually played brilliantly and might even have been Man of the Match. When Trev walked off, his girlfriend said to me, 'As long as they don't pick Leonard or Flatman, I don't care. They're both such wankers.' I said, 'I agree completely. Good evening to you.'

I've also got a worst-day story with a confrontational theme. I was 24 years old and about to start my 100th game in the Premiership. I was playing for Bath, by the way, and the game was against Saracens. Until then, nobody in the front row had ever seen me off, so to speak. I'd certainly had a few bad days but, without wanting to sound conceited, I was as good as pretty much everybody I played against in the Premiership. During this game I ended up diving on a ball at the back of a line-out and when I landed my shoulder came out of its socket. It's called a subluxation and I seem to remember it smarting somewhat. Even so, when the physio came running over we had different ideas as to what should happen next. 'You've got to come off, Flats,' he said. 'It's come out.' I looked him in the eyes. 'That's not going to happen,' I replied resolutely. 'I'm out of contract next year and have been injured for most of this season. If I come off now, I'm finished.' Against the physio's wishes, I ended up staying on but about five minutes after the incident Saracens brought on Cobus Visagie.

DURDERS – Cobus the Barbarian? Oh my God! Why do you have to bring my worst nightmare into the conversation again? You're a heartless bastard.

FLATS – Grow up. Anyway, you'll have to pardon my French, but he gave me an absolute fucking hammering. I conceded my first-ever pushover try. It was awful. These days props get hammered all the time, but back then it was different. I'd played Test matches on top of my 100 Premiership games and, genuinely, it had never happened before. Unfortunately, the effect it had on me was far-reaching and it played on my mind pretty consistently for a good while.

All I could think about, in addition to what had happened, was the corresponding fixture against Saracens. It seemed like my only way out, as it would give me an opportunity to atone for what had happened and basically exact some revenge. About a week before the fixture, I got a niggle in my back. I remember saying to the doctor that I would rather slip a disc afterwards and never play again than miss the upcoming fixture. The coaches wanted to rest me for a week and even told my replacement that he'd be playing instead. 'Then you'd better un-tell him,' I said when they informed me. 'I'm coming to training and if you haven't told him, I'm going to make sure he can't play. Then you'll have to play me.' This had been my life for the best part of a year and although there was no guarantee that I wouldn't be humiliated again, it was my only chance of peace.

DURDERS – What happened?

FLATS – I played, I stood firm, and the ghost was finally exorcised. It was redemption. I played against Cobus a few more times after that, most of which were quite even, but during our final battle I probably won on points. It wasn't the hammering he gave me, not by any stretch of the imagination, but it was a satisfying finish. Quite cleansing really.

DURDERS – You're my hero. That's a lie for avoidance of doubt. Now, I know we haven't got onto the best days yet, but I'll wager they won't be anywhere near as easy to recall as the bad ones.

FLATS – I remember the negative anecdotes, such as the one I've just recalled, infinitely more clearly than I do the happier ones. This might sound melodramatic, but one of the reasons I didn't enjoy the good days as much is because I was often preoccupied with the bad ones. Not to the point where I obsessed about them (or at least not all of them), but enough to hinder me appreciating the good times as much as I should have. John Connolly, who was our director of rugby at Bath and who went on to become head coach of the Wallabies, said to me one day, 'When you retire, Flats, it's mainly a blur, but you'll have crystal-clear memories of the worst days of your career.' At the time I probably had an idea he was right but now I know that he was absolutely on the nail. It's a shame really. I don't care, but it's a shame.

DURDERS – It's exactly the same for us amateurs, of course. The only thing I remember from my playing days with the same kind of clarity is when I missed a kick for our school one day. We were playing one of our main rivals, Wellington College, who we hadn't beaten away in 11 years, so the pressure was enormous. The reason I was doing the kicking in the first place was that at the end of practice one day a friend of mine, Westie, now known as Drill-Bit (long story), bet me a pint of cider that I couldn't kick a ball over from the touchline. The wind effectively picked up an off-course kick and it went over. Unfortunately, our brilliant coach, Peter Johnson, had witnessed this feat of sporting genius and there and then he decided I would become our place kicker. Three games and some very haphazard kicking later, my moment to be elevated to godlike status arrived: the kick that would secure Radley's first win at Wellington for 11 years. I'd be hoisted aloft, carried on the shoulders of adoring and grateful peers all the way back to OX14 2HR.

FLATS – Get to the point, waffleboy.

DURDERS – The kick was right in front of the posts. One swing of my admittedly spindly leg, a clean connection, and I'd be loved for ever. The grass at Wellington was really long and I'd done what I thought I'd seen Jonathan Webb do hundreds of times – I'd dug my heel into the turf and created a dent so the ball would sit upright. I remember thinking it looked a little odd as the grass was so long I could only see the top third of the ball. I should really have done something about that – but that's how Jonathan Webb did it, I thought, so it's good enough for me. Anyway, looking back, it had disaster written all over it. With the crowd hushed, and the away supporters primed for a triumphant pitch invasion, I kicked the ball at its highest peak and sent it skimming along the grass. The humiliation! This next bit isn't going to win me any fans, but I was also head boy of my school at the time. Being the born loser I am, I'd actually stayed on a term to have my Biden moment.

FLATS – That is truly tragic. Were you not consoled by your team-mates?

DURDERS – Not exactly consoled. Quite a few of my disgruntled team-mates lit up a cigarette in the changing rooms afterwards, knowing full well that as head boy I would get the blame. And I did. The smoke was pouring under the dressing-room door and before you could say Benson and bloody Hedges a detachment of teachers came charging into the changing room. I'd been pleading with them to stop but they obviously wanted to punish me.

FLATS – What did you get. The cane? The slipper? A ruddy good talking-to? Did they spank at Radley?

DURDERS – It wasn't *Goodbye Mr Chips*, you gargantuan buffoon. No, just a whole heap of shame and embarrassment, of the eternal variety. A few years later I managed to better that by dropping a ball behind the posts while playing for Durham University's third team. Had I managed to hold on to it we would probably have reached the final at our level for the first time in over 20 years. I came, I dropped, they scored, they won. Another hefty dose of self-loathing and crippling embarrassment.

FLATS – There appears to be a bit of a running theme with these stories of yours.

DURDERS – Incompetence? Yes, you're right. There's no escaping it.

FLATS – We could probably claim this about the majority of subjects we're covering in our tome, but we could fill an entire book with 'worst day' stories. I've actually got a 'worst week' story, if you'd like to hear it.

DURDERS – Does it involve any level of incompetence on your part?

FLATS – No, sorry. If I can add any, though, I will. I'll also keep it brief. I forget what year it was, but I'd been picked to play for England A against France A. Not an easy game, as I'm sure you can imagine. The match was taking place on a Friday, I remember, and we were flying out from Manchester on the Thursday, having gathered at a hotel on the previous Sunday. On Monday morning after breakfast we had to hand in our passports, except I couldn't find mine. I'm usually pretty good when it comes to keeping forms of identification safe, but on this occasion I appeared to be lacking. 'But we need you to play,' said the manager. 'Sorry,' I said. 'I messed up.' After making some calls, one of the administrators told the manager that if I hightailed it to the passport office in Liverpool they should be able to sort me out in a few hours, so off I went. Providing they were correct, I would only miss a few hours of training. I ended up spending the whole of Monday and the whole of Tuesday at the passport office, which infuriated the coaches. Monday and Tuesday were our two training days and, although I wasn't present, they'd committed to playing me by sending me off to the passport office.

In an attempt to ingratiate myself with the coaches even more, I ended up missing the internal flight from Charles de Gaulle to Toulouse on the Thursday, having been distracted by a large hot chocolate and a selection of pastries. Andy Sheridan and Josh Lucy were complicit in the transgression and, while most of England A and our 'entourage' (a timely bit of French there) were in a minibus ready to be taxied to the plane, we three were in a café enjoying a massive sugar rush and putting on a few pounds. Seconds before the minibus set off, Jed Glynn, our coach, who speaks fluent French, managed to persuade the driver to let him off so he could go back into the terminal and grab us. The driver let him off and he managed to get back in and, after finding his three erstwhile players, he asked to be let back out again. '*Non*,' said the attendant, who'd obviously run out of patience, '*Ils ne partent pas, et vous non plus*,' which means 'They're not going, and neither are you.' That's right, the head coach wasn't allowed to fly. Needless to say, Monsieur Glynn was not *un lapin heureux* and we ended up having to catch a flight about eight hours later. We missed the team meeting and, worse still, the evening meal.

The period between being sent to our rooms and the match went reasonably well, on account of the fact that we were in our rooms and, save for us either trashing them, slipping on the bathroom floor, or coming down with an incurable disease, nothing could really go wrong. Seventy minutes into the match, normal service had resumed when I decided that, in our own 22, an over-the-top basketball pass was going to be just the thing to get us out of trouble. To be fair, had it not been for the towering Yannick Jauzion, who is about 6ft 5in and has arms like an orangutan, I might just have got away with it. As it was, he just plucked it out of the air, trotted under the posts and scored the winner.

DURDERS – Hang on, you told me there was no incompetence in this story. It is riddled with it!

FLATS – You shouldn't believe everything you're told, should you? Anyway, after losing us the match, I was then drugs-tested and after donating a sample of urine I discovered that the team bus had left without me. I then had to call Monsieur Glynn, who it's safe to say wasn't my biggest fan, and ask them to come back for me, which they did. That night we had a few beers, as you do, and after forgetting to alter my alarm clock to French time, I missed the team recovery session. I never, ever used to miss training or recovery sessions, but while the lads were all out 'recovering', I was in bed watching telly and feeling nice and relaxed.

When I finally went downstairs at what I thought was

9 o'clock but was in fact 10, the first thing I saw were the lads walking into the hotel looking knackered. As if things couldn't get any worse, straight after breakfast I rang my parents, who were supposed to have been at the match. 'Where the hell were you?' I asked my dad. 'Oh, we were there,' he said. 'But your mother's appendix burst halfway through the first half and I had to rush her to hospital.' *What the . . .?!* Fortunately she was okay, but at the time I genuinely thought I'd been cursed or something. Fast-forward three days and a letter arrives for me at Saracens from France Rugby which I can't read because it's in French. After locating Thomas Castaignède and asking him to translate, he kindly informed me that I'd been banned from playing in France for two years after failing a drugs test. My asthma inhaler had a steroid in it, but we'd declared that, so I didn't know what the issue was. I hadn't injected heroin into my testicles for weeks.

DURDERS – So, let me get this straight. First you lose your passport, then you ensure that you, two of your colleagues and the head coach all miss your connecting flight before losing England A the game and then asking the team coach to come back and get you because you've been urinating into a bottle. You then miss the following morning's recovery session before finding out that your mum's appendix burst while watching you play, and to top it all off you receive a two-year ban from France Rugby for failing a drugs test. That is literally untrumpable. What happened about the drugs test?

FLATS – Fortunately Clive never picked me again so it never became an issue. I served my time and moved on.

DURDERS – So you're the Justin Gatlin of English rugby?

FLATS – Indubitably. How about our worst day presenting the highlights show? I think we're both agreed on that one.

DURDERS – Are we? I think your worst day would have been turning up at Exeter Chiefs to find the hog roast counter under that stand at the end of Sandy Park was closed. You were like a child running down to the Christmas Tree on Christmas Day morning to find no presents. My worst day on the other hand was the day it took us 68 takes to record what is literally a seven-take television programme. I blame the sub-zero temperatures. Our brain tissues must have frozen, so it wasn't our fault. Our poor cameraman – was it Jamesy, Hydey or Herdy that day? They sound like pet squirrels . . . Whichever of this fab three it was, I remember they couldn't feel their fingers. We must have taken a vow of ineptitude the night before or something. It reminds me of the time I was presenting top-flight Spanish football La Liga for Sky Sports and after a half-hour build-up to this key game, I threw to the break: 'It's a pivotal contest in the context of this season. Coming up after the break it's . . .' and I completely forgot the name of the two clubs playing. I knew it was Sporting something against Real something – so I went for 'Heehon' spelt Gijon and 'Thotheeeodad' spelt Sociedad. My pronunciations were awesome. I could have been mistaken for Penelope Cruz. The only negative: neither team were playing.

FLATS – I pronounced the word hyperbole 'hyper-bowl' six times during a show once and I was hammered for it on social media. I tried to persuade the haters that I was referring to a new American Football tournament, but they were having none of it. I suppose we'd better do 'best days' now. Let's keep it short, though. I take it you don't have many?

DURDERS – Surely you mean 'any'? I do have one from my school days – I seem to keep harping on about school days but, tragically, that's when I peaked as a human. It starts off with me crying in front of my housemaster and then moves on to me wishing somebody dead. A touring Welsh side was coming to play my school, Radley, but because Radley wasn't thought to be a strong enough team to take on the Welsh on its own, a combined side was put together with Wellington – inventively called Radwell. I was 18 years old and in the sixth form, and as you can imagine everybody wanted to be in that team. The evening before the match, I rushed up to the notice board where the team sheet was posted, certain that I was going to be full-back. I wasn't. The name Durden-Smith was nowhere to be seen.

At that moment, some mates of mine passed me and I just managed to hold it together. My housemaster, a first-rate schoolmaster (and also father to one of my godchildren, William – work that out) Mike Spens then walked past and, realising I was upset, invited me into his study. 'You must be very upset, Durden-Smith,' he said, but before I could answer the floodgates opened and I bawled my eyes out. That was probably the first proper epic fail of my life – many have followed of course – and the pain I felt afterwards was acute. Almost as acute as the embarrassment my house master must have felt at having a 6ft 1 1/4 inch, 18-year-old full-back crying like a baby in his study – a proper shoulders-heaving, snot-inducing blub.

That night I put a curse on the Wellington full-back who'd been picked for the match (who wasn't called Rupert Wiggin, FYI – a good friend who has spent the last 30 years scandalously and falsely claiming that he was the original pick). But whoever it was, I spent the next two nights praying that some kind of injury would befall him. Nothing serious, of course, but enough to render him unable to play. I genuinely lay there for three nights wishing injury on a perfectly innocent teenager whose only crime was having been considered by some to be a superior full-back to me. The day before the game, the original actually did get injured so I ended up playing. I felt a bit uncomfortable at first, as I believed it was my fault – the curse had obviously worked – but I soon got over that. He was out, I was in; all was well in the world. It was about to get better, though. The match ended up being one of those ones where everything just aligns – and get this, Flats: at the end of the match the touchline supporters could be heard chanting, 'Markie Durden walks on water'. I kid you not. Greatest day of my young life.

FLATS – Naaah, I don't believe that. 'Sinks in water', perhaps? Or 'cries little drops of salty water in front of house masters at very posh schools'.

DURDERS – Not even you can kill the memory of that day. To go from such a low ebb to such a high one was stuff that dreams are made of. You remember I told you about that kick earlier on. The one I fluffed? A couple of games before that, we were playing Marlborough College, who were another of our big rivals, and I had another penalty this time to draw the game. In an attempt to put me off, the Marlburians, who'd finished their games and were now supporting their 1st XV on the touchline behind me, started blowing raspberries as I took the kick. I love a raspberry. Big fan of the whoopee cushion, so it had the desired effect. I kicked the ball into a different county. Nowhere near the intended direction of the posts.

'Hang on,' said the referee addressing the phantom raspberry-blowers. 'I heard what you lot were doing. That's unsporting. Not the way things should be done. Take it again, boy.' This time the ball went sailing through the middle of the posts and we drew the game. That must be the only penalty in the history of rugby that had to be retaken because of raspberry-blowing offences.

FLATS – Don't tell me, and they all chanted, 'Markie Durden walks on water'? That's got to be one of the poshest sporting stories I've ever heard. Right, it's my turn. In terms of rugby, the best day was playing against Argentina in 2002.

DURDERS – Get you. Argentina, hey? Are you deliberately trying to belittle me after I've just bared my sporting soul?

FLATS – I'm just a different level, Marko – suck it up. Anyway, it was a game that we weren't supposed to win, really. France had won the Grand Slam and Argentina had crushed France the week before. We watched that game from the stands thinking, *Holy shit, we're in trouble!* We were also going to be resting a lot of our top players, which is why I was there, and without wanting to sound defeatist or any-thing, we were expected to put up a fight and lose. After all, the Argentinian pack were monstrous.

Alongside me in the England team were Steve Thompson, Ben Kay, Phil Vickery, Alex Codling and Charlie Hodgson, to name but a few. I still think Charlie Hodgson's one of the best fly-halves England's had. He was just unlucky to be the same age as Jonny. The match itself was quite low-key in comparison to some other matches, but it meant a huge amount to those who were there and those who were taking part. None more so than me. As a kid I supported Bath (to a point), Toulouse and Argentina, as well as England, of course.

DURDERS – Why Toulouse? Are you descended from a long line of Gallic truffle hunters?

FLATS – Kings of Europe who played the best rugby. Simple as that. They also had amazing props, which is why I also supported Argentina – they had the best props in international rugby at the time. People still talk about Argentina in the same vein, but it's a reputation that is based on former glories. Or should I say, former props. Being Argentinian isn't enough these days and their current crop aren't in the same class.

DURDERS – So the attraction for you with regards to rugby has always been watching front rows doing their thing? How about a side-stepping rugby genius with jet boots playing on the wing, for instance – doesn't that get your rugby juices flowing?

FLATS – Yes, but I could never relate to it in the same way I can the front row. One of my absolute favourite players when I was a kid was Chris Oti, the Wasps and England winger. Every time my dad and I played rugby in the street or in the park, I had to be Chris Oti.

DURDERS – That is a bit incongruous. It takes a significant leap of the imagination to see little bowling ball Flats taking on the persona of an electrifyingly quick and nimble Chris Oti. I would love to have seen that.

FLATS – One day you shall . . . but back to my true love: the props. My favourite prop was a guy called Omar Hasan, who played for – would you believe it? – Toulouse and Argentina. He had a neck like a rhinoceros and was also an opera singer, which impressed me. I got to play against Omar in a pre-season match once. It was only half a game and he wasn't really trying, but his strength was still absolutely Herculean. I remember Steve Thompson asking me about Omar the week before the Test. 'What do you think of him, Flats?' he said. 'Actually, he's my favourite prop,' I replied. 'Oi,' said Thommo. 'Don't you go easy on him just because you love him. We're gonna batter the c**t.' Phil Vickery looked up and said, 'Good luck with that, mate.'

DURDERS – So tell us about the Test. How did it pan out?

FLATS – It's was probably one of the best games I ever played, if not the best. It was similar to your game at school really, in that everything just clicked. A load of posh boys with multiple surnames didn't start chanting my name at the end or likening me to our lord Jesus Christ, but you can't have everything. At some point during the game, I remember seeing an opportunity in the middle of the field, which didn't normally happen. 'Give it me, Chas,' I said to a somewhat shocked Charlie Hodgson, and after he'd passed me the ball I then stepped around Omar Hasan and got the offload away after being tackled, which resulted in Phil Christophers scoring the winning try. I've never watched it back, but it started somewhere around the halfway mark. God, I was good. I had feet like Fred Astaire. My parents flew out for that and every single one of my mother's internal organs remained intact throughout the entire game. As I said, everything just clicked. The England scrum coach,

Phil Keith-Roach, who is a hero to everyone who's ever met him, ran onto the pitch at the end of the game crying his eyes out.

DURDERS – Tears of joy, I assume.

FLATS – Oh, absolutely. You see, we weren't supposed to have survived that game. They had Omar, Mauricio Reggiardo, Freddie Mendez, Roberto Grau. Grau was the world's greatest loosehead prop at the time. They should have marmalised us. Towards the end we even shoved them off the ball in a scrum and gave them a bit of a hiding. I remember after about 60 minutes feeling a little bit battered and thinking, *I am so comfortable here. I love this level of competition. This is exactly where I belong. I'll do anything to stay here.* In order to remain in shape, I even went running on holiday, which is something I'd never done before and have never done since. I thought, I cannot let this moment die.

DURDERS – And did it?

FLATS – Of course it did. I never played for England again. I got a shoulder injury a few weeks later and missed almost the rest of the season. The next thing to go was my Achilles' two seasons later, and then, after missing 20 months, I played a season, did both shoulders, and was out for 10 more. I also snapped my bicep somewhere along the way.

DURDERS – I'm glad we've managed to finish on a high.

Friendship

DURDERS – I can't imagine anybody has played rugby for any length of time and not made friends for life. It's why the players play and why the mums and dads cook bacon butties or go out there and coach. Whether it's behind a trestle table, out on a rugby field or in the stands, friendships are the fulcrum of this sport we love.

FLATS – I notice you said mums *and* dads when it came to the bacon butties and didn't just say dads when it came to coaching. Good move.

DURDERS – Mock on if you wish, but I mean it. Friendship is at the core of what this sport is all about, in fact what all sport is about. The ability to share an experience, get a job done as a collective and then either celebrate together or commiserate together, depending on which way it's gone. There's no greater feeling than standing on a rugby field and freezing your balls off while taking the mickey out of your mates. That's the stuff that nourishes the soul.

FLATS – I am of course in complete agreement. I'm paraphrasing here, but I once heard Gary Neville say something like, 'You can only judge a career on the amount of trophies you've won.' Does that mean my career meant nothing because I only won one European trophy in 14 or 15 years? To Bob and Sue down the road it probably does. And I'm fine with that. To me, that one win of mine represents more than just some silverware, or a gauge for how successful I was. I don't remember the game that won us the trophy. I don't even remember who we played. I don't care.

What I do remember, and what I'm grateful for, is celebrating with my team-mates afterwards. I'm at pains to quote somebody as intellectual and influential as your good self as it'll make me look pretentious, but you hit the nail on the head. Rugby is all about an ability to share an experience, get a job done as a collective and then either celebrate together or commiserate together. I actually think I can better that quote. Get this for a lovely piece of schmaltz – this is going to be used by every loser and also-ran in every sport until the end of time: 'I might not have won many trophies during my career, but I won an awful lot of great friends.' David Flatman, Bath, 2021.

DURDERS – I'm feeling a little queasy.

FLATS – That's the simple truth of it, though. I came out of rugby with one winner's medal and a load of fantastic mates. Mates who I know I'll be close to for life. Unless they find out about my murky past. Anyway. In pro rugby you're together all day five or six days a week and quite often for years at a time. In fact, you probably spend more time with these people than you do your own family, at least for certain parts of the year. Sure, we won some great games and played in some great stadia and in some great parts of the world, but that takes up about 3 per cent of my rugby memory. The other 97 per cent is all about the laughs, the bus journeys, the nights out, the characters, the hotel room pranks and the incessant piss-taking. That, to me, is what it's all about and is where I derived at least half of my enjoyment as a rugby player (the other half coming from the field of play, of course).

Despite all that, I believe rugby likes to think it has a bit of a monopoly on things like bonds and friendships and good team values, etc., which is just not true. One brother-in-law of mine has got mates coming out of his earholes through playing football for Maidstone – many years ago – and supporting Millwall. My other brother-in-law has the same thing through cars and mountain bikes and they've all been mates for 30-odd years. Rugby doesn't have a monopoly on bonding people together, but it is very good at it. As a pro, it's different as you're together all the time so it tends to happen automatically, whereas everything below that, which represents the vast majority of the sport, is because you often go to places with one another that are particularly difficult. It's also about relying on people you know and them coming through for you, and vice versa.

DURDERS – From my own point of view, it was often about letting people down unintentionally and them forgiving you. As I have well illustrated already. Although, if you ask any of my team-mates on that day at Wellington – not one of them has forgiven me. They're all bastards. I think the age you start playing rugby has an awful lot to do with what you get out of it long term, both in terms of forming bonds and friendships, but also in terms of how you play the game. Let me try a canine analogy on you. If you kept a Rottweiler in a cage for 10 years and then suddenly took it out into a field with lots of other dogs, it'd probably result in a bloodbath. Right? Get it out there early, however, and you can teach it when to be playful, when to be submissive, and when to employ its power, etc.

FLATS – I'm not sure I've ever heard you use a dog analogy before. It's a bit weird. I know what you're getting at, though. Rugby is like this wonderful socialisation experiment and it tends to knock the hard edges off you. It also forces you to be humble because anyone can be outplayed and overpowered. It's full of valuable lessons.

DURDERS – So if you'd had an opportunity during your career to sign for a club that could potentially have offered you greater glory, but meant you would have to leave your Bath bosom buddies, would you have been tempted?

FLATS – Good question, and fortunately one that I can answer from first-hand experience. Leicester were in for me at one point and, based on what they went on to achieve after that, I would definitely have won more trophies. Unless having me in the team would have buggered things up, of course, which is always possible. I'm so glad I didn't go to Leicester, though, as all my best friends were people I'd played with in really shit teams, and had I gone to a good one it would have spoiled it.

DURDERS – Remember you talked about going to places with each other that are particularly testing? Well, I once stumbled across the undulating silhouette of a mate of mine losing his virginity in a golf bunker during a rugby tour to Canada. Talk about testing the strength of your friendship!

FLATS – Funny you should mention Canada. I remember seeing an ex-team-mate of mine, who will have to remain nameless, being pursued down a street in a Canadian city during a rugby tour by an Alsatian and a pick-up truck full of incandescent gentlemen, he having jumped out of somebody's hot tub three minutes earlier. He had his shoes and jeans under his arms and he must have been going at least 25mph. I remember some girls were standing at a crossroads and when the Alsatian and the pick-up truck came past them, they said, 'They went that way,' and pointed in the wrong direction. By this time the player in question had gone off-road and was hiding behind some bins.

DURDERS – You seem to know an awful lot about this particular incident. Are you absolutely sure there weren't two players hurtling down a road starkers being pursued by an angry dog and some Canadian rednecks?

FLATS – You've found me out. I knew I hadn't told you this story before and I was attempting to keep myself out of it. I was there, though. We had a great afternoon, I must say.

DURDERS – I take it this was discussed at training the next day?

FLATS – It might have been mentioned in between tactics. But it's situations like these where friendships are formed. Most people will see their friends at weekends and in established social environments such as pubs. We, on the other hand, will see each other in hot tubs that perhaps weren't ours and in which we perhaps shouldn't have been.

DURDERS – We're almost suggesting here that rugby teams are basically friendship groups full of people who all get on like a house on fire and who would lay down and die for one another. But that isn't always the case, is it?

FLATS – No! Well, at least the first part isn't. I played rugby with guys who, if my daughters brought them home, would make me think very seriously about committing homicide.

DURDERS – You mean murder?

FLATS – I mean homicide. Homicide is the killing of one person by another and is a broad term that includes both legal and illegal killings. For example, a soldier may kill another soldier in battle. Murder is when you kill somebody unlawfully. This wouldn't be unlawful on account of them, A, being completely odious, and B, going out with one of my daughters. Rugby has its fair share of average human beings I'm afraid, as have, I'm sure, the vast majority of sports.

DURDERS – Even bowls?

FLATS – All depends on whether it's indoor or crown green. There's a bit more niggle with crown green, or so I've heard. Plus, it's outdoors. The fresh air gets to them. Anyway, what makes the undesirable elements in our sport palatable is respect. Regardless of what they're like as a person, if somebody is prepared to give you everything on a rugby field and be there for you no matter what, how can you not respect them? It wouldn't work the other way around, as in having somebody in the team you like but who doesn't give a shit about the game. No way. You don't have to like everybody you play alongside, but you sure as hell have to respect them. Amateur sport in particular is actually just a vehicle by which we find out what kind of people we are, as well as what kind or people we like and what kind of people we don't like. It's a selection process.

DURDERS – I didn't know we were writing a self-help book, Dr Erasmus Flatman?

FLATS – But some people are beyond help. Aren't they, Mark?

Retirement

DURDERS – Are we limiting this to rugby, because when I was retired (fired) from *I'm a Celebrity . . . Get Me Out of Here! Now!* on ITV2 for being way beyond the target demographic for the channel and looking very silly in skinny jeans – in fact my co-presenters out in Australia, Emma and Matt Willis, got the props department to make a Mark Durden-Smith doll using a huge uncooked turkey for the body and a pair of drumsticks, of the percussion variety, for the legs – that hurt. The firing, not Turkeygate.

FLATS – This is essentially meant to be a rugby book, posh boy. There are lots of different versions of retirement in rugby. You have 18-year-old kids who spend years forgoing their schoolwork in favour of the gym and the rugby field only to get told that they're not good enough. In some ways you're more vulnerable in that situation as you're obviously a lot younger, but at least you have time to fix it. Then you have those who are forced into retirement through injury, like myself, and those who just can't do it any more and are too old.

When I was playing, the average salary would have been

about 80 grand in the Premiership, whereas now it would be about 100 or 120. Depending on where you live, if you earn 120 grand a year for 10 years and you're careful, you can come out of it with, at the very least, a nice home. If you're playing for either Leicester, Newcastle, Sale or Northampton, for instance, that could be an entire street, whereas if you're playing for Bath or the London clubs it'll be, at best, a two-bedroom flat with a courtyard and no parking.

DURDERS – That should get the hate mail flowing nicely, you Southern snob.

FLATS – The point being that, regardless of where you're based, unless you win the lottery or sell some of your children for scientific experiments, you won't be coming out of the game set up for life. I'm excluding international players, by the way. The vast majority of pro rugby players will neither win the lottery, live in a way that will allow them to pay off a mortgage during the lifetime of their career, nor sell their children to science, which will subsequently leave them wondering, in just their mid-thirties, what the bloody hell they're going to do. You go from being an authority on what you do to the opposite at whatever it is you decide to do next, which in itself is a potential problem. And it doesn't matter how confident you are as a human being. That can only get you so far in an alien environment, because ultimately, you still won't know what you're doing. I'm in no way decrying these kinds of jobs, but let's say you're an estate agent, for instance. If you lose your job through no fault of your own in your early to mid-thirties and you're good at it, the chances are you'll be able to find something similar pretty quickly. And it's the same with most jobs. You'll retain your identity, your status, your friends and your financial position. Even if you have to change industries, there's a very good chance you'll be able to find another that you'll be able to transfer at least some of your skills to.

DURDERS – I've never really thought of it in that way, but you're right. Despite being in their thirties, their lives will have been defined by rugby.

FLATS – Abso-bloody-lutely. At the age of 15, I was in the gym on my own five nights a week after school lifting and rowing, trying desperately to get my body in better shape for rugby. It was an obsession and I loved every second of it. That carries on with rugby pros, to some degree at least, until the day you retire, when, all of a sudden, it no longer matters. It might still matter to the pro, of course, but it won't to anyone else. Nobody cares. Actually, that's not strictly true. People still care about your wellbeing, it's just that your reason for being has had a massive chunk taken away from it. You're no longer Joe Bloggs, rugby pro. You're just Joe Bloggs. In addition to that, people have their own shit to deal with so the fact that you're no longer playing rugby for a living and earning good money will be of little or no consequence to them. You simply have to dig in. The Rugby Players' Association do a great job in helping players to adjust and they're always there if you need them. Even so, there'll be an awful lot of suffering that they don't know about.

DURDERS – What more could the RPA be doing?

FLATS – Not a lot, really. They were incredibly pro-active when I was nearing retirement, and couldn't do enough to help. Every time I asked them for or about something, they were there. You have to remember that they're not The Samaritans. There's also a limit as to how aggressive they can be in offering you help. It sounds a bit clichéd, but in order for them to help you, you have to want to be helped. I also think they're an easy target for criticism.

DURDERS – Come on, then. How did you cope after retiring?

FLATS – I was one of the lucky ones, in the sense that I went straight into a job that was well paid. I still found it very hard, though, as I was doing something that I didn't enjoy and had no sense of purpose. Perhaps I'd been spoiled but for over 10 years I'd been paid handsomely for doing something I loved and had always worked hard at it. I didn't love this new job, far from it. In fact, one of the things that scared me the most after retirement was the thought of never doing something I loved for a living again. I had 30 or 40 years of work ahead of me and I kept on asking myself, what on earth am I going to do? Just to get a sense of perspective, some people absolutely breeze through to retirement, so it's not all doom and gloom. I was probably somewhere in the middle.

DURDERS – I'm not sure if this is correct, but I'd assume that footballers have it slightly easier, in the sense that they will have earned a great deal more money. At least the ones playing in the top two divisions. It's not an exact science, of course, but that's what you'd expect. How about the guys from Saracens who set up their own brewing company, or Olly Kohn from Harlequins, who started making sausages with his brothers? Having something already in place must be the best option to help ease the transition at the end of a career.

FLATS – Yes, it must be. But the thing is, if it's a start-up company, you're taking a big risk. It's not going to pay out immediately, is it? If at all. That said, I expect it provides a new sense of identity, which must be nice. One of my biggest mistakes was not confronting beforehand what was going to happen, which meant I didn't prepare. I'm an expert at burying my head in the sand and that's the worst thing you can do. I don't know if it's true or not, but if I were a betting man I'd say that's probably quite a common trait. It got to a point where I was wondering whether or not I'd have to sell my house for the simple reason that I'd failed to address what was happening. I actually remember telling people that I hadn't expected it and they all said, 'Why not?'

DURDERS – I suppose that can befall anybody really, can't it? I once messed up the negotiations of a proposed move from ESPN to BT Sport and went from thinking I was going to have a four-year contract in the bag to absolutely nothing. It was terrifying. Out of sheer desperation I almost did an Olly Kohn and started my own company. I wasn't going to make sausages, though; I was going to have my own rotisserie chicken van.

FLATS – You're taking the piss?

DURDERS – I most certainly am not. That was my great idea, to have vans selling rotisserie chickens throughout the land.

FLATS – Cock-U-Like?

DURDERS – Remind me not to employ you in my marketing team. They were going to be like ice cream vans, but instead of playing appalling versions of 'Half a Pound of Tuppenny

Rice' through an awful tannoy, I was going to play chicken noises instead. *Cluck, cluck, cluck, cluck*, etc. 'Here comes the rotisserie chicken man! Quick, Mum, can I have a five-pound note?' Genius. I did actually go as far as asking the council about it, but was told that carrying hot coals in the back of a van wouldn't be a good idea. Or even a legal one.

FLATS – It *was* Cock-U-Like then, as in the idea was cock.

DURDERS – Can you drop this cock thing please? It's unbecoming and my mother will be reading this. I'd been a freelancer all my working life and this was the first time I'd been faced with a prolonged period of unemployment. I became the desperate entrepreneur. I also spent a few months with a friend trying to get his idea called The Flying Grocer off the ground. We never managed take off.

FLATS – I'd give *Dragons' Den* a wide berth if I were you.

DURDERS – In all seriousness, as a trustee of a mental health charity, The Charlie Waller Trust (set up after one of my greatest mates and one of the very best people took his own life in 1997), which I have been for a number of years, those transitional periods in people's lives, like moving from school to university or from one job to another, can be so precarious and so damaging. My advice would be to focus on the smaller things more, which often act as a reminder that there's more to life than just the issues dominating our thoughts, such as work. Or lack of it.

Anyway, what did you miss about being a pro? Or should I say, what *didn't* you miss?

FLATS – The things I didn't miss are probably the things you think I did, such as the camaraderie, running out in front of big crowds, tours and actually playing.

DURDERS – I'm not sure what you did was technically called 'running'. More like rapid waddling. But are you seriously telling me you didn't miss running out in front of big crowds? I'd have thought that would have been one of the first things you'd miss. A huge weekly adrenaline shot?

FLATS – Honestly, they were never cheering for me anyway. They were cheering for Butch James and Olly Barkley. That's not to say I didn't enjoy it, though. I did, the same as I enjoyed the camaraderie. They were just never my motivation. Not at all.

DURDERS – Did you get to the point where you weren't actually enjoying playing any more? And, if so, that must have had an effect on you.

FLATS – Absolutely. It was massive. It made the decision to retire easier, but it didn't help the overall situation. I still identified as being a rugby player, and always had.

I used to absolutely love training, and the only aspect I didn't like about it was the repetitiveness. As Axl Rose from Guns 'N Roses once said when describing how bored he gets on tour, despite having thousands of women who want to sleep with him, 'When there's always biscuits in the tin, where's the fun in biscuits?'

DURDERS – I would never lose the love of a biscuit – I'm talking Oat Flips or an orange Club. Did he really say that?

FLATS – No, of course he didn't. Shall I tell you what I used to do to keep myself on my toes? I used to buy cars that I couldn't afford. Seriously. I'd go out and buy one and then shit myself because I couldn't afford it. The problem is that when you're a pro sports person you do not have permission to be bored or uninspired. Nor do you have permission to operate at 93 per cent. People don't like it when you admit that it happens, but we're only human. Well, ish. Anybody can get bored and anybody can have an off day. Then you have the travel, of course. Look at Marcus Trescothick. He got hammered by some people when he went home from that tour to India back in 2006, but it turned out he'd had a nightmare. Some people are fine spending months and months away from their homes and loved ones and doing the same boring shit day in, day out, but some people aren't. In Trescothick's case, it had obviously been bubbling away for a while, and it's hardly surprising. The boredom's bad enough, but if you also have to leave your family and your home for six months of the year it'll affect you all the more. Or at least it might. I couldn't have done that. Not for as long as cricket players do. It's ridiculous.

DURDERS – So game participation, which is ultimately why you're there, doesn't fully compensate?

FLATS – To some people it will and to some it won't, which is why you have to treat sports people as individuals. Don't get me wrong, it can be a great life being a professional sports person and I feel privileged to have managed to be one for over a decade. You have to take care of yourself, though, especially these days.

DURDERS – Quick question. Before you took that job after retirement, did you ever consider doing a Victoria Pendleton and becoming a jockey or something?

FLATS – A jockey?! Funnily enough, no. Elephant racing might have worked. I'd have had to move to India and that would never have worked. I did take a few Brazilian jiu-jitsu lessons once which I thought I could get into. I even spoke to the coach about it, but my shoulders let me down – again. I assume your version of this would be dressage or three-day eventing?

DURDERS – I'd consider anything that earned me a few guineas and prevented me from driving around London in a van selling dead poultry. What would you have been, by the way, if you hadn't become a rugby player? I'd have become a barrister, or I'd have at least tried. Wearing a nice wig, questioning people, and putting down the bad guys. Who was the really dour one from TV? John Thaw played him.

FLATS – Kavanagh QC?

DURDERS – That's the one. I didn't want to be anything like him. I wanted to be dynamic and effervescent. Like a legal David Hasselhoff. My school even arranged for me to do some legal work experience. It was sent to a man called Mr Page. He sat me down in front of a pile of case papers on the first day and said that if I wanted to be a lawyer I'd need to understand every page of what's in front of me. I started quite brightly, but after two days I'd changed my mind and wanted to become a stripper. When I'd finished, Mr Page came in and asked me to list five key points from the case, which I did.

He then asked me to remind him who I was, which was a bit strange. 'I'm Mark Durden-Smith, Mr Page,' I said. 'My school sent me to do some work experience.' 'That's funny,' he said. 'I wasn't expecting anybody.' I'd spent two days in his office after telling him I wanted to become a barrister and he hadn't even bothered to ask me where I was from. I assumed he knew. 'Are you sure it's not Mr Page the barrister you want? I'm Mr Page the solicitor.' I'd spent two days with the wrong person. Apart from not having the intellectual capability or the desire to read thousands of books and bits of paper, I think I could have been an amazing barrister.

FLATS – In hindsight I would have had to do something physical, I think, although that wasn't the plan. Had I not become a rugby pro I was going to go to Durham to read English, or should I say, read some English, and then go to London and become a psychologist like my dad. I find human behaviour and the human mind fascinating, and it was kind of nailed on really. Or at least an attempt to become a psychologist was. What might have scuppered the plan was a very short attention span and a reluctance to study, which I expect is a prerequisite when it comes to, erm, studying. My verbal IQ is probably fine, but when it comes to retaining information I'm subnormal.

DURDERS – I have a hypothetical question for you. Had you become a psychologist, which player, who you either played with or against would have spent most time on your psychologist's couch?

FLATS – Julian White keeps himself very much to himself and spends his entire life surrounded by animals, but I think that soothes him. He's got a beef farm now in Leicestershire somewhere.

Julian's probably the last person who needs help. He knows exactly who he is and he knows exactly where he wants to be. I think there's no point in speculating as to which players in a rugby team would need the most psychiatric help, because these things don't pick and choose, do they?

DURDERS – Here's another question for you then. If you'd known as much about mental health when you retired as you do these days, might you have done anything differently?

FLATS – The first thing I need to ask myself is what kind of state my mental health was in when I retired, and to be honest it wasn't good. The first couple of years, especially, were very hard and had I been more aware of what might have been going on with my mental health I'd have gone to see a doctor, definitely. I'd have told them that I don't feel fulfilled by the job I'm doing and that I can't understand why I'm not enjoying being a parent of two young babies. I'd also have asked them why I felt so stressed all the time and why I always assumed that everything I was doing was wrong. I couldn't see the good in anything or anyone at the time, least of all me. Fortunately that didn't last very long and once I quit the job things started to improve. In fact, you came to my rescue.

DURDERS – I was about to mention that. There you have it, ladies and gentlemen, if you're ever looking for somebody to blame for David Flatman having made the transition from head of communications at Bath Rugby Club to rugby presenter and commentator, look no further than yours truly.

FLATS – It's true. Seriously, though, that first job presenting the highlights show on ITV4 was a massive shot in the arm for me. ITV could have chosen anybody. There were a few former England captains up for the job and they all did a screen test. I didn't. Being chosen above people like that, whose pedigrees both on and off the pitch would have been more impressive than my own, gave me the confidence I needed to quit the job I was doing and try to forge a career doing something I enjoyed. It was a massive risk, though. As I just said, I had very little experience as a presenter and commentator, and had it gone tits up I'd have been left with less than nothing.

DURDERS — It's such a shame it didn't work out. You could always apply to be the man at the bottom of the Cirque du Soleil human pyramid. Or an elephant trainer. Or the elephant.

FLATS — I actually believe that I'm quite good at what I do. I'm not the best by any means, but I'm improving. Just as importantly, at least from my own point of view, I absolutely love it. Best job in the world, mate.

DURDERS — You know I don't like the word mate, mate. It's lazy. And though it pains me to compliment somebody whose ego is so frighteningly vast, I have to admit that when we first worked together on ESPN it was like a breath of fresh air. You hadn't long since retired as a player and in addition to being quite original of thought, together with your rugged good looks and your ability to eat quite literally your own body-weight in venison, you were also still very close to the game. Which is why, when the powers that be at ITV4 asked me who would get my vote to be the pundit, I said Flatman gets my vote. Don't get me wrong, as a human being you're quite reprehensible and odious, but I do respect you as a pundit.

FLATS — I wish I could say the same.

Perks of the Job

DURDERS – The reason I've decided to introduce a chapter on perks is because my beefy colleague here, David Luke Flatman III Jnr, is even more adept at procuring them than I am at fluffing my lines, which is quite a feat. He is the undisputed heavyweight champion of the freebie. My interest is born purely out of envy, by the way. Anyway, where did it all start? How did you become the Artful Dodger of the digital age?

FLATS – Are we talking blags in general or just in my capacity as a sporting and broadcasting superstar?

DURDERS – I think we'll stick with just the latter, if that's okay, or the Trade Descriptions police may be having a word.

FLATS – Well, the first time I realised that free stuff was better than expensive stuff was when my first-ever agent gave me his car to drive. I was in my first year at Saracens and must have been complaining that I didn't have a car. 'Don't worry,' he said. 'You can have mine. My wife and I have two cars and I can use hers.' He then gave me his little

Rover 200 to use for as long as I wanted. I must have had it for the best part of a year. He did that out of pure kindness, by the way. There was nothing in it for him.

DURDERS – Apart from having you as a client, of course. Worth your weight in sawdust.

FLATS – As I said, there was nothing in it for him. I love that guy and we've remained close ever since. He's not my agent any more. He's useless. But he's a great guy and he knows everything about poor-quality British hatchbacks. Fast-forward 20 years and I'm just in the process of specking up my new Land Rover. Truly, this is the best day of my year. Might even go full knob and get a private plate.

DURDERS – What will it be, then? AR5E 1?

FLATS – You're just jealous.

DURDERS – I've already admitted that. I don't know if you remember this, but we once turned up to work and you confessed to me that you hadn't bought a single thing you were wearing. You went bottom up, so from the shoes, to the socks, to the pants, to jeans, to the belt and to the shirt. You'd even blagged your accessories, for crying out loud! I was literally green with envy. The shirt was from Joules, I think, and the gloves were from Caspar. The bag was from Aspinal. That was nice actually.

FLATS – I've still got it somewhere. I might give it to you. Like a hand-me-down. Actually, why don't I do that? When I've finished with all of my endorsements, or when they're replaced, I'll hand them on to you.

DURDERS – You're the gift that keeps on giving. That's in addition to being the gift that keeps on being given to.

FLATS – It's nice to give something back occasionally.

DURDERS – I haven't finished yet. In addition to your attire and accessories being FOC (free of charge for those not familiar with blaggers' acronym speak), the car you arrived in was a freebie – obviously – as was – wait for it – the diesel in the tank! How the hell did you manage to get free diesel?

FLATS – I can't remember. It must have been true, though. As you know I'm incapable of lying. Come on, you must have been offered some freebies or endorsements over the years. Come to think of it, I can't think of any and I've known you for a while.

DURDERS – I did get given a nice Schöffel–like gilet just before Christmas from a great man called Jimmy Hibbert, who is taking on the Germans with his British gilet company.

FLATS – Ooh, toasty. That was probably just a Christmas present from your wife, though, and they don't count. Anything else?

DURDERS – Years ago I was invited to appear on a TV show called something like *Your Favourite Gadget*. It was on the channel Dave, and I spent a good half an hour espousing the virtues of my most cherished possession, my awesome, dual-speed, dual-action electric toothbrush. Back then they were still quite novel and I was ahead of the game. I was a big, big fan. The fact that a toothbrush could not only brush your teeth for you without you having to try but also tell you when to stop brushing your teeth, and even when you're pressing too hard, was just too much for me to bear. At the end of the show I was presented with a brand new – yes, that's right – a brand new Philips electric toothbrush. They also gave me a perforated plastic banana-shaped container for holding bananas. Anyway, after we'd stopped filming I asked one of the producers what the other guests had been given and she said, 'Last week we had John Cleese on and he got an electric car.' I know Johnnie C and I are at different poles when it comes to celebrity status and global renown, but my balls instantly began to ache with regret.

When the people at Dave rang up and said, 'Hi, Mark, we'd like you to choose your favourite gadget and then come on our show and talk about it,' I had no idea they were going to present me with a new one at the end. Had they done so, I would have made like John Cleese and gone for something with four wheels. Maybe a sit-down lawnmower – even though there may have been a few awkward questions about why I needed one of those for my 3x2-metre patio in Clapham. Why did I go for a *rotating toothbrush*? It still rankles as possibly the greatest regret of my life. I think that tells you all you need to know about my prowess at procuring free stuff. Not only am I backward in coming forward, but even when I'm forward, I'm a bit backward.

FLATS – I see what you did there. Bastardised a popular idiom. Clever.

DURDERS – Aren't you the Imelda Marcos of barbeques?

FLATS – You're misrepresenting me slightly. I'm only part obsequious, oleaginous, freeloading reptile. The other part is a genuine enthusiast. I'll give you an example. This very day

I have been contacted by two brands via Instagram trying to offer me free stuff. The first one asked me if I would like them to send me a few T-shirts and hoodies for me and my kids in return for a couple of posts on Instagram. I said to them, 'That's really kind and you're lovely people, but no thanks. Our drawers are full at the moment.'

DURDERS – Flatman has small drawers. Who'd have thought? So you actually turned down some buckshee apparel?

FLATS – I do it all the time. I told you, I'm really choosy about who I get in bed with. Anyway, a bit later on another brand got in touch and said that they loved my posts on barbequing and grilling and they would like to send me a box of seafood.

DURDERS – In exchange for? A post of you in the buff with a strategically placed clam hiding your delicacies?

FLATS – Nothing. The man who got in touch said there was no obligation to do anything in return. He also said that I'd been really nice to his brother-in-law at an event in Harrogate a few years ago and he'd been meaning to send me something for ages. That one, I said 'yes please' to. Partly because it had a nice story attached to it, but also because I have a genuine interest in the product. I know you joke about me being king of all endorsements, but I honestly don't go looking for them. It just happens. I'll give you another example. When I started posting stuff about barbequing, a company got in touch and asked me if I'd like a grill, and I said yes. Now look at me. I'm already thinking about what I'm going to be cooking on my grill tonight, and how I'll be cooking it. I've also been thinking about the rub I'm going to make to go with some pork shoulder I've got that's being smoked this Thursday. Last week somebody offered me a beautiful new barbeque worth over £4,000 and I had to turn it down.

DURDERS – Why would you do that?

FLATS – Because I just wouldn't use it. I then said as a joke, 'I've got a mate who'd like it,' and they said, 'Okay, we'll take it to him.'

DURDERS – Nothing's arrived yet.

FLATS – I said 'a mate'. It's in the small print.

Brands are looking for two kinds of people. They're looking for superstars who couldn't give a shit about their product but have millions of followers, and they're looking for lesser mortals like me who have far fewer followers but might just develop a genuine passion for what they do. You won't believe this, but I probably turn down – very politely – 70 per cent of the things I'm offered. A few weeks ago a supplements company sent me a message that was clearly just a generic cut-and-paste job that they'd probably sent out to hundreds of people, if not thousands. 'Hi there,' it said. 'We'd really love to work with you.' I don't need protein powder at my age. It was completely the wrong approach, or the wrong approach for me. I only ever accept things from companies that I can either use on a day-to-day basis or that I can sell on eBay. That's my rule when it comes to endorsements and I will not deviate.

DURDERS – Is there anything you're wearing at the moment that you paid for yourself?

FLATS – Yes, my Rolex. I paid for that myself, although I did try and get a discount.

DURDERS – How do you go about trying to get a budget Rolex, for goodness sake?

FLATS – I went to the top, mate. To the top. Zara Phillips, who is obviously a close personal friend of mine and confidante, is sponsored by Rolex, so I decided to give her a call and see if she could sort me out mates rates (or better) with a nice Roller for the arm. Needless to say, she was incredibly gentle in her delivery, but she did suggest politely that I work harder and buy one for myself.

DURDERS – What did you do?

FLATS – I ended up going to a shop in town and buying one, which didn't feel right. What's the point of being mates with Zara Phillips if you can't get free Rolexes? She let me down there. I won't forget.

DURDERS – Elephants never forget, do they? Despite being found wanting in the old affirmation department, I actually think I can make you jealous with one of my perks. As part of a TV series I was recording a few years ago, I had to taste what was then the world's most expensive hamburger. It was in New York and the hamburger cost a mouth-watering $110. Wagyu beef – from the beer-drinking cows – the best truffle oil, the perfect bun. It was amazing.

FLATS – Funnily enough, and this is no word of a lie, before we met up today I ordered something off the internet called the Ultimate Wagyu Burger. It's basically a kit that gets sent to your home with everything you need to make one. It had a quote on the website that said, 'Possibly the best thing I have ever put in my mouth.' That was good enough for me. I also ordered a new pair of jeans this morning and both were paid for using my own money, so up yours.

DURDERS – Send those jeans back – you're going through a mid-life-jeans-too-tight-want-to-look-like-a-member-of-a-boy-band phase. Sorry, that will have been really hard to read but it had to be said.

One line we haven't touched on yet is meeting famous people, or people who we admire. That's a perk, right?

FLATS – Absolutely. I remember going to an event that you were hosting once. You interviewed Prince Harry and because he'd grown a beard you kept taking the piss out of him. You called him Prince Hairy, I think. It was very funny. I remember thinking to myself, *Wow! I'm watching the Queen's grandson being mocked by the son of Judith Chalmers.* It was a privilege.

DURDERS – That was the Sports Industry Awards. A great night. I think I also called him Your Royal Hairiness, which wasn't, apparently, following royal protocol to the letter. I also told him in front of 2,000 people that it was his royal duty to marry Cheryl Fernandez-Versini, as she was then – just Cheryl these days, I think. As it happens, I think he'd just secretly started dating Meghan so the headlines about Cheryl the next day may not have been greeted with great enthusiasm as he was served his kippers and marmalade the next morning. In the fleeting moments I had with him, though, I thought he was a top man, and I was convinced we'd be friends for life but he never calls. Do you ever get nervous or excited meeting famous people?

FLATS – Very rarely. It just doesn't register with me normally.

The only time I can think of where I've been genuinely nervous was when I met Frank Bruno. He was always a big hero in our house and one day I had the pleasure of doing an event with him. I was sitting in the green room beforehand, having a cup of tea, and when he walked in I had butterflies in my stomach. That had never happened to me before and I don't think it's happened since. Better still, Frank was just the loveliest man. They always say you should never meet your heroes, but I disagree. Ricky Hatton walked in a bit later and he was lovely, too. I did an event with Bradley Wiggins the following week who I also admired, and guess what?

DURDERS – Was he lovely?

FLATS – He was! I actually love that side of what we do. Not just meeting famous people, but meeting interesting people.

DURDERS – I would have to concur with you there. In fact, I'd say that's my version of blagging free stuff really. And I'll prove it. If I were offered a free pair of jeans and a new watch or a 15-minute audience with Rebel Wilson, I'd choose the latter.

FLATS – But as a child you must have been surrounded by famous people. The son of Judith Chalmers and Neil Durden-Smith? Come on.

DURDERS – It never seemed that way, although I was obviously a slightly clueless and gormless child. I do have a photo from my dad's 50th birthday party at home, where I'm sitting in the garden on a bench with Eric Morecambe. I don't actually remember it being taken, which is a shame, but I love the photo. In those days the entertainment industry was a lot smaller and far more incestuous, so everyone seemed to know everyone else. My parents were also big supporters of the Lord's Taverners charity, which was quite starry. The only downside to it all was that some people used to confuse my mother with Gloria Hunniford, including me. It's quite disconcerting, that – having two possible options for the role of your mother.

FLATS – I bet it is. Who's Gloria Hunniford?

DURDERS – WHO'S GLORIA HUNNIFORD? Wash your mouth out with soap and water, and novichok while you're at it. Gloria Hunniford is a broadcasting legend and Northern Ireland's premier Judith Chalmers impersonator, although not necessarily in that order. How ignorant are you? What about *The Goon Show*'s Harry Secombe? I know that's a bit retro, and I'm still only 27, but surely you've heard of him?

FLATS – Yes, I think so. My parents were fans of his.

DURDERS – Well, he invited our family to a Sunday lunch party. He was a big star in those days and I remember being quite excited at the prospect of going there. While the adult guests were all getting warmed up prior to lunch a few of us children decided to have a look around the house, and after going upstairs I came across Mr and Mrs Secombe's boudoir. I've always fancied myself as a bit of an adventurer so I boldly set foot in the Secombe bed chamber and there, before my very eyes, was the showbiz equivalent of the Turin shroud – an enormous pair of Harry Secombe's jockey Y-fronts. They were vast. They could have been deployed as a mid-sized wedding marquee. They also contained a little brown streak. I think in modern parlance it might be referred to as a mark akin to a skid.

FLATS — Why can't you just say there was a skid mark in Harry Secombe's undercrackers? What's wrong with you?

DURDERS — I have sensibilities and sadly he's no longer with us to defend himself. He may have used this undergarment to clean up a Nutella spillage after breakfast, we don't know, do we? So I feel compelled to soften the language I use. I don't want to cause offence to the Secombe family.

FLATS — Spare me!

DURDERS — Anyway, as opposed to chucking them on the floor and fleeing the scene, I stood there, showing off to my new friends, holding my trophy aloft, pretending to be sick. 'Errrr! Look at Harry Secombe's manky pants!'

I was only about eight or nine years old at the time and didn't really know who he was. I also had no idea you could get pants in this size, and I'd had very little experience of skid marks. He may have been a Goon and a comedy legend to some people, but to me he was just a nice smiley man who had failed to wipe his bottom properly. Just then, as I was standing by the window still holding aloft the well-soiled thunder crackers, Harry himself walked in the room. Have you ever seen a Welsh entertainer and all-round legend lose his shit with the errant child of a travel presenter and a sports commentator? It's not pretty, believe me. I remember Harry shouting at me very loudly and then snatching away his shreddies. At which point I burst out crying and ran down the stairs shouting, 'I'm sorry, I'm sorry!' I shudder to think what might have happened had I found a pair of Mrs Secombe's harvest festivals or a brassiere.

FLATS — Harvest festivals?

DURDERS — Bloomers. That was a golden era for the Lord's Taverners. I had my first crush on the actress Suzanne Danielle, who was a Taverner. A proper tongue-on-the-floor job. She's married to Sam Torrance now. I felt it should have been me. But what's a chubby 11-year-old got to offer a successful actress of the 1980s? In hindsight I think she made the right decision. One of the first jobs I had after leaving university and doing radio training was as a researcher on *The Clive James Show.* That was one of the best jobs on God's earth as I was basically sent off to meet a lot of very famous people and ask them a few questions. One of the first people I had to go and see was Joan Collins.

FLATS — I knew it! When you mentioned *The Clive James Show* I was just about to make a joke and say, 'Mark, you must tell us about the time you had cocktails with Joan Collins in her New York apartment,' but you beat me to it.

DURDERS — I think she lived in Knightsbridge, actually. Although I don't remember coming across any cocktails while visiting Miss Collins. Clive James was so thorough, though. As was Clive Anderson, who I also researched for. In fact, I worked for anybody called Clive — except Clive Sinclair, who made lie-down electric vehicles — the C5. I didn't work for him. Anyway, for Clive Anderson we not only had to go and meet the week's guests and do a full research interview but we also had to 'be' them in rehearsals so he could work out a few cheeky one liners — the ones he became famous for. I'm pretty sure I was Goldie Hawn for a week.

FLATS — Of course you were.

DURDERS — Well, she definitely came on the show and I

definitely remember being in the Green Room after she'd been interviewed by Clive and I definitely remember falling madly in love with her. I was never more than an average ant's length away from her. 'What a nice interview,' she said. 'He's such a lovely man.' Trying to be humorous, I parried with, 'Oh, you like bald men, do you?' to which she said, 'Oh yes, I love bald men.' I must admit this threw me somewhat, and in an attempt to bring the conversation back to me and her, I said, 'I'm bald.' She looked at me as you would a small child who's let one go in front of the vicar. 'No, I am,' I said. 'Look at me. I'm bald.' There wasn't a hint of irony in my voice and I honestly don't know what possessed me. I had even more hair than I do now. It was probably just a desire to get in her good books.

FLATS – Or her underwear.

DURDERS – Don't sully this memory with your filth. This is true love we're talking about. The following day I was told that Miss Hawn had left her coat in the green room and I was asked to take it to her hotel. My heart literally leapt when I got the instruction. I believed that she'd deliberately left her coat so that I would take it round to her room and that we'd live happily ever after in a beachfront villa in Malibu. Suzanne Danielle would become a distant memory. Truthfully, that's what I thought. Kurt Russell was going to be history and Goldie and I would live out our days together. When I arrived at the reception desk at Goldie's hotel my heart was beating like a drum. 'Good morning,' I said to the receptionist, trying to appear composed. 'I have Miss Hawn's coat. She's expecting me.' The receptionist then rang up to Goldie's room and, after putting the phone down, he said, 'Miss Hawn's PA has asked you to leave it with us.' That was the end of my affair with Goldie Hawn.

I was heartbroken. Truly I was. She led me on and then just cast me aside.

FLATS – Like an old coat. Have you fallen for any other women who were barely aware of your existence?

DURDERS – Oh yes, loads. Princess Diana being one. Clive James was a friend of hers and she came to a recording of his show. I never actually talked to her, but did hover within a metre of her for at least four minutes. That was enough for me to convince myself that her bodyguard was going to whisper in my ear, 'Princess Diana would like you to come back to the palace for crumpets.' Maybe with a knowing wink thrown in. My ears were on high alert to receive said instruction, but it never came. Everyone in that green room that night was totally mesmerised by her cheeky, flirtatious charm, including Stephen Fry, who was one of the guests. Princess Diana had that often-talked-about mischievous twinkle in her eye and was keen to question Stephen Fry about the horse sex scene in the book he'd come on the show to promote, *The Hippopotamus*. A great read, by the way.

FLATS – As much as I'm enjoying hearing these tales, we should really try and pull this back to sport at some point, and even – dare I say it – to rugby?

DURDERS – Do we have to? I'm just hitting my stride. No, of course we will. We must. It's just the one chapter though, for my riveting showbiz stories.

FLATS – Not having it. It's a sports book.

DURDERS – Well, horse humping is a sport to some people. Okay, I'll reign in the luvvie stuff and bring it back to sport.

There's a cricketer called Fred Rumsey who played Test cricket for England in the '60s. Anyway, one day at our house I squirted his daughter Claire in the face with a water pistol, and after chasing her downstairs I then squirted Fred in the face too. I was probably about four or five years old and it's the first and only time I remember being given a clip by my father. I didn't think squirting a little girl in the face with a water pistol was a terrible crime, but I suppose taking out an international cricketer on my watery spree was the straw that broke the camel's back – my father being the camel in this instance. 'Not in my house,' said my father. It's a very vivid memory, that one.

FLATS – So your dad had very high standards when it came to you attacking international cricketers and their offspring with water, but didn't mind you getting stuck into Harry Secombe's thunderpants? Astonishing. I had a very, very different upbringing to you. While you were meeting Joan Collins and playing happy imaginary families with Gloria Hunniford-slash-Judith Chalmers, I was being attacked by people with screwdrivers. I was leaving school one day when somebody came up to me and said, 'There are three Travellers waiting for you out there with a screwdriver and one of them's going to stab you with it.' 'Okay, cheers,' I said. 'I'll go out the back way,' which I did. Once I'd got on the bus, it passed the front of the school and standing there by the gates were three Travellers, one of whom was indeed carrying a very large screwdriver.

DURDERS – How do you know they weren't just DIY enthusiasts? And why have you just chimed in with that possibly made-up story?

FLATS – To try to demonstrate the differences in our upbringings.

DURDERS – Hang on. I experienced some pretty harrowing times too. At the end of every day at my primary school, Gospel Oak in north London, I had to walk past a classmate's older sister demonstrating her snogging prowess with her boyfriend outside the school gates. Those memories stay with you. That's how it was on the mean streets of Kentish Town.

FLATS – You can't seriously be equating a couple of teenagers snogging with three Travellers brandishing a screwdriver?

DURDERS – Nobody got hurt though, did they? Whereas I had to stand there open-mouthed and watch two young people tongue fighting. I was also wedgied once and then hung up by my jockey Y-fronts. You see. Not that different, is it?

FLATS – Beat this, then. My two best mates and I once had a gun pulled on us outside the Warehouse Nightclub in Maidstone by a bodybuilding dwarf. I remember what he said as if it were yesterday. Two of the areas in Maidstone are Tovil and Shepway, and after pulling the gun he said, 'Are you Tovil?' 'No,' we said, looking confused. 'We're not Tovil.' 'Are you Shepway, then?' inquired the dwarf, thinking he'd got us. 'No, no,' we said. 'We're not Shepway either.' 'Where you from, then?' he demanded, clearly becoming annoyed. 'We live up from Safeway's,' we said. 'Really?' said the dwarf. 'Fuck off, then.' After that he just put the gun into his jeans, pulled his shirt over it and walked into the club.

DURDERS – How on earth does a chapter that was originally going to be about perks, and no more than a couple of pages long, suddenly morph into an opus featuring armed body-building dwarfs?

FLATS – You're hardly doing the description justice. We've also got Harry Secombe's skiddy drawers, soaked England cricketers, French kissing outside school gates, Travellers with tools and intent, famous imaginary parents, and Goldie Hawn – the love that never was. Do better, Mark. While we're here, we may as well stick with school for a page or two. Okay, what was your worst experience at school, apart from crying in front of your house master and watching a live snog? The reason I'm asking is because I have a feeling it's going to read like something out of a *Just William* book. Does it involve nettle stings followed by jam roly-poly and lashings of ginger ale?

DURDERS – Funnily enough, it does have a touch of the Enid Blyton about it. It's still quite shocking, though. When I first started boarding, at the age of 13, I used to get picked on by a boy in the year above. This will shock you, but I think it might prove cathartic for me to get it out there after all these years. This boy – he will know who he is – used to make me go and pinch matron's tadpoles out of her tadpole tank, decant them into a cocoa mug and then bring them back to the dormitory. That was tough. He also used to make me sit on top of a wardrobe and then pull my legs. 'You can't retaliate, Durden-Smith,' he used to say. 'Don't you dare retaliate.'

FLATS – Did you also have a friend called Moonface who lived in a big tree? Go on, I bet you did. Were your best friends called Dick and Fanny? You actually lived out an entire Enid Blyton book. That's incredible.

DURDERS – I haven't told you about the cheeks and newspapers yet, though, have I? Despite you having a screwdriver and a gun in your tales-from-your-childhood armoury, I would urge you to consider this piece of fresh hell. When I started at Radley the boys in my year all had to take a test about how well we knew the school, and unfortunately, but somewhat predictably, I came bottom. As a result, I had to arrive at the school shop at 6.55 a.m. every morning to collect the newspapers for my house. The man who ran the shop, Wing Commander Bowen I think he was called . . .

FLATS — Of course he was.

DURDERS — Don't interrupt while I'm dealing with previously buried childhood trauma please. Anyway, Wing Commander Bowen would plonk this enormous pile of newspapers in my arms, I would then stumble out of the door to be met by two other boys, from the year above, who would then each grab hold of one of my cheeks — we're talking cheeks-attached-to-the-jaw variety, before you say something childish and smutty — they'd then pull my chops to their peak elasticity and order me to run back to the house as quickly as I could while they held said cheeks. I think that happened every single morning for my first term and is the reason why I don't have nice, chiselled cheeks. You may laugh, you heartless bastard — that's Flats, not you, reader, for avoidance of doubt — but the main difference between our upbringings is that you almost suffered, whereas I *did* suffer. Anyway, this is all getting a little bit too traumatic for me. Any more and I'll have to see a psychologist.

FLATS — Was it the tadpoles that pushed you over the edge? It was, wasn't it? You poor little mite.

DURDERS — It was the cheeks actually. Let's finish off with a predictable and rather hackneyed double-headed dinner-party question, shall we? Is there anybody you'd like to meet who you haven't?

FLATS — My God, you're right, that is hackneyed. I really don't want to say the first person that springs to mind, purely because he seems to be someone who people love to think of as an ogre.

DURDERS — Is it Darius from *Pop Idol*? Nasty Nick from *Big Brother* Series One? Robert Mugabe?

FLATS — Close. I would love to have an extended lunch, blending into a long dinner, with Mr Jeremy Clarkson.

DURDERS — Despite us never having discussed this, I knew you were going to say that.

FLATS — I know it's obvious, which is why I was trying to think of somebody else. I think he's great, though. One of the things I like about Clarkson, apart from being very bright and very funny, is the amount of tosses he doesn't give. He's a consummate not-give-a-toss-er. I also love cars, which is probably where my admiration stems from. Apart from animal cruelty, cars are the least cool thing in the world to love. Seriously, nobody thinks it's cool to love cars, especially people who you wish were attracted to you. Jeremy Clarkson turned a car programme, which, let's face it, was fairly dull and car-centric before he got hold of it, into the coolest television programme on the entire planet. Over 150 countries broadcast *Top Gear* and it was all down to him. In my opinion there's an element of genius to Clarkson, although by claiming so I'm probably in danger of being ostracised by half the country.

DURDERS — Do you care?

FLATS – No, not at all. He's also one of the few journalists I've read who can turn a dull subject into something interesting. I caught myself reading an article he'd written about the Nissan Leaf the other day – a car that I have absolutely no interest in and will never buy – and I found it fascinating. I certainly don't agree with everything he says and writes, but I love the way he does it.

DURDERS – I almost met Jeremy Clarkson once. I was at a party given by one of my wife's friends. David Cameron had been standing behind me and . . .

FLATS – Hang on. David Cameron? Was he prime minister at the time?

DURDERS – No, he'd exited and was in his shepherd's hut phase by then. I don't normally mix in those kinds of circles and 'mix' would be an inaccurate description in any case. As always, I was lurking on the periphery of the circle where the top-end mixing was going on. I'd been biding my time to walk up and introduce myself to him for some time. I'd been presenting the brilliant and important Police Bravery Awards for quite a few years, which he'd attended a couple of times as PM, and had given him a bit of light-hearted stick about slashing the police budget as part of the austerity measures. I thought I'd remind him of that and was sure we'd then slip into easy and casual bonhomie as though we'd been lifelong friends.

FLATS – I'm getting increasingly worried about the extent of your delusions.

DURDERS – Don't lose sleep over it. Knowing that he was going to find me a great addition to his inner circle, I berthed alongside DC as he was reclining on a double sunbed-type thingy.

FLATS – Of course he was ... why have a sofa or a few chairs when you can have a double sunbed-type thingy.

DURDERS – Stop getting hung up on the minor details. Anyway, I knew we'd be on nickname terms before the night was out – we started with a bit of small talk, at which I excel, and just as I was about to cement this bromance and just as DC was about to share some really juicy state secrets that the rest of you would have to wait 50 years for, Clarkson walked in. 'DAVID!' he bellowed, after spying his mate. Cameron then turned around to greet his fellow Chipping Nortonian and from that moment I was dead to him. I stood there for about five minutes just behind him in full hover mode, hoping he'd remember that he'd just met one of life's great men and that he'd introduce me to Jezza, but he didn't. Like you, I'm a big fan of Clarkson's and the prospect of mixing it up with him and Dave over a gin and tonic was so near ... yet so far.

FLATS – It's a pity that thought wasn't reciprocated. He's also made *Who Wants to Be a Millionaire?* watchable again, which is good. Once again, a low level of concern for what people think of his behaviour and opinions have been key to his success on that show, and long may it continue. Let's have your choice, then.

DURDERS – I've decided I'd most like to spend a bit of quality time with Caitlin Moran. I think she'd loathe me from head to my haphazardly clipped toes but her mind is the gift that will never stop giving.

FLATS – Brilliant writer. I was expecting you to say David Cameron.

Nutrition

FLATS – I went pro in 1998 and even back then things were pretty advanced behind the scenes. We had full-time physios and full-time messieurs.

DURDERS – Full time Frenchmen? Don't you mean masseuses?

FLATS – Them as well. It was all relatively new, though, so things have moved on a pace in recent years. The only issue was that, unlike today, we didn't always do what they told us to, which probably explains the state of my shoulders. In hindsight, I should obviously have done things differently and had I been turning pro now, in addition to following their advice, I would probably take an active interest in it.

When it came to nutrition, we were again just advised to do certain things. Don't eat too much crap, don't drink too much, don't go overboard on carbohydrates, and take in as much protein as you possibly can. If only somebody had told me 20 years ago to monitor the calories I was eating, I'd have had much less body fat to cart around the field. My diet then wasn't brilliant, but it wasn't bad. I was also training my arse off and eating loads of protein. We'd always have a big lunch at the club and then George Chuter, who I was sharing a house with at the time, would cook most nights. He was a bit older than me so was like my dad. During the afternoon we'd drive down to Asda and get a large rotisserie chicken each and then eat it with some mayonnaise while watching television in the flat.

DURDERS – I was doing something similar in the late '90s, just without the physical activity.

FLATS – That wasn't it, though. After dinner we'd sit and watch more television and then at about half past nine we'd have six Weetabix each or a bucket of Alpen. I remember one of the nutritionists with England once saying to me that you cannot eat too much protein. I now know that that's complete and utter tosh. It's not like I would have been shredded or anything had I realised, but I probably would have carried five or six kilos less around all the time, which would obviously have made a difference. A positive difference.

DURDERS – I'm not sure how I'm going to shoehorn myself into this chapter on pro athlete nutrition, but in 2014 I did a 300-mile charity bike ride and on the first morning I got really bad cramp. Somebody said that if I didn't want it to happen again, I should eat as much as I could the whole time. Even when I was on the move. Being both greedy and gullible I decided to follow this advice to the letter and while all the other riders ate in order to keep their engines going, I basically flooded mine. They'd all lost at least half a stone when they arrived home, whereas I'd put one on.

FLATS – Did it prevent you getting cramp though?

DURDERS – Yes, it did in fact.

FLATS – Then it did the trick.

DURDERS – But overeating has been a talent of mine from a young age. My mother, being a travel presenter, was away a lot, so couldn't guard the fridge or – more relevantly, in my case – the freezer. She used to buy my love with ice cream. More specifically, with toffee and almond ice cream from M&S. I think it was her saying, 'I'm sorry for abandoning you again but tuck into dangerous levels of E-numbers and calories and you won't have time to miss me.' Before flying off to film *Wish You Were Here* she'd leave four tubs of the stuff in the fridge. That was for a five-day shoot. I'd get more if it was longer. Sorry, this is slightly off the point.

FLATS – Slightly? Far be it from me to try and trump your myriad achievements in the saddle, but I once did three times that for a charity bike ride, having never even ridden one before.

DURDERS – Your Land's End to John O'Groats mission you're always wanging on about? Didn't you have to have some adrenalin injected into your testicles?

FLATS – Correct. It was John O'Groats to Land's End actually. We did 996 miles in nine days and I lost no weight whatsoever. Everyone said it would come off the following week but it didn't. Not a single, solitary pound. Even the blood that left my body on account of the racing saddle didn't constitute any weight loss.

DURDERS – That is tragic. I know we're going to talk about nicknames later, but you remind me a little bit of the kid from *Grange Hill*. What was he called? Roland? That's it. It was pronounced 'Ro-Land'. 'We're only trying to help you, Ro-Land.'

FLATS — Yes, it must be my mop of black hair, my north London accent and my thick-rimmed glasses that do it. Funnily enough, that's what we used to call Duncan Bell. At least he had the mop of black hair, in addition to having not been able to see his penis for several years. Anyway, getting back on track, I remember returning home from school one day and complaining to my mum that I was two stone lighter than one of the other props. It was the first day of pre-season training and I was just 15 stone, whereas one of the other props was 17 and these things mattered then. I didn't have to say any more. From that day on, after I arrived home from school at about 5 p.m. every weekday, Mum would cook me a big steak, which I'd eat with some bread at the table. Then, at about 7 p.m., I'd sit down with the family and have my evening meal.

DURDERS — That sounds heavenly. How about during the day?

FLATS — It was non-stop really. As well as having school meals, I'd also take a big tub of tuna pasta to school with me and a few snacks. During break or between classes I'd wolf something down.

DURDERS — And for breakfast?

FLATS — Ah, breakfast. The most important meal of the day. At that age mine consisted of a bucket of porridge, some fruit, and a lot of toast. I used to make myself a 4,000-calorie breakfast when I was a pro, which is a lot of calories.

Eating can lose its appeal, especially if you're doing it mainly through necessity and over a long period of time. My two daughters are both big fans of the strongman Eddie Hall. I don't expect for a moment you'll know who I'm talking about, but he won World's Strongest Man back in 2017.

DURDERS – You seem to underestimate both my grasp of popular culture and my understanding and appreciation of the strength and fitness zeitgeist.

FLATS – Okay, then. What is Eddie Hall's nickname?

DURDERS – Edward?

FLATS – No, it's 'The Beast'. When he was at the height of his powers, he would have to consume no fewer than 13,000 calories every day. I read about this in an interview a while ago. He'd basically have to graze all day, so if he wasn't training, sleeping or competing, he'd be eating. He even used to take flapjacks and pieces of steak into the gym with him. I think the most alarming example of extreme eating I've ever heard about is when Eddie was attempting to become the first man ever to deadlift half a ton, which is roughly the same weight as a well-fed racehorse. A few hours before the attempt – which was successful, by the way – he visited a restaurant and asked to speak to the chef. 'Do you have a side of ham or a very large gammon?' he asked. 'We've got a gammon,' said the chef. 'It's huge.' 'Could you take the fat off and have it served to me on a plate please?' asked Eddie. I believe the chef thought that he'd escaped from somewhere at first, but after explaining what he needed it for he eventually said okay.

DURDERS — So, let me get this straight. Shortly before attempting to deadlift a fat racehorse, Eddie 'The Beast' Hall actually sat in a restaurant and ate the fat from the hind leg of a big pig. That is inspiring.

FLATS — Isn't it just. Shall we talk about nicknames for a bit? The only nickname I have at the moment is Flatypus, which is the one you gave me. Flats doesn't count as it's just an abbreviation.

DURDERS — You have to have more than one, surely?

FLATS — There is definitely a misconception that the game of rugby is teeming with witty and imaginative nicknames, which is probably the reason you suggested we cover it. The reason that isn't the case, apart from rugby players being thick and unoriginal, is because when you're communicating on a rugby field it's what comes quickest. You must have more nicknames than me. I like calling you Jacob Rees-Mogg.

DURDERS — I don't like that one. For a start I'm a centrist politically and am not a practising Catholic. I also don't wear a monocle or write books about Victorians, and my childhood nanny left the household staff donkeys ago. The front row forwards were the ones in my school and university teams who had the most nicknames, and they were usually apt but unimaginative ones like Bonehead or Grevious. There was also Pig, Bucko, Gibbo, Priesto and Brawler. Yup, your theory stacks up. Pretty unoriginal or a derivative of the surname. Although my surname, unfortunately, lends itself quite nicely to reinterpretation. I remember being really wounded when I was at the pink-blazer-wearing Hall School in Belsize Park in north London. My nemesis, who shall remain nameless . . .

FLATS – Why don't you just call him an arsehole? You'll feel a lot better.

DURDERS – No, I'm happy to call him my nemesis, thank you, you arsehole. One day, in front of everybody, he turned around and called me Fart Doo-dah Piss. I went home in tears and said to my mum, Judith or Gloria, who just happened to be in residence for a change, 'Somebody at school called me Fart Doo-dah Piss, and now everybody's doing it.' As her name was still Chalmers for work reasons and not Durden-Smith, she couldn't have given two hoots and quickly soothed me with some ice cream. Unfortunately, this nickname then morphed into Fart Turd 'n' Whiff, which, to be fair, sounds a little bit more like my actual name.

FLATS – It's actually quite catchy, and thank heaven for small mercies, eh, Markie?

DURDERS – Exactly. If only I'd had the self-deprecation skills to deal with this at the time. Alas, I did not, and I remained wounded for quite a while. I was also called Dudley, at one point, which may or may not have had something to do with it rhyming with the word 'cuddly' and me being a bit rotund. 'Durders' was my dad's nickname and my usual nickname is Durds, but as you rightly said that's more of an abbreviation.

FLATS – Imagine if we'd decided to use our actual nicknames for this book: 'Flatypus and Fart Turd and Shit on Rugby.' That would have looked great on the cover.

DURDERS – It was actually Fart Turd 'n' Whiff, not shit – to be accurate.

FLATS — Pedant. We used to call little Lee Mears 'Piglet' at Bath. He started off as Pygmy, then became Pig, and ended up as Piglet. As well as Ro-Land, Duncan Bell's nickname was Ender, as in bellend.

DURDERS — Thank you so much for explaining that.

FLATS — It's a good job I'm here, isn't it? I don't know if you've ever listened to the award-winning podcast I do with Tom Shanklin called *Flats and Shanks*, but we once dedicated an entire episode to the nicknames in the Welsh dressing room. You've got Bonkeye, Bus Head, Columbo . . . Everyone who plays for Wales has got a nickname. Unlike England. I can't remember one decent nickname from the England dressing room.

DURDERS — You're trying to tell me that Danny Grewcock doesn't have a nickname?

FLATS — Cock.

DURDERS — Really? That was the extent of your imaginations? He's called Grew-Cock, for heaven's sake. Couldn't you have called him 'Erection', or 'Viagra', or 'Semi'?

FLATS — You're right, it is a bit lame.

DURDERS — I don't like smut in general but this seems like a major dereliction of duty. How about Borthwick?

FLATS — Nope.

DURDERS — Jonny Wilkinson must have had a nickname.

FLATS — Wilko.

DURDERS – Pathetic. I'm starting to lose patience here. Wasn't Lewis Moody called Mad Dog?

FLATS – Nope. He was called Moodos, which is obviously unoriginal. The Mad Dog thing's a bit of an urban myth as far as I know because nobody ever called him that. It's a bit like John Eales, the legendary Australian second-row. Everybody in the dressing room was supposed to have called him Nobody, as in Nobody's Perfect, but I don't think they ever actually did.

DURDERS – Phil Vickery. Raging Bull?

FLATS – Another one. That was just a T-shirt brand he had. He was called either Vicks or Phil.

DURDERS – Bloomin' 'eck! You really were the Stock, Aitken and Waterman of nicknamers. You should be ashamed of yourselves. In order to try to atone for your collective sins, and to try to elongate this chapter a bit, why don't we try some retrospective nicknaming? I've thought of one for Grewcock. He'd be Boner or Bonerman.

FLATS – I've just remembered, Danny did actually have a media nickname. They used to call him Robo-lock, which would have been more fun had it been Robo-cock. Steve Thompson was called Wal, I remember, on account of his surname once being Walter.

DURDERS – You see, you're getting there now. All it took was a little nudge. How about Lawrence Dallaglio? I take it that was something like Lol or Lollipop.

FLATS – Spot on. Lollipop mainly. I remember Tim Payne

used to call him The Ruffler, because no matter who you were, he would always ruffle your hair. 'Well done, boy,' he'd say, giving you a ruffle. He is without doubt the biggest alpha male I've ever met in my life. I always say that you could put Lawrence Dallaglio in a field full of silverback gorillas and 10 minutes in they'd be picking nits off his back and eating them. He doesn't have to try, you see. It's completely natural. The ruffling thing's part and parcel of that, although no one ruffles Lol. He is The Ruffler.

DURDERS – What about the coaches? Andy Robinson, Jack Rowell.

FLATS – I used to call Jack Rowell 'Shooting Stick', as in the things you sit on outdoors, because he was 6ft 7in and had size seven feet. Robbo was called Growler, on account of him being so miserable and aggressive. He's the opposite when he's not coaching. That's just his style, though.

DURDERS – How about Sir Clive? I wasn't going to ask, out of respect for a Knight of the Realm, but what the hell. His middle name is Ronald so you had plenty to go at. Sir Clive Ronald Woodward, OBE.

FLATS – I didn't know that. Nope. Nothing. I remember Dave Alred looked exactly like Jim Rosenthal.

DURDERS – Fascinating. Matt Perry?

FLATS – The Weapon.

DURDERS – Because?

FLATS – I never quite worked that out. He wasn't good on the pull, he wasn't a dickhead ('Weapon' often being the nickname of choice for people who fit into this category), and as far as I know he doesn't have a particularly memorable member. So, I don't know is the answer. That's slightly disconcerting as I've been calling him that for donkey's years. Dan Luger never had a nickname, apart from Loogs, which is surprising.

DURDERS — Were things any more imaginative at Bath or Saracens?

FLATS — Yes, massively. George Chuter was Georgie and Paul Wallace was Wally. See! Tim Horan was called Helmey because he looked like he was wearing a helmet. Seriously, his hair was like Lego. It looked like it had been stuck on. Francois Pienaar was Frankie or Frankie Peanuts. If anything, that helped to humanise him as he's actually part cyborg. Kyran Bracken was Kyran Broken.

DURDERS — That's probably the best yet. Or at least the most imaginative.

FLATS — Thierry Lacroix was known as Terry the Cross. How's that for imagination?

DURDERS — You mean translation. Richard Hill?

FLATS — Hilda.

DURDERS — I think we need to stop now. People will be asking for refunds. It could have been worse, I suppose. In cricket, you just stick the letters 'ers' onto the end of everyone's surname. Hang on, what about the full-back who went to play in France? Went from Bath to Clermont. Nick Abendanon.

FLATS — Bendy Knob. There was a player at Bath once who had the most ropey pulling technique you've ever seen in your life. He used to get very nervous and would walk up to a woman he liked the look of, grab her by the hands and pull her towards him so he could chat her up. 'Come with me,' he used to say. 'Come with me.' He probably thought he was being romantic or humorous, but the women thought he was trying to abduct them. It never worked. In the end I bought him a pair of oven gloves and whenever he got the urge to go and pull somebody towards him I'd make him put them on. It worked, too. Mike Tindall's nickname is 'Lord' and I think he gave it to himself after he married Z. He even signs his WhatsApp messages with it. I got one the other day and at the end it said, 'Cheers mate, Lord.' Do you know what my all-time favourite nickname is, though?

DURDERS — Go on.

FLATS — Fart Doo-dah Piss. Winner.

Front Row

DURDERS — Okay, we're back to your specialist chosen subject: the front row. Give us a personality profile of your typical front rower.

FLATS — It's a little more complex than that. The two main groups of people you get playing in the front row are people who were built a certain way — i.e., those who are too dense and slow, or too massive, to play anywhere else — and decent rugby players who aren't tall enough or fast enough to play in a certain position and have been convinced by a coach to convert.

DURDERS — Rejects, basically.

FLATS — Not necessarily. There have been, and are, some brilliant rugby players in the front row. Look at Christian Califano 20 years ago. Look at Ellis Genge and Kyle Sinckler now. Those three could not play at pro level anywhere else because of their physiques. They might have been good at an amateur level at No. 8 or inside centre, but they'd be torn apart at either pro or Test level. You also get people who come into the game late as they're usually too immobile to play anywhere else.

DURDERS – I honestly wasn't expecting that. I was expecting you to say what I was thinking, which is basically a bunch of psychos. No normal human being would want to do what you lot do in the front row, which is basically smash into another person's head and shoulders, gouge somebody's eye out, grab hold of a pair of testicles or nibble another person's ear (most of which you're obviously not allowed to do these days and I'm sure never, ever happens). I think the nicknames we give these people merely adds to the mystique, don't you? As I mentioned in the previous chapter, at Durham you could field a front row of Bonehead, Grievous and Pig and the one thing they had in common was that they all had at least one screw loose.

FLATS – It's like boxers walking out to fight in front of tens of thousands of people on their own. When I was a kid I used to think, *God, they're so brave.* Far braver than rugby players. Then, when I was 18, I played against Darren Garforth at Welford Road. From that day on, every time I was having a bad day or a rough match I would say to myself, 'Oh well. At least it won't get as bad as that day at Welford Road,' and it never did. Playing against Darren was as aggressive as the game of rugby union ever got for me, so it provided me with a benchmark. A benchmark that, in a perverse sort of way, often kept me afloat.

DURDERS – Were you ever scared?

FLATS – Oh, absolutely. Don't believe anybody who played on the front row who says they were never scared. Take all the screaming and shouting that goes on before a match. Some people at home might think it's just rock-hard rugby players being super-aggressive prior to battle. You know, 'Let me at 'em' kind of stuff. Often these players will be either nervous, petrified, or both, so by shouting, screaming and hitting things prior to a game they'll hopefully quell some of the fear and summon up a bit of much-needed aggression. If you believe that pre-match rugby dressing rooms are awash with nothing but anger, aggression and testosterone, then you're miles out. What generates the fear and nervousness is the prospect of confrontation. Not the pain or injuries that might result from it, but the prospect of it actually happening. The vast majority of human beings would be scared of playing against Darren Garforth or Julian White, and therefore they wouldn't do it, which would be understandable. We, on the other hand, as in people who play in the front row, obviously have no choice – and we rather enjoy it – and if it takes a bit of shouting and shrieking to get you there, that's fine.

DURDERS – It's obviously a very different kind of fear to what a full-back or a winger might experience. If you're a full-back you might be scared of dropping a ball in front of everybody, in which case it's really your ego that's creating the fear. Here's a question, though. Say you do make a mistake in the front row, would you feel it as much afterwards as, say, a full-back who dropped a ball under the posts to lose his team the game? After all, a mistake made by a player in the front row would be seen by far fewer people. Less noticeable, I suppose.

FLATS – I made loads of skill errors during my career and I couldn't tell you about one of them. I couldn't give a toss. All my thoughts would have been about the confrontation that had taken place. Nothing else mattered apart from the result.

There's an innate level of confrontation within all front rowers. Sometimes it'll have to be summoned or coaxed, but it's always there. It's an essential ingredient.

DURDERS – Have you ever tasted the flesh of another man?

FLATS – You mean did I ever bite anybody on a rugby field? No, I didn't. I much prefer pig or cow to human. Nope, I never understood that. I was certainly bitten a few times. What really annoys me about this is the reaction on social media to violence on a rugby field from people who I know have been guilty of it in the past. It's just a touch sanctimonious for me.

DURDERS – What was your vice, then? Were you a testicle squeezer? A gouger?

FLAT – Was I a gouger? Habitually, no, but I did do it more than once; many of the lads were at it at the time, in truth. It was just far more common then. I'm not saying that makes it right, of course. It most definitely doesn't. It's a fact, though. I remember a game when I was 18. A scrum went down and George Chuter had his head stamped on deliberately, which tore his ear. I was going to try to help him – or at least get my body between his skull and the other chap's boot – but was then kneed and kicked in the face, so the game then was hugely different.

DURDERS – Because you're a man with a conscience, did you ever think to yourself, *Why on earth are we doing this? Are we not meant to be a little further down the evolutionary path?* Or did you just go, *Sod it. If we don't do it to them, they'll do it to us.*

FLATS – Oh, the latter, definitely. That's not to say I didn't occasionally walk away after matches wishing it had been different, but that's just the way it was. I remember playing against Northampton Saints at the Rec once. They were in a good bit of form and in order to stand half a chance we had to try to get to their fly-half and their flanker, Darren Fox (a very good chap by all accounts). He had this thing where'd he'd race around the corner during a line-out and take the ball off the No. 9 and it was my job to stop him. When the opportunity came, I got off the line quick, raced him round the corner and tackled behind the gain line. Job done.

My only other task during that game was to knock Darren Fox off any rucks and make sure he didn't turn the ball over. The first one I hit I misjudged, and after effectively skimming over the top of Darren and missing him altogether, he nicked the ball. Everyone looked at me, as if to say, 'That was your job, and you've let us down.' I felt so ashamed of myself. At the next ruck I did exactly the same thing again, except before he could nick the ball I reached back grabbed him by the face and eyes. I remember him saying to me, 'Watch where you put your fingers, old chap.' In the moment I was terribly regretful, but after the game I apologised. It just used to happen all the time.

DURDERS – What, you flying over rucks?

FLATS – Yes, that too. It was actually used more as a deterrent really. When people put their fingers in your eyes, you shit yourself and move. It probably happened to me 20 times during my career and I can honestly say it never hurt me once, for the simple reason that I always shat myself and got out of the way! I'm obviously not condoning it; I'm just explaining how and why it was used. I remember playing

Biarritz once in the semi-final of the Heineken Cup. They had a hooker called Benoît August and during the match he gouged Danny Grewcock. Danny was properly terrified as he thought he'd done him some serious damage, but that's the only time during my entire career that I saw anything like that happen. As I said, it was mainly used as a threat.

DURDERS – 'Move out of the way or I'll gouge your eyes out.' Yep, that would probably work with me. Although I'd be more worried about my hair – take a clump of that and I'd go on the warpath. Let's move on from the eyeballs to the more intimate pair of orbs, shall we?

FLATS – Testicles? Why not. Always happy to talk testes, as well you know. I never did any ball-grabbing during my career but I was often on the receiving end. In fact, I once had my balls grabbed so hard that my ball bag got lacerated by the grabber's fingernails. The perpetrator went through my Lycra shorts and actually tore the skin. If he'd just squirrel-gripped me or even punched me I would have released the ball, but he wasn't trying to get me off the ball. He was just trying to hurt me.

DURDERS – By removing your testicles?

FLATS – Yes, sorry. That's what he was trying to do. He was trying to unceremoniously remove my testicles in the middle of a rugby match.

DURDERS – Before having them mounted on a nice piece of mahogany, no doubt.

FLATS – I wouldn't settle for anything less than a nice piece of African Blackwood.

DURDERS — Was it mildly erotic? You know, did you experience a little *frisson* when he tried to deconstruct your manhood?

FLATS — We had a causal relationship for a couple of years after that. What can I say, though? He was a man who knew what a man wants. Did you never experience any rough-housing on a rugby field?

DURDERS — I very nearly became the hardman of our school team, believe it or not.

FLATS — I think I'll choose not to, on this occasion.

DURDERS — No, this is God's honest truth. The rugby master at school was a top man called Pete Johnson, PMJ, who was on the RFU committee. One day he said, 'Guys, we're too soft as a team. What we need is a hard man.' I remember thinking, well, that obviously isn't me. I was playing at No. 7 and we had a guy called Chris Sheasby playing at No. 8 who went on to play for England. He had one cap fewer than you I think, Flats, which takes some doing. Before our next match, Pete Johnson gave us a 'Once more unto the breach, dear friends' kind of speech, which turned me into a spitting ball of blood and thunder. *Perhaps I will become the hard man,* I thought to myself.

Sure enough, as opposed to playing my usual game, which was to feign injury whenever contact seemed imminent, I decided to get among it. During a ruck, somebody on the opposing team incurred my significant wrath and, seeing Peter Johnson standing on the sidelines looking on, I decided that this was my chance. After clenching my hand into a fist, I started to wind up a punch that would have floored a rhinoceros, and just as I was about to deploy my haymaker, Chris Sheasby grabbed me by the collar, pulled me back and threw me on the ground. There was a bloody fight going on and I was lying on my back having been removed from the scene by my own No. 8 and not having thrown a punch. It was the most humiliating moment of my life on a rugby field.

FLATS – I'm sure you've claimed that somewhere else in this book.

DURDERS – Good point. I'm prolific, if nothing else. Anyway, that was the closest I ever came to any argy-bargy. Actually, I did get knocked out once after a game of cricket on a tour to South Africa. Does that count? It was in the car park of a bowling alley and when I came round everyone had buggered off. It was a hell of a punch.

FLATS – So you almost threw a punch during a match and got floored by one after a match? What a contribution. My first punch-up in a game was England schoolboys versus Wales schoolboys. A newspaper the following day called it the dirtiest game in schoolboy history. It wasn't our fault. They had a lad called Dean Colclough at hooker and Gary Powell at tighthead who ended up playing for Gloucester, Cardiff and Leeds. A fight broke out during the game and I remember thinking to myself that nobody could have Dean Colclough, because he was basically a monster, but Gary Powell seemed fair game. Also, Powelly, who is now a good friend of mine, was a proper gobshite, so he needed decking.

Right in front of the main stand I flew in with an epic

right hand, missed his head completely, lost my balance, spun around like a hippo from *Fantasia* minus the tutu, and fell over. I thought Powelly was going to stamp on me or something, but he just held me down by my chest and laughed his tits off. 'That's fucking class, that is,' he said in his smooth Welsh brogue. Then he just gave me his hand and helped me up. About five minutes later, Powelly got the ball from a line-out and ran straight into Alex Sanderson, which was the end of his match. Alex hit him very, very, very hard, which he did to a lot of people. It doesn't matter how streetwise you are at that age, there are always going to be some people who are just harder than you, so it's best to leave the hitting to them, really. You don't walk around like you're carrying carpets when Mike Tyson's in the room, do you? After that I just left it to Al.

DURDERS – Alex Sanderson exudes menace. As the new boss of Sale Sharks, he was interviewed every week for our show and I always watched him and thought, *God, you wouldn't mess with him.* He's got a steely but smiley gaze. I find that really disconcerting.

FLATS – Alex Sanderson is a lovely, gorgeous man, but if you ever got into a situation where you needed to beat him in a physical confrontation, you'd have to kill him. That would be your only way out.

DURDERS – So how do the front rows of yesteryear compare with the front rows of today, then?

FLATS – Well, I can only really go back as far as my own era, but the front rows of today have significantly more involvement in the game for one thing, which, as a rule, makes them better rugby players. They're also every bit as strong as we were, because the training's obviously improved, as has the nutrition. All that's just straightforward evolution, and in 20 years' time the Genges and Sincklers and Mako Vunipolas of this world will look old-school, which is how sport works. The way the scrum is set up now means that it's effectively impossible to get into an awkward body shape, which is very handy if you ask me. If I'd been playing these days I'd have loved it because there's an emphasis on static strength, which was my forte. I would love to have played with a pre-bind as my shoulders effectively stopped me swinging my arms up into position post-engagement.

DURDERS – You played in the era that was arguably the most physically damaging to the front row. In the 1970s it was more of a form, lean in and push, for instance. I watched a video the other day of England's 1980 Grand Slam and during the scrums they flopped, the ball was put in, and then it was away. You lot engaged with full-on force, though. What are the stats on kilos going through your neck and spine, etc.?

FLATS – Oh my God, there are loads, probably. We used to try to get as far away from the other team as we could so we could hit them as hard as possible. Unless we were playing against somebody really tall, in which case we'd close the gap. We were big guys, so we'd always go for maximum impact. Now and again you'd absolutely nail it and feel somebody just buckle, and on other occasions you'd nail it but *you'd* buckle. I remember absolutely nailing a few engagements against the mighty Census Johnston and basically my ribs got rear-ranged. I remember thinking to myself, *Mmmmm, we might have to address this.* I was giving it everything I'd got and he was bending it in half like a fucking deckchair. I remember Lee Mears saying to me, 'What the hell are you doing, Flats?' and me saying, 'What I'm doing, Lee, is not being as strong as Census. That's what I'm doing.' We had to get as close as the referee would allow in order to prevent me from having to eat my own ribs.

DURDERS – You wouldn't mind that – well marinaded and slow-cooked. I remember asking you some time ago whether there was anything you missed about playing rugby and you said the confrontation.

FLATS – And that's the honest truth. I'm not trying to present myself as a hard man here, but the only part of the game of rugby I miss, apart from the training, is the confrontation. I obviously watch a huge amount of rugby live and on TV, but the sports I watch most, apart from rugby, are all confrontation – and aggression-based combat sports. I appreciate that these kinds of sports are supposed to be the reserve of beer-swilling morons and thugs, but if my shoulders were in better nick I would, at least once a week, be taking part in something like jiu-jitsu or boxing. Without any contact to the face, of course. Failing that, if I could find a local club of a half-decent standard that did live scrums once a week, I'd go and do it. I wouldn't play rugby again on account of having no interest whatsoever in running, passing or catching. That's what made me anxious about rugby: the athleticism. I hated that. Head-on tackling and scrummaging? Yes, please.

DURDERS – You do feel pain, don't you?

FLATS – Of course I do, but if you have enough adrenalin flowing through your body you don't. Or at least not as much. The natural instinct for human beings is to remove themselves from potentially violent or confrontational situations, whereas if you play in the front row the instinct is to do the exact opposite. This is achieved by conditioning and one of the things that drives you is how it makes you feel.

DURDERS – You mean you gradually become addicted to acting violently and being confrontational?

FLATS – Kind of, but not just for the sake of it. The reason it works is because it takes place within, and is part of, a sport that you enjoy playing. I never got endorphins from doing exercise. Or not knowingly. The thing is, if you're forced into a confrontational or violent situation and you survive it, you feel more confident going in again, to the point where you actually look forward to it. That's what I miss the most. As I said, if my shoulders had the range, I'd be part of something like a jiu-jitsu club. Some of my old buddies who I used to play in the front row with go to my local place. They love nothing more than having a bit of a grapple while their faces are being torn and abraded. Who wouldn't?

DURDERS – That all sounds very noble and even vaguely heroic. Reading between the lines, however, the overriding impression I get is that you're a psycho. Isn't there a Fight Club or something you could join in Bath?

FLATS – What do you think? I'm not even sure you're allowed to use the word 'club' in Bath. I think they prefer 'society'. Here's a curveball for you. Even in the throes of battle, I never wanted to hurt anybody, nor did I enjoy it when I did. Generally speaking, I'm a lover, not a fighter. For instance, if I see a video of somebody being beaten up gratuitously, say on some CCTV footage, I'll turn it off immediately. That kind of violence really upsets me.

DURDERS – Okay, it's kind of making sense to me now. What made it possible for you and your fellow front-row primates to put yourselves in that situation was the environment you were in, and each other.

FLATS – Exactly. To paraphrase a horribly hackneyed saying, we were all in it together, and if we hadn't been, it wouldn't have worked.

DURDERS – As you have a penchant for what is basically masochism, have you ever thought about going into politics?

FLATS – Too much confrontation. It's just sadomasochism without the sex. Or without as much. That's the front row, by the way. Not politics. There's obviously loads of sex in politics. Just look at John Major and Edwina Currie.

DURDERS – I would really rather not. Disturbing imagery. Now, the front row stereotype, which I know is balls, but it has the 123s struggling with their ABCs and basically incapable of stringing full sentences together. Despite those perceived limitations, was it a chatty place down there during the game?

FLATS – Not really. We're too knackered. There's also not a lot *to* say. There's also very little sledging, which might help to dispel a few myths. Some people assume that because we're in a physical battle we must also be in a verbal one, but not in my experience. You'll get the odd gripe. You know,

'You bugger, that hurt, I'll scratch your eyes out.' That sort of thing. That's about it. You've also got to be careful where sledging is concerned. You might have a good scrum and the fly-half might tap you on the back and whoop and holler, but you're only ever one bad scrum away from being introduced to your own colon. You really do have to stay humble if you can. It's like boxers who show off at the end of rounds during close fights. I always cringe when I see that because I know exactly what can happen.

DURDERS – So the front row are generally quite a humble bunch?

FLATS – During a match, yes.

DURDERS – I guess you do have to be fully focused and you told me that the concentration required to focus your power in the right place and at the right time is considerable. It must have impressed me as I remembered it and as a rule I don't listen to a word you say. It's a very precise art, though.

FLATS – It is. If you're at full-back you have to see everything, so you almost have to zoom out, whereas at prop you have to zoom right in. You also have to be totally in the moment.

DURDERS – It can go wrong quite easily, then.

FLATS – Oh, catastrophically. And I'm not talking physically. There's obviously physical danger present, but what worries you on a rugby field is letting your team-mates down.

DURDERS – So if we were to equate this to a movie, you'd probably be Ben Affleck in *Armageddon*. Isn't he the one who has to blow up the meteor?

FLATS – I'm more like Gollum looking for the ring.

DURDERS – Yes, a blown-up Golem. I can see that. How is the BMI these days?

FLATS – It isn't too bad at the moment. Or at least I didn't think it was, until I went for my first Covid vaccination jab last week. As a sprightly 41-year-old, I was quite surprised when I received my text just a short while after my parents, and I assumed it was because of my asthma. Off I wheezed to the clinic like a good little boy, but when I got there I immediately realised that every single recipient, bar one person, was morbidly obese. Because of that one person I held out hope that it wasn't because of my BMI, but then he spoiled it. 'Hello, Flats,' he said through his mask. 'I used to work for the magazine you write for. We met a couple of times?' 'Oh yeah,' I said. 'I remember. Hello, mate. What are you doing here? You're a bit smaller than the rest of us?' I was then hoping he'd say that he was an asthmatic or something, but I was out of luck. 'I'm a type-one diabetic, mate,' he said happily. 'Oh bollocks,' I muttered. 'That means I've joined the fat club.' I went in to see the doctor, and after glancing at my notes he said, 'You're a bit young to be having this, aren't you?' 'Well,' I said, 'my girlfriend thinks it's because I'm a fat bastard and I think it's because I've got asthma.' 'Could be both,' said the doctor, looking at me seriously.

DURDERS – How much did they inject. A pint? I imagine it would take some effort just getting through your hide.

FLATS – I don't understand it. For lunch today I had a tin of sweetcorn, a lump of cheese, a six-egg omelette and a tin of plum tomatoes. I should be losing weight.

DURDERS – Six eggs? That would have been considered a killer back in the '80s, which unfortunately has just reminded me of Edwina Currie and John Major going at it.

FLATS – Good luck to 'em, I say.

Injuries

FLATS – I think you should start this chapter, for the simple reason that you're basically the Six Million Dollar Man without the bravery and ability to fight.

DURDERS – Hang on, let's do the stats. How long were you a professional athlete?

FLATS – About 15 years.

DURDERS – You hung around way too long. I remember going to Bath in your final season and shouting, 'Get that man off, he's knackered!' I even considered buying a little tranquiliser gun and putting you out of your misery. Or deploying a taser.

FLATS – Imagine if it had been your body going through it. I wanted me to stop as well!

DURDERS – So, numerically, how many injuries did you have in 15 years?

FLATS – Well, quite a lot. When I was considering retiring, I rang my dad and said, 'Dad, I've just seen a doctor called

Grey Giddins and he says I can't play any more.' 'Really?' said Dad. 'Thank God for that.' He knew it was all over.

DURDERS – I guess you were in denial for ages so you could eke it out? Anyway, you still haven't answered my question. I know that Terry Biddlecombe, who was a very famous National Hunt jockey who won the Cheltenham Gold Cup, suffered no fewer than 47 broken bones during his career. Forty-seven! I'm fairly certain that most jockeys would be able to tell you off hand how many bones they've broken or how many operations they've had, so how about you?

FLATS – Well it's nowhere near 47, thank God. I had 10 general anaesthetics during my career, but as I said, that was over 15 years. As for my bones, they're actually made of wood.

DURDERS – My bones are made of tungsten, but my tendons on the other hand are pure candyfloss, which is why I think there's an outside chance I might just pip you on this one. I'll certainly slaughter you on the ridiculous front, that's for sure. The only thing I can talk about with any kind of bravado is how many stupid injuries I've suffered over the years. The earliest ones were down purely to irresponsible parenting. Have you ever been to Hampstead Heath? For a stroll or something?

FLATS – No. I'm too cool and sexy for heaths.

DURDERS – Well, there's a place on Hampstead Heath called Kite Hill, which is the highest point. I was about five years old and had recently graduated from a tricycle to a bike. After putting stabilisers on it, my parents took me up to Kite Hill for a try-out. 'Off you go, son,' my father said. The first thing that came into my mind as I began to move was, 'How the hell do I stop this thing?', but it was too late.

My tricycle didn't have brakes and my parents had omitted to tell me that a) my new bike actually had some brakes, and b) how I should use them. As I was picking up momentum – completely against my wishes, it has to be said – the 1970s and '80s television icon Judith Chalmers and the less famous and less iconic but equally charming commentator Neil Durden-Smith looked on as I hurtled to my doom. These days I suspect that omitting to inform your five-year-old child that their new bicycle has a device on it for making it stop before pushing said child down a large hill in north London would be classed as a form of child abuse, but this was the '70s, remember. Little things like that mattered not in those days and, despite me trying to improvise by using my foot, I ended up going straight over the handlebars. The result was one of three broken collarbones I have suffered – so far – during my life. If only Childline had been on the go then. If they had, I'd have put in a call. Collarbone Break, The Sequel, was courtesy of my unnamed, aforementioned prep-school nemesis, who made up the nickname Fart Doo-dah Piss, you may recall, and was a little over-exuberant during a playground game of British Bulldog.

FLATS – Do you want me to duff him up for you? Actually, given he's the person who invented the nickname Fart Doo-dah Piss, I'm not sure I can. In fact, I might have to buy him a pint instead.

DURDERS – If you make friends with the villainous man whose name shall not be spoken, I will never speak to you again. The collarbone trilogy was completed by one of my teachers, Mr Corbett, who was also a bit heavy-handed during a game of British Bulldog.

FLATS – There's a joke there somewhere, but I shan't go looking for it.

DURDERS – Anyway, this trio of clavicle catastrophes will pale into insignificance when I tell you about the boil on my chest. A boil that the 1970s, '80s and '90s television icon Judith Chalmers promised would be expunged from my person without me suffering any pain.

FLATS – Was Mumsy fibbing?

DURDERS – Yes. I know I'll be shattering the dreams of at least a handful of people with this revelation, but that's the way of it. The 1970s, '80s and '90s television icon Judith Chalmers lies to small children. Shattering! I went into the Royal Free Hospital in Hampstead and I remember my mum saying to me, 'You're being so brave, Markie.' Actually, my parents used to call me Bomber in those days.

FLATS – Why?

DURDERS – I think it was because I used to bomb around the whole time. They stopped using that nickname around the start of the jihadi era, though. She continued by saying that if I let these people who I'd never met before come at me with a scalpel and lance my revolting chest-boil, she'd buy me a dog.

FLATS – Lied to *and* bribed by Judith Chalmers.

DURDERS – As I said, shattering. It did the trick, though, as I'd been wanting a dog for ages. The only downside was it was a stuffed one from Harrods. I ended up calling him Waffles and he still shares a study with me at home. When the doctor lanced the boil, I screamed and screamed until I was almost sick. My mother was incredibly embarrassed. And the truth, that my parents must never discover, is that it didn't actually hurt in the end but I don't want them to take Waffles back.

FLATS – I'm not sure about Harrods' returns policy but I don't think they'd accept a stuffed toy that was bought in 1978.

DURDERS – I also had to have some warts frozen off my thumbs around that time, at the same hospital, with the same level of screaming. The medics must have hidden in the canteen when they saw me coming. And since then I've continued to collect an impressive array of injuries. In fact, it's been a kind of theme in my life. I've got two patched-up tendons in my knees, having ruptured the old ones while playing extreme sports – Dad's Wednesday-night football and Dad's elite tennis. I suffered a very bad shoulder injury while tobogganing in Finland. I was trying to catch the Northern Lights and ended up having a general anaesthetic, which resulted in no lights at all. I'm lucky to be alive really, and I'd say your injuries are probably minor by comparison.

FLATS – They certainly weren't as dramatic, that's for sure. And there were probably fewer tears and fluffy dogs and less screaming. I was playing for Saracens against Ulster years ago when Paul Wallace suffered a horrible injury. It was his knee that went and I remember hearing him scream. I hadn't had an injury at that point, nor had I really seen anybody suffer one. Wally was in a massive amount of pain and after the game I remember walking into the dressing room and feeling tears bubble up in my eyes, purely because I'd seen my mate so badly hurt.

Danny Grewcock walked in and with a look of mild disgust said, 'What's up, mate?' 'It's Wally,' I said, wiping my eyes. 'Yeah, shit that,' said Danny. 'He'll be all right.' Danny and I went in to see Wally later on and before I could express any sympathy or even hold his hand, Grewcock pushed in and said, 'What happened, then, Wal? Fucking stinker that.'

My first serious injury happened while I was playing for Saracens. I'd suffered a few knocks before then but this was the first biggie. We were playing against Bath and they had this French tighthead prop called Alessio Galasso, who was massive. For some reason I was convinced he was soft so decided to get into him. We'd been scrummaging really well in the match and during the next one I went for him and he just caved in.

DURDERS — You were right, then. He was a big softie.

FLATS — He was in that particular scrum. He just bottled it and fell over. As he did so he took me with him and I ended up wrenching my shoulder. I remember thinking it felt a bit funny but had no idea how bad it was so I played the rest of the game. I was out for six months after that and my shoulder was never the same again. We did a lot of very heavy weights in those days, which definitely didn't help. A few years later, when I was playing for Bath, they asked me if I'd like to play tighthead for a week. I was a loosehead but said I'd give it a go and luckily I survived it.

Four or five weeks later I was still playing tighthead and while playing against Bristol one day I went down in a scrum and felt my left shoulder go. I immediately came off, and after going to see the surgeon he said that, in addition to having to have my left shoulder operated on, the right shoulder still hadn't healed properly so they decided to do that one as well – again. Because I'd had so much work done on my right shoulder, the mechanism in there had weakened so my bicep tendon snapped, came out of the top of my shoulder and shot down towards my elbow. After that was fixed, they cleaned out my elbow, but it made little to no difference. In fact, despite that surgery I still can't straighten my arm completely and it still causes me a certain amount of pain. I wish I'd never had it done.

DURDERS – I'd forgotten how detailed your shoulder and elbow injury stories become. Are your Achilles' injury stories any better? Less sleep-inducing?

FLATS – My Achilles' story is great! A proper page-turner. It started off as a sore heel that wouldn't heal, so to speak, and when I went to see the doctor he decided to stick a cortisone and steroid injection in there. 'Will that stop it hurting?' I asked him. 'It most certainly will,' said the doc. What I should have asked was what would happen once the injection wore off. Or, more specifically, if there was anything he could do to actually fix the underlying problem. Unfortunately, I didn't and when the pain came back, he injected me again and then a third time. After that the injections stopped working, which is when they decided to operate. There was a big bone spur down there, but while trying to remove it I caught an infection which resulted in me having to spend 10 days in hospital with a drain coming out of my leg. A year later I still wasn't even running, let alone playing. I remember going to visit my parents one day and when I walked through the door my mum almost burst into tears. Still being on crutches after a year out was hard for all of us to take.

DURDERS – I think I might prefer your shoulder and elbow story. But let's feign interest for the sake of good form. I take it your foot was still painful, then?

FLATS – That's the thing – it wasn't. I remember my mum asking me the same question. I just didn't feel anything really. Even today, if I try and stand on tiptoe, nothing happens.

DURDERS – How often in your life do you get the urge to deploy the tiptoe? You are not a man who should *ever* tiptoe. Surely the risks involved are way too high. I'm thinking pure physics here.

FLATS – As I was about to say before I was rudely interrupted, the nerves are just dead. I went to see a specialist, who said to me, 'I'm afraid you definitely have osteomyelitis.' He was an Italian man who had operated on Lee Sharpe's knee (a fact that he seemed keen to repeat every few minutes), and he finished off the consultation by saying, 'Your bones are like cheese, my friend. They are like cheese.' 'Brilliant,' I said. 'So my bones are crumbling?' 'Yes,' he said. 'Very, very bad. Excellent, excellent, very, very bad.'

DURDERS – That was all delivered in a beautiful cod Italian accent, FYI. I just thought you, the discerning reader, should know.

FLATS – *Grazie.* On the train back with the physio I said, 'Shit, that's not good,' and he said, 'Yep. You're right.'

DURDERS – He tried his best to cheer you up, then.

FLATS – He did, bless him. A few weeks later I got a nudge from a couple of the Wasps and England players. 'We hear your Achilles' is still bad,' they said. 'Yep. I think that's it,' I replied. 'I can't see a way back.' 'We've got this bloke in London,' they said. 'He's called Kevin Lidlow and there's no one like him in the world. If you can be fixed, he'll fix you.'

DURDERS – That must have given you some hope?

FLATS – Oh, it did. I first met Kevin a few days later in Regent's Park. I was doing an England appearance there and shortly after arriving I felt a tap on the shoulder. 'Are you David?' said the tapper. 'I'm Kevin Lidlow. Lawrence Dallaglio and Will Green have told me all about you. Have you got a minute?' 'Of course I have,' I said. He took me into this marquee, where all the tables and chairs were. 'Take your shoe and sock off and lie down on that table,' he said. After then taking my foot in his hands, he closed his eyes and spent 10 minutes or so digging his fingers into my foot. I remember thinking, *Who the hell's this weirdo?*

DURDERS – I must admit that the thought of you arriving in Regent's Park and being approached by a man who wants to massage your foot with his eyes closed does strike me as being a little strange. At least he let you keep your shorts on.

FLATS – To be honest I would have whipped them off if he'd just said the word. Anyway, after opening his eyes and putting my foot down he said, 'We can fix that, David. The trouble is, it's going to take a long time.' I said, 'I've been out for over a year and I'm nearing the end of my contract. I haven't got another year.' 'Well,' he said. 'I'm afraid it'll take as long as it takes.' I felt thrilled that he thought he could help me but gutted about the amount of time, but I felt I had no choice. 'Okay, let's do it,' I said finally.

DURDERS – What a bittersweet moment that must have been. I take it the road back was a hard one?

FLATS – Incredibly. After having two operations, which Kevin observed, I went to London three days a week for physiotherapy. That alone went on for over eight months in total, but he fixed me. Bath Rugby didn't love me going to see Kevin because he wasn't on the staff. Ultimately, though, the person they'd sent me to see had told me that my bones had been turning to cheese. When I first started talking to Kevin, I told him what the Italian surgeon had said, and although he didn't agree with the diagnosis, he investigated it as if I did actually have osteomyelitis. That was the way he did things and with that in mind I was sent for all kinds of CT scans and X-rays. I remember him calling me about this. He said, 'Can you get to London tomorrow morning? I want to get these scans and X-rays sorted.' I was on a train at 6 a.m. the next day and at lunchtime he sat me down and confirmed that I did not have osteomyelitis. With that out of the way, he was then able to explain to me what he thought had happened and what he thought needed to be done. He was the zenith of professionalism.

DURDERS – What was the problem, then?

FLATS – It turned out that my nerves were basically just encased in scar tissue. He basically saved my career. No doubt about it. Even to this day I have a sore Achilles' tendon, but

I still managed to play another 150 games after that point. Actually, it was probably over 150. Funnily enough, when I mentioned Kevin to the England physios – this was before he treated me – they said that I wasn't to go and see him under any circumstances. I remember thinking that was really weird, but in hindsight I think it's because there were so many England players going to see Kevin as their primary physio and it obviously put their noses out. That's obviously understandable, to a point, but when the vast majority of your players are going elsewhere for treatment – and are being treated successfully – there has to be something in it. You can't just dismiss that person outright. Almost everyone I know, in and out of rugby, who has come back from a serious injury has been to see Kevin. Rio Ferdinand, Danny Cipriani, Lawrence Dallaglio, Gordon Ramsay.

DURDERS – You know Gordon Ramsay? I think that's a name drop that won't stand up to scrutiny. I taught him how to swear, FYI. On another of my TV breakout hits, *Hell's Kitchen: Extra Portions* on ITV 2.

FLATS – Your CV is an abomination. Okay, I know of him.

DURDERS – Like the rest of the world. Let's move on. Is Kevin still around?

FLATS – Yes, Kevin's still around. He's very under-the-radar, so you'll only ever come into contact with him if you have either a serious or long-standing injury.

DURDERS – He's not like Eileen Drewery, then, Glenn Hoddle's faith healer?

FLATS – You've completely lost me now.

DURDERS — She was a faith healer brought in by Glenn Hoddle to help the England football team in the late 1990s. He caused controversy by omitting Paul Gascoigne from the squad and then installing her as part of his coaching staff. Legend has it that during one of her one-to-one sessions with the England players she asked Ray Parlour what she could do for him and he said, 'A short back and sides, please.'

FLATS — That's lovely stuff from Ray. Kevin's certainly good at instilling faith, but he doesn't use it to heal people. The day before one of the operations that Kevin arranged, a member of the England Rugby medical team rang me, seemingly just to let me know that I didn't have his blessing for the operation. I said to him, 'But I've been told to retire, for heaven's sake! I've got absolutely nothing to lose, have I?' He said, 'I'm ringing you to let you know that I don't approve of the operation.' It was completely nonsensical, not to mention incredibly unhelpful. I said to him, 'Thank you very much indeed. I'll be taking the op.' As I said, eight or nine months later I was back playing for Bath again. I was fat and not running very well, so was completely back to normal, basically.

DURDERS — How was it long-term?

FLATS — As I said, I played over 150 more games and never missed one game or one day's training again because of my Achilles'.

DURDERS — There was an amazing amount of detail in that story, including the time of your train to London. I've got a nagging suspicion that this is the precise point in our groundbreaking literary masterpiece that people have downgraded our tome from the bedside table to the pile of books in the loo that sit there simply gathering dust.

FLATS — The reason I remember the train time is because Kevin always asked his clients — or at least clients whose bills were being paid for by their respective clubs — not to take rush-hour trains as they cost too much money. I remember saying to him, 'Who cares? The club hate you anyway,' but he was adamant. 'You're costing the club too much money in expenses,' he said. 'You cannot take rush-hour trains.' He never charged me for the eight months of physio, by the way. Not one single session. Sometime later I contacted him again about my shoulder and, to cut a long story short, he recommended some more physio. The club weren't willing to pay and when I told Kevin, he said he'd do it for nothing. 'You can't do that,' I said. 'It's not fair. You have to get paid.' In the end he and the club came to a compromise and they ended up paying half, but he fixed my shoulder and I never missed another game with it.

DURDERS — We're back to free stuff again. Why does it always happen to you? Bearing in mind I had a ruptured knee tendon a few months ago, when were you going to tell me about this secret Mr Fixit who could get me back to gliding like a catwalk model rather than limping around like a buffalo that's just survived being mauled by a lion (but only just)? It's taken a book for me to get it out of you.

In penance, you have to allow me one more of my compelling injury tales. I think the scariest procedure I've ever had to have because of an injury is an aforementioned cortisone injection. It was back in the early 1990s and the needle was about the size of a Polaris missile. I was desperate to play in the Durham University v. Newcastle University fixture and it was the only way I stood a chance. It was going to be the biggest crowd of the season — a show-off's dream.

Those occasions were never primarily about the rugby for me. Unfortunately, the cortisone injection, which I had for a haematoma, didn't work, so I had to stand on the touchline aided by crutches as the girls cheered on their 'rugby heroes' on the pitch. That hurt way more than the haematoma. But the morale of my epic haematoma story is that these so-called miracle treatments are usually anything but. At best they just paper over the cracks and at worst they make you stand on a touchline as your mates become the 1990s northern university equivalents of One Direction.

FLATS – Didn't you suffer a bizarre injury in New Zealand once? I'm sure you told me you did.

DURDERS – You're making this easy for me. I genuinely think I'm slaughtering you in this chapter, certainly in terms of my vast smorgasbord of injuries. There's something for everyone. Sporting injuries are all variations on a theme really. Mine are too, I suppose, but at least the theme is usually either incompetence or negligence shown by either myself or my parents. Have I mentioned my parents? Big icon and little icon? I think I have.

FLATS – Your dad should have changed his name to Chalmers really. I'm surprised you didn't.

DURDERS – Children of real icons rarely do. Look at Norah Jones and Ravi Shankar, or Kate Hudson and my former squeeze, Goldie Hawn. Anyway, New Zealand. It was during my gap year and I was in Rotorua on the North Island, south of Auckland.

FLATS – Don't tell me, you were helping out at an orphanage and had dreadlocks?

DURDERS – Absolutely not. I was visiting a geyser park with
my oldest friend, called Huw Thomas, known as Spewie
for fairly obvious reasons. I was wearing a poncho and sun-
glasses, and after finding a geyser with some steam billowing
out of it, I asked him to take a photo. I thought I looked a
bit like Clint Eastwood in *A Fistful of Dollars* with the get–up
I was wearing. 'Hang on a second,' I said to Huw at the last
minute. 'There's more steam over here.' With that I walked
towards a geyser with slightly more steam coming out of
it and with a much better bubble factor, stood over it, held
out my arms and told Huw to take the photo. As he was
doing this, part of the bank I was standing on collapsed and
I whooshed down into the geyser, just managing to cling on
to a bush so that I only went in up to my knees. 'Did you get
the photo?' I asked Huw. 'Nope. Sorry,' he said. '*Whaaat?*'

So I have no photographic evidence, but you'll have to take
it from me, I looked smoking. Literally, as it turned out. At
first, having not really fully understood the ramifications of
dunking your feet into 200-degree boiling sulphuric water,
I was just a little peeved that I'd got my jeans wet. Huw, the
Welsh sadist, found the whole thing very funny. 'Hang on
a second,' I said to Huw. 'This is getting a bit painful now.'
'What is?' asked Huw, who at the end of the day was just
the other half of what was a Tim Nice But Dim double act,
albeit a Welsh half. 'My legs,' I said. 'They really hurt.'

Fortunately, somebody who knew what we were dealing
with had seen my fall into this geyser and came running
over. 'Come with me now,' she said, before marching me
off to the ladies' loo. I thought, *Crikey, this is exciting!* When
we were inside the loo this woman said, 'Take your trousers
off, quickly.' 'Whaaat?' I said. 'I can't do that!' 'You have to,'

said the woman. With the pain becoming overwhelming, I decided to do as I was told and seconds later I was standing there in a ladies' loo in a geyser park in New Zealand wearing a threadbare, tight-fitting pair of jockey Y-fronts (all my very nice pairs of pinstripe boxer shorts that don't hug your testicles too much were awaiting a trip to the laundrette), with a woman I'd never met before looking at my legs and feet.

'Now take off your socks,' she ordered. *Very domineering*, I thought. Is she a bit kinky? Is she a bit *Fifty Shades of Grey*? Once again I did as I was told, but as I began to pull my left sock down my leg, I realised that the skin was coming with it. 'Oh dear,' I said. 'That's not supposed to happen, is it?' I was staring at raw pink flesh. 'Okay, you need to stick that in the basin now,' said the woman. 'Really?' I said. 'How? I've never been that flexible. I'm always out first in the "pick the Frostie packet up with only your teeth" game.'

FLATS – You have lived the weirdest life. You do know how far from normal your existence has been, don't you?

DURDERS – There's no time for that now, we're in the middle of high drama. So, the basin was quite high on the wall and you'd have been hard-pushed to bathe a kitten in it. I tried for about five minutes to get my feet and ankles under the water, hopping from one fleshy foot to the other. The pain at this point was, even for the pound-for-pound hardest man in British broadcasting, excruciating. The sink wasn't working out for me, so this woman/angel, whom I never saw again to thank for her incredible mercy mission, took me at high speed to hospital. I walked into a very busy Rotorua General Hospital A&E department, naked but for my ill-fitting jockey Y-fronts, with skin flapping around my ankles.

They were brilliant, although I did have to be restrained as the pain was so acute I was writhing around on the floor of A&E like a chicken that's just had its head lopped off.

FLATS – I think you have the pain threshold of a toddler and you're obviously embellishing for dramatic effect, but I concede it does sound a little uncomfortable.

DURDERS – A tad. It wasn't just the pain of my skin burning that affected me, though – it was the pain of my embarrassment, too. Why did it have to be that day, the day when I'd run out of my sexy boxer shorts, that this happened to me? I'm sure there are people who were waiting in that A&E who must have been traumatised by the images of a burned, brief-wearing Englishman slithering around the floor beneath them. Obviously screaming a little too. We've established that's my go-to reaction upon any hospital admission.

FLATS – How long were you in for?

DURDERS – Just under a month. They put me in the prostate ward, so there were lots of people farting and losing control of their bowels. I did see all kinds of things while I was there. One guy came in with a beer bottle literally sticking out of his forehead. He looked like a rhino. It was extraordinary. It's quite a frisky place, Rotorua.

FLATS – A month's a long time.

DURDERS – I think I suffered some second-degree burns and had to have a lot of rehab. You know, learning how to walk again. That sort of thing. You had to do that after your Achilles', didn't you? It's weird.

FLATS – Yes, I did. The thing I remember most about it is not being allowed to walk with a limp. You'd teach yourself bad habits doing that, so you just had to walk slowly. You're right, it's a very strange experience.

DURDERS – Well, after I was discharged from hospital wearing rather more clothing than I had on when I entered, I went to stay with some friends of my parents. 'Go and see them for a bit,' said my iconic parents. 'They'll look after you. No point you coming home in that state.' They'd known these people since their early twenties, when my father had been ADC to the governor general of New Zealand. They were amazing and came and picked me up as I was still on crutches.

I'm not sure quite what they made of the 19-year-old Pom hopping around their beautiful stud farm in Okawa pumped up on morphine, but I shall always be eternally grateful that they big-heartedly took in this wounded stray. Do you think we're done with the injuries stuff? I think we're in danger of becoming injury bores.

FLATS – I do have one more to add our catalogue of broken bones and chargrilled flesh. I was on tour in Canada with England. It was a capped tour but it was a bit second string. We went out on a rig boat one day and the man in charge asked us if we'd like to see some killer whales. 'Ooh, yes please,' we said. As we were flying along, he asked us if we'd like to go faster and naturally we said yes again. After ramping up the power, we ended up hitting this wave and we landed with a hell of a bang. *Fucking hell,* I thought. It felt like my stomach had literally hit my chest and for the rest of the trip I felt awful. Something was up.

When we got back to the hotel the rest of the lads got

changed and went out for some sushi, but I decided to stay put. I was feeling even worse now and just wanted to be left alone. A couple of hours later, the pain became excruciating, to the point where I genuinely thought I was having a heart attack. I ended up having to text a couple of the lads and fortunately they came back to the hotel. It turned out I'd popped one of my ribs. In fact, I remember the doctor saying to me that I'd managed to pop a rib whale-watching, which made me feel better. I said, 'You're joking. For God's sake don't tell anyone.' He said, 'Never mind that. You're not going to be able to play on Sunday.' 'I am definitely not missing a game because of this,' I said. 'I've got to play!'

The following morning we had scrums with the legend that is Phil Keith-Roach. 'Flats,' he said. 'I'm going to play you at tighthead and loosehead this weekend. We're just going to swap you over, okay?' 'Yeah, no worries,' I said. In those days the scrum machines were basically anchored into the ground, so instead of hitting something that resembled human beings, it was like scrummaging against a tree. I hit the first one at loosehead fine on the machine, but when I went in for one at tighthead it felt like my rib had cut through my skin. I stood up and started choking as if I'd been strangled, so Phil asked me what was the matter. 'Oh, nothing,' I said to him. 'I'm fine.'

After that, we had a quick drink on the sidelines and he asked me again if I was okay. 'Are you sure you haven't done a rib or something?' Phil asked. 'Actually,' I said, beckoning him towards me. 'I have done a rib. Thing is, I did it while I was whale-watching.' 'What?' he said. 'Whale-watching?' There was a look of horror on Phil's face. 'If you'd done it scrummaging, then fine,' he said. 'But *what*-watching?'

Fortunately Phil seemed almost as embarrassed as I was, so I knew my secret was safe with him. 'Get back in there,' he said, pushing me towards the machine. 'Tighthead first.'

DURDERS — Your stories always make you out to be like Rambo, mine make me sound like Shaggy from Scooby Doo. It's not fair. Surely you had a jab or something to dull the pain before the match, or are you just so hard you didn't bother?

FLATS — I did. I asked Simon Kemp, the England doctor. 'What kind of jab would you like?' he said. 'I'd like an anaesthetic jab, please,' I replied. 'We're not allowed to give you one of those,' said Kempy. I said, 'I don't care about that. Can I have one anyway?' 'No!' he said. 'I'll get struck off.' 'Fair point,' I said. 'I tell you what, I'll just crack on.' I consoled myself with the fact that I probably wouldn't be on the field for more than 50 minutes and it would all be over within the hour.

DURDERS — Don't tell me. You stayed on for the full 80.

FLATS — Correct. I have never been so resentful about playing a full game of rugby in my life. I was fuming. That night I went to bed in absolute agony and didn't get a wink of sleep. Another embarrassing one was the Achilles' injury I mentioned earlier. It happened right at the end of the domestic season in 2004 and afterwards England were off on tour to Australia and New Zealand. Clive had selected me to go on this tour, but at the time we didn't know what my Achilles' injury was, so I played it down. 'It doesn't feel that bad,' I said. Guess how many games I played?

DURDERS — I'm guessing none?

FLATS – Didn't put my boots on once. Not even to train. Having missed the World Cup (not that I would necessarily have gone), I was desperate to be involved but ended up spending the entire month doing rehab. Being a passenger on any rugby tour must be pretty demoralising, but when it's the national team it's something else.

About a week from the end of the tour, the doctor said, 'We might as well just fly you home.' 'But I said that two weeks ago,' I replied. 'I've gone and booked a holiday here now at the end of the tour so it makes no odds.' 'So you only want to stay because you've got a holiday booked?' said the doc. 'No, of course not. I would have gone home two weeks ago if I'd known, but as I was told to stay, I decided to stay on for a holiday. Do you want me to cancel it?' The doctor was in full-on belligerent mode, unfortunately. 'I've booked you in to see a specialist two days after we land back in England,' he said. 'So, yes. Cancel your holiday.'

DURDERS – Was his doctorate in misanthropy?

FLATS – May as well have been. Because it was all so last-minute, my girlfriend, who I was going on holiday with, had already started travelling to Australia and it was too late to stop her. She then landed in Brisbane the following day and after telling her how nice it was to see her, I then had to tell her that we were flying back in three days' time. I thought, *You absolute dick. Why on earth would you do that?* When I got back to England I went to see this surgeon and after looking at the scans he said, 'I haven't really seen that before and, to be honest, I'm not sure what to do. Anyway, thanks for coming in.' I was in there literally five minutes.

DURDERS – Did she bin you?

FLATS – Eventually, yes. But we had to get married first. It was probably a contributing factor. The doctor seemed to think that I was only there for the tour fee, but I promise you it was mortifying. I'm on an England tour and I'm not even training. Whenever the lads go out, I'm standing in the foyer watching them, and when they come back, it's the same again. It was humiliating. When I suggested going home after the first week the doctor said no because he thought I'd be able to play, but when I couldn't he tried to make me feel like I was on a jolly.

Shortly before we left for home, one of the coaches said he was thinking about going on a backpacking holiday and another coach piped up and said, 'You should ask Flats about that. He's the one on holiday.' That was it, I'm afraid. I said, 'You're a prick, mate. I'm a 24-year-old rugby player who can't play on an England tour with all these legends and you're telling me I'm on holiday? This is the worst month of my life. You really are a prick.' That kind of shut him up, but I was also told off for talking to him like that. I then made the argument that if he was going to try to humiliate me in front of the group, I wasn't going to let him, so we just left it at that.

DURDERS – When you really lose it with people, what do you do?

FLATS – I usually stab first and justify later.

DURDERS – To conclude, I think we've got more broken bits between us than Evel Knievel or the entire cast of Channel 4's *The Jump*.

FLATS – Never mind conclude, I've got one more. It involves an elbow, my nose, Francois Pienaar and a great deal of blood and pain.

DURDERS – Okay, just one – injury time extra time, away you go.

FLATS – Saracens were playing Northampton Saints one afternoon and after a little bit of a scuffle the most appropriately named French second-row in the history of the game, Olivier Brouzet, gave me a little elbow on the nose. A elbow from Olivier was probably the equivalent of a jab from a heavyweight boxer and unfortunately it caught me so flush that I thought my nose had exploded. Every fibre of my being wanted to hit him back, but instead I decided – as I could barely stand up at this point – to assess the damage, which was considerable. I remember feeling my nose and thinking, *Oh shit. I'm going to look like Mike Tindall.* It had completely gone. I didn't care about what it looked like. What I cared about was the fact that it really hurt and the fact that I was almost swimming in blood.

DURDERS – A little bit melodramatic, don't you think? Swimming in blood?

FLATS – Are you saying that I exaggerate? This man had almost literally knocked my nose bone through my brain and out the other side. I was drowning in gallons of my own blood. Fortunately, the physio came on just in time and after shoving some cotton wool up my nostrils he told me I'd be fine.

It got to half time and after looking in the mirror I discovered that my nose had migrated onto my right cheekbone, which was interesting. I know I'm not a classically good-looking guy, but I was now disfigured, and that was quite annoying. The reason it was annoying is because I knew that Francois Pienaar, who was our head coach, chief exec and bus driver, would not allow me any time off to get it fixed, so I was going to have to look like Mike Tindall for the rest of my life.

DURDERS – That's horrifying. Poor you. You were quite literally the elephant man.

FLATS – Exactly. 'I'm not an animal!' Great film. When Francois came into the dressing room at half time the doctor was with me and the first thing he said to Francois was, 'He can't go back on, I'm afraid. His nose is broken and there's far too much blood.'

(Note to reader. You have to remember that Francois is South African, so I'll be doing an impression. A good one.)

'Give him to me,' he said, taking me by the arm. 'I'll fix you, boy.' As Francois was pulling me away, I looked back at the doctor as if to say, 'Please tell my mum that I love her.' After dragging me into this cubicle, he got me in a headlock, grabbed hold of my nose and basically just yanked it over.

DURDERS – Blimey!

FLATS – He yanked it so hard that my entire head moved, which seemed to vex him somewhat. 'Keep your fucking head still,' he said. I did as I was told and he went for it again. This time my nose went back into place and he said, 'You look beautiful. Okay, Flatsy, let's go.' With that, he then grabbed me by the arm again, pulled me out of the cubicle and released me. 'Put some cotton wool up his nose, would you?' he said to the doc. 'There's fucking blood everywhere.' The following Monday I went in for training and the physios were going to send me home. 'You've got to get that re-set, Flats,' they said. Just then, Francois walked in. 'What's going on?' 'We're sending Flats to get his nose re-set,' said the physio. 'I re-set his nose myself,' said Pienaar. 'He looks lovely. He's got to train today, so let's go, Flatsy.'

DURDERS – So you never did have your nose re-set?

FLATS – Nope. Shirt by Joules, gloves by Caspar, nose by Pienaar. Lovely stuff.

Characters

DURDERS – I have been thinking about this and the mystery and myth that surrounds rugby players was so much greater when there was far less exposure, if that makes sense. I'm talking about the Willie John McBrides and the Mike Teagues of this world. Legends of the game whose myth and reputation grew because the reality wasn't there for us all to see. We couldn't see their Twitter feeds or their Instagram pages. They had a genuine mystique about them and stories of their heroics and antics on the rugby field – and occasionally off it – were almost part of folklore. Does that kind of rugby mythology even exist any more? I'm not sure social media allows it to. Everybody seems to know everything about everybody these days. I know the likes of Joe Marler, Jamie George and Johnny Sexton, for example, are big personalities, but do they have the same aura that their equivalents of bygone eras had? The accessibility to modern players is definitely a positive, but I think elevation to the pantheon of being a legendary character of the game is a lot harder to achieve because we almost know them too well. If they wreck a hotel room, it will result in a six-month ban rather than a pat on the back and a ruffle of the hair as it used to be. The other factor at play here is, is the modern pro rugby player over media-trained? Does that in itself suppress the revelation of character and encourage vanilla opinion?

FLATS — There is actually some good media training nowadays, but the majority of media training I received as a player was crap, to use a technical term. Bits of it were good but the majority was just awful. So much of it wasn't actually about media training, per se, it was about the press officer's attitude was towards the journalists. Quite often that attitude will be dictated by how much they fear or revere the chief executive, so if they're shit scared of the boss because every time something appears in the paper that they don't like the press officer gets a bollocking, that will affect who the press officer puts up for interviews and how much they will allow you to be yourself and how readily they will advise you to say nothing at all.

I remember Melissa Platt coming to do some media training at Bath Rugby after I'd finished playing and she was absolutely brilliant. She said, 'Right. So, which of you here thinks that you have to be careful around the media because if they get the chance they'll write something derogatory and stitch you up?' There were 36 players in the room and after she'd finished asking the question 36 hands went up. 'Okay then, guys. How many of you here know somebody who has been stitched up by the media?' One hand went up. 'Who was that?' Melissa asked. 'Lawrence Dallaglio,' said the player holding his hand up. 'Fair enough,' said Melissa, being very conciliatory. 'He did say some incredibly illegal stuff, though, which probably wasn't a great idea. I take your point, though.' You see, she wasn't trying to just disprove the player's claim and make him look stupid. She was trying to plant a seed. 'By the way, did you know Lawrence personally?' asked Melissa. 'No,' said the player. 'I played against him.' 'Okay, is there anybody you know personally who has been stitched up by the media and who didn't bring it on themselves in any way?' 'No,' said the player.

Another player then mentioned somebody who'd been hammered by the media for drink-driving. 'Yes, but he did get pissed and drive home in broad daylight,' countered Melissa. 'Do you think they shouldn't write about it because he plays rugby?' 'No, of course not,' said the player. Game, set and match to Melissa.

DURDERS – Melissa had your attention and you sound like you were an eager student? Teacher's pet.

FLATS – Seriously, she was amazing. 'Right, then,' she continued. 'How many of you have been on nights out when journalists have been there?' About 30 hands went up this time. 'Okay. How much have they seen that they've never written about?' The silence was deafening. 'Okay, I'll answer that for you,' said Melissa. 'Loads!' A player then put his hand up. 'Yeah, but they keep it in the bank, don't they?' 'Do they?' she said. 'Why would a journalist sit on a red-hot story when it could earn them a bonus or get them promoted? There are loads of idiots in professional rugby, the same as there are loads of idiots in journalism. The vast majority, however, are good people. That's what you need to try to remember, guys.'

DURDERS – That's an astute and clever way of making a very good point. I know we're trying to avoid referring to matches or events from the current domestic season or Six Nations tournament, as both will be ongoing when we've finished writing, but I have to mention the BBC reporter Sonja McLaughlan, who, after the Six Nations match in 2021 between Wales and England, which featured two rather controversial decisions by the referee, Pascal Gaüzère, had to ask England's captain, Owen Farrell, some very pertinent but potentially provocative questions. Thirty or forty years ago she may well have received a genuinely honest answer from the England captain, which may or may not have caused ructions, but media-trained Owen was obviously prepared for Sonja's line of interrogation and understandably brushed aside her very relevant questions. Sonja was castigated on social media for the questions she asked, which were the right questions asked by a very good broadcaster and journalist. The reaction and aftermath left her in tears. It was appalling.

I think the antithesis to this kind of conditioned and controlled response – certainly since we've been presenting the highlights show – is Sale Sharks' former director of rugby, Steve Diamond, who, incidentally, is probably one of the only people I can think of that would survive more than five minutes against his successor, Alex Sanderson. Steve Diamond knew he wasn't supposed to say certain things, but he obviously didn't agree with being stifled and on many occasions just said what he thought. To us media types, that made him the best interview out there really. On the flipside, you'd have somebody like Paul Gustard, a really good man and really forthright off camera, but who was always a lot more guarded when in the eye of a lens.

FLATS – Didn't you once get Steve Diamond banned from the touchline for a few weeks?

DURDERS – Sort of. It was actually a 12-week suspended ban and a £5,000 fine, £4,000 of that suspended, to be precise. I guess I owe him lunch one day. It goes back to Melissa and your media training, and in fact mine as well. I was seated in the stands at their old ground, Edgeley Park, watching Sale take on Northampton, and saw Diamond push a member of the Northampton Saints coaching staff. My journalistic instincts kicked in and I asked the team in our broadcast trucks if they had any footage of the incident. On a human level I felt like a sneak, but my job required me to view the incident dispassionately. They did have footage and he was subsequently given the suspended ban. His post-match interview in our ESPN studio, where he spoke candidly and forthrightly, was also part of the ban and fine. Ironically, the other aspect of the judgment on his case by the RFU was that he was ordered to do some media training! That backfired. The untrained are so much more stimulating to interview. A similar thing happened with Mark Cueto, but that was on the field of play. I saw an angle of him appearing to gouge another player that had been missed and asked our team to take another look. It would almost certainly have been picked up by the citing commissioner on review anyway, but the former England winger got a nine-week ban. Fortunately, he didn't miss out on the 2011 World Cup as a result, as I would have felt even more uncomfortable had he done so.

FLATS – Are Steve and Mark aware that you grassed them up and got them a nice ban each?

DURDERS – I have fessed up to both of them. I explained
I had been a professional sneak, and even though they
probably wanted to smash my face in, they didn't, which I
take as a major result. My bottom was squeaking slightly,
especially with Steve Diamond, but I lived to tell the tale.
The reason I mentioned these two incidents is because on
both occasions I was simply doing my job, as was Sonja
McLaughlan when she questioned Owen Farrell. My
neighbour popped round after that England game and
said, 'Wasn't that interview disgraceful?' 'No, it wasn't,' I
said. To be fair, he wasn't aware of the Twitter backlash,
so hadn't been influenced by keyboard warriors brandishing virtual torches and pitchforks! I repeat, though, Sonja
McLaughlan merely asked the questions that everybody at
home wanted answering. Some people complained that it
was the way she asked the questions that was the problem,
but he's a 6ft 2in rugby player with getting on for a hundred
caps, not a six-year-old child. Owen Farrell knows how
to handle himself. Have you ever incurred the wrath of a
rugby dressing room?

FLATS – I'm sure I have, but only for having given my honest
opinion. You don't have to be aggressive or overly critical
in my job. If somebody plays badly you have to say so, and
if somebody plays well you have to do the same. I expect
it's quite tempting for some people to try to pass themselves
off as being all things to all people, but by saying bugger all
you're not doing the sport, or the art of punditry, any favours
whatsoever.

A couple of years ago Bath were going through a bad run
of form and in my position as a pundit I said what I thought.

The following week a mate of mine who still worked at the club rang me up and said, 'Mate, you got knifed in the team meeting on Monday. One of them even said that you should never be allowed back to the Rec again.' 'Really?' I said. 'That's just ridiculous.' 'Hang on,' said my mate. 'I haven't finished yet. The head coach then stood up and said that he agreed with you. "We are in a bad run of form," he said, "And something needs to change." I think he still thinks you're a prick, though.'

DURDERS – I'm with the coach on that one. Have you ever contacted anybody in advance of the highlights show going to air after voicing an opinion that someone may not particularly enjoy hearing?

FLATS – Good question. Funnily enough, I have done that only once in my career as a pundit so far and it was just a few weeks ago. The person I contacted was Stuart Hooper, the director of rugby at Bath, who is an old mate of mine. I sent him a message saying something along the lines of, 'Just so you know, this is what I'm saying on the TV tonight, depending which version they use. Regardless of which, I absolutely stand by what I've said.' Stuart came back to me after the show had aired and said that he agreed with some of my points. Most importantly, though, he said, 'Listen, Flats, you carry on giving your opinions and carry on being honest.' I respected him massively for that. It's not his job to worry about what I think and vice versa, but if Stuart Hooper – or any director of rugby for that matter – ever asked me if I thought they should leave or be removed from their position and I thought they should, I'd say so.

DURDERS – Apart from Alex Sanderson. You wouldn't dare.

FLATS – Apart from Alex Sanderson. Sale should offer him a lifetime contract as far as I'm concerned.

DURDERS – Would you have afforded that courtesy to every director of rugby you were potentially in danger of upsetting?

FLATS – No. The only reason I contacted Stuart is because we played together at two clubs and are very good mates. That has no bearing on what I'd say, though, not in the slightest. You actually asked me during the chat that prompted me to contact Stuart whether I thought he should still be director of rugby, and I said yes. But only because I believe he's the right person for the job. If I didn't believe that I would say so, whether I thought he'd speak to me again or not. Just because I'm a pundit doesn't mean to say I know more than anybody else. It means that I've got opinions and have a platform from which to express them. Sam Vesty and George Ford will know a lot more about the game than I do. Okay, not about the intricacies of forward play, but the game as a whole. They'll know more than I do and that's fine. My job is to communicate well the opinions I have about a game I love, follow, and know something about. That might be with a former rugby pro, a fellow pundit, my gran, or a coach.

DURDERS – You've basically just listed our entire audience there.

FLATS – My gran's dead actually, but we kept her telly on Channel 5 so it would count as an extra viewer. Can't lose.

DURDERS – Is it ever tempting to be controversial just for

171

the sake of it. An agent provocateur? Do a Cowell or a Craig Revel Horwood?

FLATS – Not in the slightest, for the simple reason that if it's not how you truly feel, the chances are it'll come back and bite you on the arse at some point. I haven't been bitten yet and for the simple reason that I haven't said anything for the sake of it or because I want to get a reaction. Perhaps I could do a kind of 'cash for questions' thing, like those MPs did back in the '90s.

DURDERS – You read it first here. Questions on a postcard please, complete with a £2 postal order to Mrs D. Flatman, Seaview Cottage, Tibet.

FLATS – When I was working for the communications team at Bath Rugby after I retired, Gary Gold was the chief executive and one day he came in and said something to me about Austin Healey. Austin was on ESPN with you at the time, Durds, and Gary said, 'All Austin does is look for foul play and try to get people banned.' I thought, *That's not what he does at all.* Austin's a brilliant pundit and co-commentator. The only reason Gary was having a whinge about Austin is because he found his players out occasionally. The thing is, if they didn't commit foul play in the first place, it wouldn't be a problem.

I'm not preaching from on high, by the way. I wasn't a particularly violent player but on the few occasions I was cited – such as the time I punched Lawrence and he seemingly didn't even notice – I held up my hands. I didn't go around asking who'd grassed me up. You can fool yourself by trying to blame the police for catching you doing

100mph on the motorway but the only way you're going to guarantee it doesn't happen again is by not doing 100mph on the motorway.

DURDERS — Don't do the crime and then blame the person who spots you doing it, basically.

FLATS — *Exactement.*

DURDERS — Why do you do that thing when you slip into *'Allo 'Allo!* mode? I'm not sure it suits you. That aside, do you have any sympathy with the players when it comes to talking to the media?

FLATS — Yes, of course I do, because ultimately it's not what they get paid to do, and in many cases not what they're good at. They get paid to play rugby to the best of their ability and although they'll obviously speak to the media if they're asked, it's not their forte. Reader, sometimes Durds and I will finish interviewing a player and as he's walking off we'll say to camera, 'Maybe we'll ask one of his team-mates to do the interview next time.' It's only a joke, but it will underline the fact that the interview was probably quite staid or a bit dull and that some people are more comfortable speaking in front of a camera than others.

A dilemma we have sometimes is when the Man of the Match is somebody we know isn't a confident or entertaining interviewee. The person we want to interview might only have been on the field of play for the last 20 minutes and the question we have to ask ourselves is whether or not we can justify asking for them and not the Man of the Match. You obviously want the big names as they look good on screen, but you also want the extroverts, the entertainers and the piss-takers. As with most things, it's about finding a balance.

DURDERS – Weren't we supposed to be talking about characters in this chapter?

FLATS – You were the one who first mentioned media training. Yes, we were supposed to be talking about characters in the game. Shall we attempt get back on track?

DURDERS – Some would say that you're a bit of a character. Personally I find that notion, like the waistband of your trousers, a bit of a stretch.

FLATS – The same as they might say that you're a bit of a . . . No, I'll be nice. I don't know about that. I like to hide my light under a bushel as well you know, so half the time most people won't even know I'm there. I know we've already mentioned him a couple of times, but when it comes to characters I've met in the game of rugby I have to start with Julian White. Everybody knows that Julian was a mighty tighthead prop but he was also – sorry, *is* also – a unique character. He's actually very, very funny but you'd never know because he rarely opens his mouth.

DURDERS – Not even to breathe? Not knowing him at all, he doesn't strike me as rugby's Jack Whitehall.

FLATS – I promise you. Hands down, Julian White is the funniest man I ever played with, to the point where, during the England squad sessions at which he'd get picked and I'd be carrying the bags, we'd be separated during the meetings. I remember Clive saying, 'For God's sake, can you two young guns sit apart please?' Julian was 27 at the time.

Phil Larder, the defence coach, who wouldn't have been my biggest fan, did a presentation once and at the end of it he turned to the players and said, 'Thanks, lads. My work here is done,' and then sat down. I'm not sure if Phil was aware that he'd just pinched a quote from the *Prisoner of Zenda*, but regardless of which, it sounded quite funny. As soon as he sat down Julian shot me a quick look as if to say, 'What the fucking hell was that?' and unfortunately I started guffawing.

One of the reasons he always had that effect on me is because Julian's natural expression is a mixture of lugubrious and dour, which are perfect for comedy.

Just then Andy Robinson stood up. He's another character, by the way. I love Robbo. I saw him out running the other day and he was flying along. Anyway, Andy Robinson stood up and in full-on David Brent mode he pointed at Phil and said, 'That man . . .' – pause for effect – pause for even longer – 'Inspirational!' That was it. I looked at Julian, he looked at me, and we completely fucking folded. We were all sitting behind desks and in an attempt to try to hide the fact that we were pissing ourselves, we had to pretend that we'd dropped things on the floor. Not everybody got the joke, of course. I remember Neil Back looking over at us and shaking his head. By this time Danny Grewcock had started laughing and was also doubled up and when Lawrence leaned over and asked him what was going on he couldn't speak. He just let out a little whining noise. Things like that used to happen all the time, to the point where we sometimes had to actively avoid each other.

DURDERS – Let's have your funniest Julian White story then.

FLATS – Okay. I always try to maintain, jokingly, that this is the reason I didn't get picked for England too many times. I was standing with Julian in the foyer at England's training ground, having just arrived for training one Monday morning, when Clive suddenly walked up. Now Clive used to have a handshake that came in from above, if that makes sense – from the sky – and as he approached us I knew what was coming. 'All right, Flats,' said Clive, while turning his hand in a circular motion until it was about head height and then bringing it down to meet mine. 'How you doing, mate?' 'I'm very well, thanks, Clive.' It was almost a handshake version of dad dancing really and used to make me feel ever so slightly nervous, as Clive's hand came in so fast and from such an unorthodox angle that it was easy to mistime it.

After greeting me, Clive moved on to my uncommunicative and, at this moment, quite awkward-looking colleague. As well as being a top-grade bloke, Julian was also a very traditional prop in the sense that he never really wanted to do the running and catching stuff and was always happiest scrummaging and maiming people. 'Whitey!' said Clive, going in from up top again. Being old-school, Julian's a traditionalist when it comes to handshakes, so while Clive began performing his usual up-and-over shake, Julian stuck his hand out as if to perform a normal one. This resulted in Julian catching hold of Clive's thumb as it came down, which he then gripped onto and shook up and down while dourly wishing Clive a good morning. 'Hello, Clive,' he said, Clive's hand flapping about like a dead fish. This was just too much for me to bear, unfortunately, and I ended up on my knees – not a typical exaggeration this time – in the foyer almost soiling myself. I remember looking up at Clive and Julian, which was a massive mistake. Julian looked like he always does – impassive and bored – and Clive looked like somebody had just insulted him. Worst of all, though, Julian was still shaking Clive's thumb.

DURDERS – Did you actually soil yourself? Was there some detectable seepage?

FLATS – I honestly can't remember. It was close. It does lose a bit on the page unfortunately, but you get the idea. In the end, Clive's expression morphed from very surprised to mildly disgusted, and after Julian let his thumb go he just walked off.

DURDERS – Did you get any caps after that?

FLATS – Not one. I have claimed somewhere in this book that a series of injuries and an overall lack of talent spelt the end of my England career but it might just as easily have been Clive's thumb.

Another thing about Julian is that he was always late. It didn't matter what the occasion was, his watch was always stuck on Julian Mean Time, as opposed to Greenwich Mean Time, and if that happened to be different to the time zone he was in at the time, tough. He also used to ride motorbikes back then so when we were training for England I'd take his bag in my car and he'd come in on his motorbike.

One day he was late for a meeting at one of the England training sessions, which in those days was a massive no-no, as I'm sure it is now. When the meeting was about to start, everybody started asking where Julian was and because I was his mate and his bag carrier, everybody turned to me. 'He is here,' I said pleadingly but probably not too convincingly. 'I think he said he'd lost his boots or something.' After a few grumbles from the hierarchy the meeting began and every couple of minutes they'd look over to me as if to say, 'Where the hell is he?' About 10 minutes later, the door suddenly flew open and standing there in full biker leathers with his helmet under his arm was Julian. 'Fuck me,' shouted Mark Regan. 'Who ordered pizza?' He never even got a bollocking for being late. In fact, I recall Clive bursting into hysterical laughter. The brilliance of Julian, and the brilliance of Sir Clive.

DURDERS – Do you know how many interviews there are with Julian White on YouTube? Two. Both on his farm. In one he's holding a lamb under his arm and it's fair to say his comic genius doesn't feature heavily. When was the last time you saw him?

FLATS – About five years ago. I'd been to George Chuter's house for dinner after a Leicester game and I thought it might be nice to ask Julian along. I rang him up and I said, 'I'm having dinner at George's tonight, do you fancy coming?' He said, 'Erm, yeah, I could do, I suppose. I am lambing, though.'

We had dinner at 7 p.m. and at about half eight this battered old truck pulls up outside. 'That must be him,' I said to George. 'Shall I go and let him in?' When I opened the front door, there standing before me was what looked like the proprietor of an abattoir. The proprietor of an abattoir who hadn't been to bed for a few days. 'Looking prosperous, mate,' I said, shaking his hand. 'Hello, Flats,' he said, walking over the threshold in his massive shitty wellies. 'How are you? Ah, George. Hello, George. Nice to see you.'

DURDERS – He'd made an effort then.

FLATS — It looked to me like he'd delivered a lamb, rubbed some of the afterbirth into his wrists and face, shoved a couple of pounds of muck under his fingernails and then jumped in his truck. About an hour later, after having had a good old chuckle, a phone suddenly started ringing. 'It's not mine,' said George. 'It's not mine,' said Katy, his wife. 'Flats?' 'Nope, not me.' We all looked at Whitey when suddenly it dawned on him that it was his. 'Fucking thing,' he said, reaching inside his pockets trying to find the phone. It took him a while, but after finally locating the offending item he pulled it out of his pocket, held it out in front of him and looked at it like an epidemiologist might look at an especially dangerous disease. 'HELLOOO,' he said. He reminded me of one of my grandparents when they used to use a mobile phone. What followed were a series of about 15 yeses all delivered in exactly the same tone and at intervals of about three seconds. You know in American films people always put the phone down without saying goodbye? Well, that's also the custom of Leicestershire farmers, it seems. 'Fuck me,' he said after hanging up. 'Got to go lambing now,' he said, standing up, and after offering us all his hand again he said, 'Cheers then,' and then left. That was the last time I saw him. Just the best bloke in the game.

DURDERS — Stories involving people who are least expected to be a character are always my favourites. If I had to pick a couple of characters from my side of the fence it would have to be Dewi Morris and Stuart Barnes, who I had the pleasure of working with on the Sky Sports rugby team for a number of years. They're a thinking man's version of us, in a way. Or should I say, we're an idiot's version of them? They complement each other perfectly in my opinion. You have Dewi, who's all heart, and Stuart, who's all brain. Dewi, of course, is famous for getting the names of players wrong during commentaries. I think his record was during a game in the Heineken Cup once, where he pronounced 13 of the 15 Toulouse players incorrectly.

FLATS – One of my favourites of Dewi's is one that we actually adopted for a match against Biarritz once. He pronounced Imanol Harinordoquy 'Hardey-Nordequee', which was an absolute classic. We adopted it during the training sessions leading up the match and Martin Haag, who was our coach, assumed that was correct and started using it. I remember at half time he said, 'Can we get hold of that fucking Hardey-Nordequee, lads!' It was all Dewi's fault.

DURDERS – He actually gave up in the end and started calling him Hairy Donkey. True story! I remember hearing a story about John Wells, the Leicester Tigers coach. It might actually have been on your dodgy podcast, Flats. I think they were playing Toulouse, and Jean Baptiste Poux – pronounced 'Poo' – was one of their props. At half time John Wells stormed into the dressing room and said, 'Will somebody try and get Poo off the ball! Come on, lads. Poo's all over it!'

FLATS – I'm not adverse to a spot of scatological humour from time to time. What about Stuart Barnes?

DURDERS – When I worked at Sky Sports, Stuart was the person most people wanted to talk about when they met me. These days they want to talk about you or my iconic mother. Usually my mother. Stuart was quite a polarising character and so people would either begin the conversation with, 'That Stuart Barnes is a bit of a tosser, isn't he?' Or, 'I love Stuart Barnes. What's he like?' To be honest with you, the second of the two was less common. Stuart was so candid and so opinionated that every time he picked up his commentator's mic he was going to offend someone who believed their club or their favourite player was being grievously slighted. I was always a member of the Stuart Barnes fan club as I think he's a top-of-the-range commentator, pundit and bloke. I'd hate him to know my feelings about him though, but bearing in mind he's an Oxford Uni alumni and achingly high brow, the chances of him reading this lurid kiss-and-tell book are very slim.

FLATS — What about Dewi then? I'm sure you told me you once tackled Dewi when you were under the influence.

DURDERS — I did. It was after the European Cup final, which Bath actually won. Were you playing that day?

FLATS — I was still at school.

DURDERS — Of course, it was 1998. So long ago! After the game we all had a few drinks and in a moment of sheer exuberance I tackled Dewi Morris over a central reservation barrier on the French equivalent of the M25. We both could have died that night but somehow we lived to tell the tale. No thanks to me. Dewi didn't mind, by the way. He's about as sensitive as a rubber bludgeon in both thought, word and deed so he'd have minded more if I hadn't tackled him.

I suppose a more obvious contender for characters within rugby would be Austin Healey. Whether you like him or loathe him, he is without doubt one of the funniest and most offensive people I've ever met. He's very in your face and will wind you up mercilessly thinking it's hilarious but underneath all that bluster and bravado – and he'll hate me for revealing this – he's a very sweet-natured human being. I expect you'll bristle at me wanting to include Austin Healey in this category as he's everything Julian White isn't. Does he fit your bill as a character?

FLATS – Austin's every inch a character and he refuses to play to the gallery, in the sense that he will not compromise his beliefs or opinions. The amount of abuse he receives on 'anti-social' media is industrial, yet he keeps on saying what he believes. Bloody good on him.

DURDERS – Yes, while the Squirrel from the Wirral doesn't have the thickest of hair, he does seem to have the thickest of skin. Rather him than me. We work a lot together in The Green Room, a hospitality venue I'm involved with (top of the range, of course), and one of my favourite pastimes is to come up with new nicknames for the Irritating Little Hobbit. The Leicester Lip (stick) must have more nicknames than any other player in rugby. Why is that? Is it because he's a wind-up merchant? Is it because he's brash? Is it because he's more Shetland pony than giraffe?

FLATS – Maybe it's a bit of all of that. Austin's not a big man physically, which probably makes the whole cheeky thing easier to attribute. He's not tiny, though. What is he, about 5ft 10in? You get different characters in all the positions on a rugby field. Look at Martin Johnson. He's 12ft 6in in bare feet and because of where he played and how he conducted himself on and off the pitch you might lazily assume that he's the strong, silent type. Physically and as a rugby player, Martin Johnson was indeed mighty, yet when you played against him and got to know his character you realised that his physical prowess was complemented by a very keen intellect. He can also be very, very funny, which some people might find surprising.

Like Julian, he's a bit of a contradiction, whereas the Austin Healeys and even the David Flatmans of this world are perhaps a bit easier to read. I think what the four of us all have in common is that we don't really care a huge amount what people we don't know think about us. That makes me feel lucky as it allows me to carry on being me. Some people might not like that but, as I just said, I don't care much about the views of some people.

There are people I've spent time with in the past who have unlimited amounts of energy and are super-hilarious yet I've always ended up asking myself, is this actually you? The people I gravitate to the most are people who I believe are being true to themselves. A time-evolved version of who they were 20 years ago, basically.

DURDERS – Martin Johnson does have a glare. A glare that can even make the pound-for-pound hardest man in British broadcasting a little scared.

FLATS – But you always hammer him when we're working on stages together.

DURDERS – That's a lie! My interactions with Martin Johnson do usually take place in the corporate arena, where I ask him a series of inane questions and play the fool slightly. He gives me the eye, not in a good way, as if to say, 'My God, this man is talking absolute bollocks. Will you just give it a rest!' He has a reputation for not suffering fools gladly that doesn't work in my favour. In fact, if our chats didn't take place in such a public arena I'm pretty sure he'd just get up and chin me.

FLATS – Just like Ellis Genge almost did at a dinner we co-hosted.

DURDERS – I'm fearless – like Dr Strange or Ironman or Wonder Woman. Actually I still get flashbacks to the Genge affair. Most of the England team were there and, let's be honest, it was a tiny bit awkward.

FLATS – It really, really was.

DURDERS – I was going around the room talking to some of the England players and I came upon Ellis Genge's table. He was sitting next to one of the sponsors and I said, 'I'm sorry to interrupt you, Ellis. I'm sure you're loving the small talk and are brilliant at it.' I can't see how he could have taken offence to my comment – apart from it being very subtly laced with irony – but he immediately stood up and literally went nose-to-nose with me. He then said something along the lines of 'All right, babes', which I assume is some kind of a modern-day version of 'You want some, do ya?'

FLATS – You moved quite quickly after that. I had my own Ellis moment at that dinner. At least I think it was that one. I asked him an overly long question about something and when I'd finished he said, 'That's a really shit question, Flats.' 'Wrong, Gengey,' I replied. 'A question is only as good as its answer. It's like saying it's a shit kick in a game of rugby. You can always chase the ball and make it a cool kick.' 'No, no,' countered Ellis in a very matter-of-fact way. 'You can have a shit question and you can have a shit kick.' On reflection, he's done me very nicely indeed.

DURDERS – Ellis is another one who genuinely couldn't give a toss what people think about him, so what you see is always what you get, if you'll pardon the hackneyed expression. Which in my case was very nearly a good hiding. I agree with you, though, the terminally uncompromising are always the best people to be around and there are quite a few of those in rugby.

FLATS – I think there are in all sports really. We just happen to be talking about rugby. I don't mean this in a patronising way, but I genuinely feel sorry for people who find it difficult being comfortable in their own skin. I used to play with a full-back at Bath called Lee Best. He had to retire early, unfortunately, due to injury, but what a player. Come to think of it, I also played for England schoolboys with Lee.

DURDERS – Unnecessary and dull detail again. You're going to be even more of a crashing bore when you're older than you are now. Are we also going to get Lee's favourite train to take to a physio's appointment, with the time and platform number thrown in for good measure?

FLATS – I like detail, and I know our readers are passionate about the detail. Anyway, Lee Best is one of the most unique and wonderful human beings I have ever met and for the simple reason that he is always totally himself. Everyone else I've ever known will have altered slightly in certain situations, but Lee Best never, ever changes. This actually used to rub people up the wrong way in the early days, but when he arrived at Bath we embraced him exactly as he was and he flourished there. He used to call himself the Ferrari and would back it up by saying, 'Mate, I know I break down a lot but when I'm fit and firing on all cylinders and have just had a service, no one can touch me!' Ferrari was actually his nickname too, but not because of that. While he was at Bristol he went to test drive a Ferrari once but instead of taking it on the motorway or even an A-road he just drove it around Clifton village a few times to impress the lads, who he knew would be sitting outside having a coffee and would see him. Amazing commitment to the big show.

I remember, at Bath, him being completely broke yet outside his flat he had a Porsche Boxter and a convertible BMW M3. The reason he was broke was because he'd just bought the BMW and he hadn't got around to selling the Porsche. I seem to remember both his cars having the same number plate, which was L33 3EST. The BMW had to go in for a service at one point – this was after he'd sold the Porsche – and while it was in the garage Brendan Daniel lent him a red Mini Metro to drive. I said to him, 'How are you getting on with "Metro Love", Ferrari?' 'Awwww, Flats,' he said. 'It's shit, man. I can actually notice people not noticing me and you know I don't like that.' I bloody love Lee Best. As I said, loads and loads of front, but all completely genuine.

DURDERS – Did you ever play with or against John Bentley? He's probably before your time. I think we've both done a few corporate events with him, though. He is a *very* big character and a lovely man to boot. I once saw John deliver a speech about playing for the British Lions, as they were then, which he did in 1997, scoring a spectacular try from

60 yards out against the Gauteng Lions. I think he beat something like five men and it's still considered as being one of the best individual tries ever scored for the Lions. John opened his speech by saying – assumes a West Yorkshire accent – 'Hello there. My name is John Bentley and I'm from the West Yorkshire town of Cleckheaton. We're not twinned with anywhere but we do have a suicide pact with Dewsbury.' I loved that opening line. It may be an old classic but it brought the house down.

FLATS – Funnily enough, John had a bit of a shocker in his first Test appearance on that tour and was subsequently dropped. He put this down to the fact that he'd spent too much time playing the joker on the tour and not enough time concentrating on his rugby. After altering his behaviour he then forced his way back into the team and ended up scoring 'that' try. Jeremy Guscott had a pop at John after the match, saying he should have passed to him before scoring and I think John replied with something ending in 'off'. Jeremy went on to seal the series victory for the Lions with a dramatic late drop-goal in the 18-15 second Test win, so he didn't have much to complain about.

DURDERS – Jonny Wilkinson's quite a big character. You perhaps wouldn't think so, given the fact that he's a very softly spoken, spiritual person who can often be found levitating in the corner of rooms, but he is. Like Martin Johnson and Ellis Genge, Jonny Wilkinson became a big fan of my interviewing technique after I asked him an incisive question about the 2003 World Cup final at a corporate event a few years ago. 'That moment in Sydney, Jonny,' I said, 'as the ball went soaring between the posts, did you think to yourself, if this goes over, I could marry Cheryl Fernandez-Versini?' Why I'm obsessed with trying to marry off Cheryl I don't quite know or understand. Anyway, like Martin Johnson, Jonny decided to forgo answering my very pertinent question and opted instead to stare at me like you would a smudge of poo on the sole of your loafer.

FLATS – Metaphorically, that's kind of what you were at that moment.

DURDERS – That is a price I was willing to pay to get a light giggle from a crowded room. We're not talking raucous belly laughs obviously. Tittering I think is my comic ceiling. But you have a very soft spot for Jonny, don't you?

FLATS – He is the most gorgeous bloke, though, both to look at and to be around. I played with him from the age of about 17 and although he left me behind rugby-wise, our paths did still cross occasionally, on tours and things. As you'd expect, he's very erudite, very intelligent and, unlike us, he actually thinks before he speaks. I'll have to give that a go one day.

What you don't see on TV or at corporate events, especially when the hosts are firing off banal questions, is that he's really funny. He can make you laugh hard if he wants to, although he's not a jack the lad. He can also laugh at himself, which is very important. I think the pressures of being a successful rugby player weighed hard on Jonny's shoulders and one of the things that impressed me most about him was that he always faced it head-on. He was in David Beckham territory for a time and was probably the first rugby player in the UK to have to deal with that. I know he found it extremely difficult sometimes, but his behaviour both on and off the pitch was always exemplary. That's not to say it didn't take its toll on him from time to time, and I think these days he likes to keep his public appearances as low-pressure as possible.

DURDERS – Matt Dawson?

FLATS – I love him. You remember the tour to Australia and New Zealand I told you about, when I was injured? Well, nobody went out of their way more on that tour to make me feel less useless than Matt Dawson. Feeling like an imposter in that situation is hard to deal with, but had he not been there it would have been a thousand times worse. I can't speak highly enough of Matt Dawson.

DURDERS – You won't believe this.

FLATS – Don't tell me. You did a corporate event with Matt Dawson a couple of years ago and after asking him a series of really shit questions he looked at you fiercely, put down his drink and then insulted your mum?

DURDERS – Ten out of ten for effort. I have big-time love for him now but he actually humiliated me in front of about 500 people. It's all a bit sketchy, I'm afraid, as I've been trying to banish it from my brain. It was my first ever corporate gig, so we're going back a bit to the Year 2000 and I made a lame joke about England not collecting the Calcutta Cup after they'd had their Grand Slam dreams shattered by Scotland at Murrayfield that year. Matt Dawson didn't warm to my attempts at humour and when he came on stage to be interviewed the first thing he was something along the lines of, 'Is everybody enjoying Mark Durden-Smith's shit jokes?' I was mortified.

FLATS — I like him even more now. All rugby players are a little bit alpha male and when they retire some of them lose that urge to get one over on people all the time and some don't. Martin Johnson has definitely lost some of that and is no more aggressive on a stage than Jonny Wilkinson. Eddie Jones, on the other hand, can make your life really difficult by giving you a series of one-word answers in front of 600 people. You have to have at least 20 questions ready for Eddie, but if he doesn't feel like giving you an answer containing more than one word, he won't.

There's something inside me that says, if I was on a stage being asked questions in front of an audience who had paid to hear me speak, I would try to give value for money, regardless of whether I was being paid or not. I might not like the questions or even the person who's asking them, but I'd answer them all the same. Making somebody look stupid or feel ill at ease in front of an audience — or anywhere, actually — just because you can, is uncalled-for in my opinion, even if they're you.

DURDERS — Thank you for your support.

FLATS — As I said, that behaviour is only really an extension of how these people behave in the dressing room or on a rugby field, so we shouldn't be surprised. I had coaches and managers who went out of their way to make us look stupid sometimes. They did it to get more out of us, but I used to find it so counterproductive. They think it'll make you revere them somehow, but it doesn't.

DURDERS — Believe it or not, the howlers and periods of awkwardness I've mentioned in this chapter wouldn't even get into my own Top 20.

FLATS — You mean you're even more incompetent than we originally thought?

DURDERS — Not incompetent, just occasionally I panic and blurt. Like the time I called the amazing Duke of Edinburgh 'Your Royal Dukeiness'. I was so confused by how I was meant to address him according to Royal protocol, that's what I went for. Not my finest hour. Nor was addressing Tony Blair as 'T-Dog', followed up by 'T-Bone'. I blame the system giving these distinguished people all those titles. What's wrong with Mr and Mrs?

FLATS — I think we should leave it there before you heap more shame on yourself and the House of Chalmers.

Health, Safety and Bad Behaviour

DURDERS – Let's start this chapter by stating the obvious. Rugby isn't without its dangers. A great deal has, and is being, and will continue to be, done to make it safer, but you can't sugar-coat the fact that rugby is a full-blooded combative sport. As one of its principal attractions to participants and fans alike, that creates an incredibly fine line between what is acceptable and what isn't. Keep it safe, but keep it entertaining, being the want of most people. Imagine the game of rugby with little or no contact, though.

FLATS – It'd be basketball really, but on a much bigger playing surface and with posts instead of hoops. And a more varied shape of athlete, of course. And more swearing.

DURDERS – I would happily pay good money to watch you attempt a slam dunk.

FLATS – So would I. I'd also like to see you have a go. You might be taller than I am but you're clumsy and visibly unathletic.

DURDERS — That's not true. I'm very supple and can get into some extreme yoga poses. But back to the nitty and, more relevantly, the gritty of the game. Let's talk about the changing nature of what the late and great Bill McLaren would have called 'argy bargy' and use the Leicester v. Bristol game in Round 21 of the 2020/21 Premiership season as a starting point. A high stakes, tense game finished 26-23 to Bristol, amid great controversy. Tempers flared and there was a bit of a scuffle on the pitch; two players smashed into one of the broadcast cameras and it became the week's biggest talking point. One scuffle, though? In the olden days every match would have a full-on fist fight or three. No yellow cards were given. Or rarely. It was just a 'Come on, chaps, calm down.' As you'd expect, I was always right in the thick of things whenever a rumpus began on the field of play.

FLATS — A rumpus? Oh, I see. This is the recurring theme of you as the hardman. Yes, I bet Bakkies Botha had nothing on you. By the time I left school and became a pro, all that had changed, fortunately. You still got the odd fight, as you do today, but it's like chalk and cheese compared to the era you're talking about. The reason I say 'fortunately' is because I wasn't a particularly talented fighter. I never minded getting stuck in, but there's a big difference between someone with a thick neck and someone with actual skill. I remember playing a couple of pre-season games in France when I was at Saracens. One of the games was against Agen, which is in the south-west of the country, and it was just a brawl really. We'd taken a really young team and because it was pre-season we thought there'd be a good atmosphere and water breaks every 20 minutes. Easy-going stuff.

The French boys came out leeringly angry and you could tell straight away what they had in mind. They also had a hell of a team, which didn't help. Among their props were my aforementioned hero, Omar Hasan, and Jean-Jacques Crenca, who is one of the strongest French looseheads of all time. He's also one of the only looseheads to give Julian White a hard day at Test level. He didn't dominate him, but Julian had to work hard for it. The game was just so violent.

One of our props stood up from a scrum and was knocked clean out by a second-row for no reason. I remember hearing a sound as I ran off and at first I thought that someone had ruptured their Achilles'. It was that kind of sound. When I turned around, the prop, Romain Magellan, was lying on the pitch unconscious with a broken nose. From then on it kicked off every few minutes and by half time virtually every member of our team had either been chinned, gouged or both. Stuart Hooper was playing with me and at half time he said, 'I'll race you to the next fight and whoever gets there first has to crack the player as hard as they possibly can.' It wasn't a laugh or a game, by the way. We'd been under attack for a little over 40 minutes and with little or no protection being offered we had no choice but to meet it head on.

DURDERS – This is actually quite exciting. I know we're not trying to glorify violence or anything, but I am hoping you manage to wreak some kind of revenge in the second half.

FLATS – Well, if you stop talking, I'll tell you what happened. About four or five minutes into the second half a fight kicked off, and after arriving before Hoops, I laid one on their flanker, Philippe Benetton. Unfortunately, I hit Philippe so hard but so poorly that I ended up breaking my hand. I did knock him over, though, which was a bonus. After that, all hell broke loose for about the 50th time, but for some reason I didn't get hit.

During the next line-out, one of the French players looked at me, made the cut-throat sign and issued a threat in French. Chris Chesney saw it and said this to him: 'Fucking hell, mate. We ain't in *Predator*. He don't even speak French, you daft c**t!' I said, 'I do actually, and he reckons I'm dead.'

DURDERS — Can you refrain from using the C-word please, even if two of the four letters are asterisked? You know I don't like it when you swear.

FLATS — This isn't *Brideshead Revisited*. The physio came on a few minutes later to drag off a few bodies, but before he did that, he came to see me. 'Are you all right, Flats?' he said. 'The hand doesn't look too good.' I had no idea what he was talking about, but when I looked down at my hand it was black. 'I think that's broken, mate,' said the physio. 'Let me test it. If it is, you're obviously coming off.' It was broken and as I was walking off Stuart Hooper said to me, 'Lucky fucker.'

At the end of the game, Philippe Benneton walked past me on the touchline, saw my hand in a bucket of ice and laughed at me pityingly. It even kicked off after the game, and as it started I thought to myself, *Please don't, lads. Not now!* I would have had to get involved for the sake of honour, yet I was sitting on a chair with my feet up and had my hand in a bucket of ice. Fortunately, it was stopped before it could go too far. Agen, though. Punchy lads.

DURDERS — There are two things that struck me about that story, Flats. The first one is that you can speak French, and the second is your claim that had it all kicked off at the end, you would have had to get involved. Why would you have had to get involved? Where are all the peacemakers? Why on earth couldn't you have stood on your chair proudly and sung 'Frère Jacques' or 'Kumbaya'? *'Ne combattez pas, mes amis,'* you should have cried. That mentality is so old-school: 'My mate's being beaten up so I have to go and stick the boot in!' Why? Be the bigger man. Sing a hymn, or, better still, play the harp, the instrument of peace.

FLATS – I was generally a peacemaker, I promise you. The reason I felt obliged to enter that particular fracas was because doing my Kofi Annan impression or playing the harp would have made no difference whatsoever. In fact, I would hazard a guess that if I'd wandered over there with a harp mid-fracas and had started serenading them with a verse or two of something melodic and conciliatory, they would have taken it from me and beat me with it. Rightly or wrongly, in that moment the only language they under-stood was the language of extreme and unnecessary violence. Anyway, as I said, fortunately it was all quelled very quickly and I was able to carry on sunning my legs and feet. Beautiful part of the world, by the way. Victor Rabu was born there, the famous architect who designed hundreds of Uruguayan churches. 'Lord of the Churches' they used to call him.

DURDERS – You've obviously just googled that to make your-self sound less like the psychotic gorilla you obviously are. Or are you really not a fighter? Did you not have a switch that could be flicked that would send you into Hulk mode?

FLATS – No, I genuinely didn't enjoy scrapping and if any-thing that was secondary. There just wasn't all that much of it by then, really, and by then red cards were no longer seen as terribly cool. There were a good few scraps that I really enjoyed, actually, but most of them were quick and unpleasant. I don't think the French lads enjoyed it and they were the main instigators. It was cultural – within the game, that is, not the country. When the game was really violent, I think people who didn't play it assumed that all rugby players were born fighters who enjoyed knocking the shit out of each other, but that can't have been further from the case. Some might have been okay with it, but you can guarantee that a lot weren't. The term 'contact sport' is often directly associated with violence, and if violence is an essential ingredient of that sport, such as boxing, then that's permissible. In rugby it isn't, though. It's a by-product of practising the sport, which makes it preventable and therefore inexcusable. It'll always happen to some degree, but it can never be excused. Not these days.

DURDERS – How was your disciplinary record?

FLATS – Bearing in mind where I played, not too bad really. As I said, I was always very conscious about cards and figured that a ban might result in me losing my place. I only received one ban during my career, which was down to an accumulation of yellow cards. A few of those were for punching and these days would be reds. I never got one of those, by the way.

DURDERS – I think that's enough about violence and general wrongdoing for the time being. Let's move on to the health-and-safety aspect of rugby, which is a fairly broad subject but is an area of the game that is under the most intense scrutiny at the moment.

FLATS — We were always looked after brilliantly when I was a player and despite the negative connotations that will always inevitably accompany subjects like health and safety within rugby, I actually consider it a success story. Compared with when my dad played rugby, the game was infinitely safer when I was playing and is obviously even better now. We also didn't know anything like as much as we do now about the damage playing rugby can do to the human brain. Not that we know that much now, to be perfectly honest. A lot of us are just sitting and waiting. It sounds melodramatic, but it's true. Just going back to the way I was treated, though, some of the people who looked after me, medically, as a player are some of the people I love most in the world. There are three in particular who I would genuinely do anything for. Not just because they looked after me as part of their job, but because they actually cared about my wellbeing and always went above and beyond. Rugby is full of people like that and it needs them.

DURDERS — So are World Rugby doing enough to protect the modern player with the tweaking of laws and the implementation of protocols?

FLATS — They never stop, and a lot of the time it's down to safety. Some of it can be anti-spectacle, though, which is what we said at the start of the chapter. Finding that balance. The scrum, for instance, is less attractive than it used to be because it just takes so long to set up. It's safer, though, which is very hard to argue against. You asked about changes to the elite game? World Rugby are there to protect everybody and the changes they make are as much, if not more, about the amateur players and the kids as they are the pros. We get all the care, remember, and make up a tiny percentage of the rugby-playing population. I once did my shoulder in during a night game on a Saturday and had it reconstructed late the following morning. I received a text that evening saying, 'Don't have any breakfast – you're coming in for an operation first thing.' It was that quick.

DURDERS – During the pandemic there have been some odd rules deployed. Of course everything had to be done to try to stop the spread of that miserable virus, but I could never quite get my head around the logic of banning try celebrations when the players had spent 80 minutes rolling around with each other. I guess it was necessary tokenism.

FLATS – You could write a lot of small gestures off as being tokenism, and in life, not just in sport. But there is a practical benefit to them sometimes, and huge societal change can indeed begin with supposed tokenism, so don't knock it so readily. If there are 20 ways in which players can come into physical contact during a rugby game and you have an opportunity to remove two of them, why not do it for a few months? With regards to them not celebrating, what if Mike Brown has Covid and doesn't know? Him and Joe Marler could possibly only come into contact during a game if and when they score and celebrate, so what's wrong with separating them for a while? By not celebrating, players remember the restrictions.

DURDERS – That's actually a very powerful point. You've turned the tide of the argument. How do you feel?

FLATS – In the right, as always.

DURDERS – Just going back to discipline for a second, a question I forgot to ask you earlier was: who is the most ill-disciplined player you ever played with? As in, who caused the most trouble? It has to be Danny Grewcock, surely, as in theory he was the most ill-disciplined rugby player of your generation. More cards than a croupier and more bans than Ben Johnson, Marion Jones and Lance Armstrong put together.

While we're here, let me just remind you of Danny's record when it comes to bans. He started off with a five-week ban after being sent off for kicking All Blacks hooker Anton Oliver in a Test in Dunedin in 1998. Next up was a two-week ban for punching Lawrence Dallaglio in 2003. I have no idea if Lawrence noticed or not, but I'd say he might have on this occasion. After that he got a two-month ban for biting All Blacks hooker Keven Mealamu during the first Lions Test in 2005 and then six weeks for punching the French lock Thibault Privat in 2007. Rounding things off is a cosy seven-week ban for stamping on Ulster flanker Stephen Ferris in 2010. It's an extensive and impressive list of thuggery.

FLATS – Yes, I suppose Danny could misbehave from time to time. During the second half of my career it was academic really, because the rules changed and so did the behaviour. Players still get angry, of course, but these days it's mainly just posturing. They know they can't hit anyone, so they don't. If a thief walks into a car lot and sees a hundred CCTV cameras, he's going to walk out again. The same thing applies. If you do it, you'll get caught, so don't. That's obviously a good thing, not least because getting injured through being punched is shit. There are enough ways to get injured in this game and being punched shouldn't be one of them.

The problem you had with Danny Grewcock was that he was actually quite good at fighting. Once you've been walloped by somebody like that you think, *Okay, I'll try to avoid that in future.* On the field he was very aggressive, although off the field he wasn't. He was easily riled, though, which could cause the odd issue. The thing is, we didn't think of Dan in those terms. Yes, he was hard, but the things that come to mind when I think about Danny Grewcock the rugby player are his scrummaging ability, his line-out work and his defensive play. That's what epitomises Danny Grewcock the rugby player, not him punching somebody and getting a red card.

I have a friend who played in the second row in the Premiership and he says he hated playing against Borthwick and Grewcock because Borthwick nicked all the line-out balls and Grewcock physically hammered him all the time. I remember smacking him once during a game and he said, 'Not you as well!' I said, 'I'm just trying to mix it up for you, mate, that's all.'

DURDERS – Come on, name and shame. Who was your poor victim?

FLATS – Never in a million years. Alex Brown. Alex is really posh. Class player, though. Danny Grewcock actually became a really skilful rugby player, but what got him picked to start with was an ability to, as Francois Pienaar used to say, 'smash rucks and smash c**ts'.

DURDERS – Powerful words there from the man who helped the Rainbow Nation emerge from isolation. Brings a lump to the old throat.

FLATS – I know you're not supposed to pursue a balanced position on anything these days, but I feel comfortable saying that I want rugby to be a safe as possible. I also feel comfortable saying that rugby will and must always have an inherent physical risk. That, as we've already stated, is why people love it. Since time immemorial, human beings have loved watching other human beings produce brilliance while under massive physical pressure. It's nothing new. Look at the exponential growth of the UFC over the past 10 years, which is basically just gladiatorial Rome for the 21st century. And look at how popular boxing's been for what seems like for ever. People love it. It's like watching Ronnie O'Sullivan hit a 147 in 11 minutes. It's otherworldly.

DURDERS – I'm not a snowflake by any stretch of the imagination, but the other day I was watching a documentary about the Frank Bruno and Mike Tyson fight and it occurred to me that it's very odd that evolution's greatest success story, we humans, still get so much pleasure out of watching bestial violence.

Surely, if we keep evolving – and, being an anthropology graduate, I can confirm that is definitely the long-term plan for the species – at some point we'll go, *That's too base. Watching two human beings knock seven bells out of each other isn't right.* Though perhaps I'm slightly further down the evolutionary path than you are?

FLATS – I wrote an article years ago for *Sport* magazine in which I talked about my love of boxing. I don't watch the second-division stuff but I will happily pay 20 quid to watch the big fights. I love it and always have. I remember Tyson v. Bruno and Eubank v. Benn very well indeed. Regardless of all that, I genuinely do not see how boxing is still allowed. There's just no sense to it.

DURDERS – What if one of your daughters wanted to take up boxing?

FLATS – There is no way whatsoever I would allow one of my children to practise the sport of boxing. Never. Even if they were 25 and had moved out of my house, I would find them and stop them going. I absolutely love boxing, but it scares me.

DURDERS – You're on my side, then. Maybe you're further up the evolutionary scale than I thought, even though you do look like the second one in those 'Evolution of Man' posters.

FLATS – I suppose I am, except that I still love watching it. I'm a contradiction. A lovely one.

DURDERS – By far the biggest story within the realms of what we're discussing here is the dementia issue. Just a few months ago, Steve Thompson, who is only 42 years of age, revealed he is suffering from early-onset dementia and probable traumatic encephalopathy. One of England's great sporting heroes confessed that he can't remember much about winning the World Cup in 2003. One of the greatest games ever involving an England sporting team, which he took part in, and he has very little memory of it. That fact is as sad as it is it sobering.

Steve went on to say that he would not want his own children to play the game as it is at the moment and that he regrets ever taking it up himself. And he's not alone, unfortunately. He and a group of seven former players, who are all under 45, are proposing to bring legal proceedings against World Rugby, the RFU and the WRU over what they claim was a failure to protect them from the risks caused by concussions. Stories don't come much bigger than this, in any sport, and again we're back to that fine line. Where on earth do you draw it? The contact they're talking about is fundamental to the very existence of our sport. In that respect, rugby obviously has a similar problem to boxing, and if the prosecution against the three governing bodies goes ahead, the very existence of rugby, as we now know it, will be challenged. Does it worry you at all, Flats? The dementia, I mean. You're sharp and your memory's good but I know you occasionally worry about it.

FLATS – I'll come on to that in a second. This is all about adults making educated decisions, but until we know a lot more about it, there isn't really an educated decision to be made. Or, should I say, a conclusive one. If it's proven beyond reasonable doubt that there's a high chance you'll cause damage to your brain by playing full-contact rugby, it'll be difficult to make a case for it. Boxing, you'd imagine, would be a lot worse, but then how often do boxers fight, and how often does an amateur boxer fight compared to a professional? It's such a nuanced conversation.

DURDERS – But we are dealing with something different to the usual conversations you might have with former rugby players about sore knees and creaking joints. This is taking us to a whole other level of concern, isn't it?

FLATS – Yes, in a word. That said, a lot of ex-pros are peddling the narrative that we knew what we signed up for, which I respectfully but stubbornly refute. We did not know. What they're referring to are the broken bones, the concussions and bad knees and backs you talked about, etc. No one ever spoke to us about brain damage or dementia. No one ever spoke to us about the possibility of being in a home in your forties or fifties. No one ever sat us down at 18 years of age with our parents and said, 'Imagine from the age 10 not being able to communicate with your father because he's in a home and has dementia and you have no money to pay for his care. That's because your dad played for Streatham and Croydon for 10 years in the front row. Anyway, do you still want this contract for five grand a year?'

Either there was information kept from us, which I find very unlikely, or they just didn't know. Either way, the subject of brain damage and early-onset dementia and the dramatic impact that can have on your partner, your children, you parents, your siblings and your friends was never part of the conversation. We weren't glib. We didn't ignore it. We were just completely ignorant of it. And I mean completely ignorant. For those of us who played in that generation, it really is a waiting game. You just sit and wait to see if you get dementia.

DURDERS – If those conversations were had with young players and their parents, if they were warned that in 20 or 30 years' time they could end up suffering from a serious neurological and/or psychological illness, what do you think would happen? I think the majority would get up, walk out, and never play the game again, wouldn't they?

FLATS – What you're forgetting is that a large proportion of the parents sitting with these young players will have played the game themselves, as will many of their own parents. Sure, they might have some physical niggles from having played the game, but the vast majority will not have experienced any serious neurological or psychological issues, and rightly or wrongly that will count for something.

Something positive that's happened in recent years is always erring on the side of caution and not allowing players to decide whether or not they should stay on the pitch. We got asked that question all the time – 'I think it's broken. Can you carry on?' – and the answer was always 'Yes.' Not because we were being macho. We just didn't want to let our team-mates down. Removing the final decision from players and leaving it with a medical professional is obviously common sense and will already have done a massive amount of good.

What will be a game-changer on the other end of the scale is if the people who are studying this are ever able to put a percentage-chance on you suffering from neurological or psychological illness in later life. If that happens, the parents of the young players will be able to make an informed decision, and unless the chance is very small, they'll probably take their son or daughter out of the game.

DURDERS – Despite the alarm bells ringing quite loudly at the moment, there hasn't been a spate of players retiring immediately. How many times has George North been knocked out over the years? Players obviously still think that it's a risk worth taking and, by association, a price worth paying.

FLATS – There are three reasons players haven't retired. Number one: nobody knows what the risk is – yet. Number two: they all know far more players and former players who haven't complained about symptoms relating to early-onset dementia than we do who have, and three: they're earning hundreds of thousands of pounds a year and are heroes to millions of people. I'd play, given that argument. One hundred per cent. Put simply, when you don't know what the risk is, it's a risk worth taking.

DURDERS – Okay, so how many of your ex-pro mates are free from any physical or mental issues? A rough percentage.

FLATS – Let me put it like this. Last night I saw Matt Powell and he's 100 per cent. I spoke to Danny Grewcock this morning and so's he. Ollie Barclay's coming over to mine in a couple of hours and he, too, is as fit as a fiddle. Tomorrow you and I are meeting up with Topsy Ojo and Paul Grayson, who are both fine. The answer to your question obviously isn't 100 per cent, but you get my drift. Ollie Barclay, Danny Grewcock and Topsy Ojo could play a game of rugby tomorrow if they wanted to and they all had super-long careers. A lot of players come out of rugby with nothing whatsoever wrong with them, and because there's nothing wrong with them there's no story to tell and nothing to report.

DURDERS – Does the possibility of you developing a neurological illness scare you? I assume it must do in light of all the recent noise on the subject?

FLATS – I don't lose sleep over it, although I have lost sleep over it in the past. In the early days of the lads coming out and going public I had a few moments where I thought, *Holy shit, this is going to be happening to me one day. What the hell am I going to do?* Some people are more prone to catastrophising about these things than others, and fortunately the worries I experienced then have settled. The closest I get to it affecting me is that once or twice I day I'll have a thought lasting literally a millisecond that it's happening. It'll be triggered by me not remembering where something is for a few seconds or forgetting to ring somebody back.

DURDERS – Has the transition to bigger, faster players had an impact, do you think? Also the change in tactics, as in seeking contact, whereas before players tried to avoid it.

FLATS – The notion that rugby players have only started looking for contact in the modern era is a bit like calling modern-era pro tennis a power game. If it's only happened in the modern era, what the hell were Goran Ivanišević and Pete Sampras playing? As well as being a power game, rugby is ultimately an evasion game and always has been. In fact, some of the best players on the planet at the moment are lauded for their evasion skills. That said, because of the way things have evolved, the players are now bigger, faster and fitter than they've ever been and in the context of this conversation that isn't going to help matters. If you get punched in the head by Ricky Hatton, it's not going to do you any good, but it's going to be worse if Anthony Joshua does it. There's also very little space on the field these days and that's because the players are so fit and mobile. Everything goes through the middle.

DURDERS – In terms of junior rugby, I think the New Zealand model has to be the way forward, i.e., if you're bigger and stronger, you should only play against bigger and stronger players, regardless of your age. My son Freddie, when he was 12, got steamrollered by a much taller, bulkier fellow 12-year-old, lost consciousness for a few seconds and spent six weeks on the sidelines. I think until you get to the age of, say, 16, you would ideally play against boys and girls of similar height, weight and strength.

FLATS – I like the New Zealand model. I'd love to see the data, if there is any, on the potential damage that massive kids can do to small kids. It certainly won't do your evasion skills any harm and players like Shane Williams must have benefited from it. I obviously wasn't small as a kid but even I got unnerved when I came across a giant. If someone's that big you just stick them in the year above. Equally, if somebody's ridiculously quick and is making a fool of everyone else, you do the same. It's not an exact science, though. Everyone's seen the photo of the 12-year-old Billy Vunipola at school where all his mates could fit in his pocket? If you'd put him in a team full of 15- and 16-year-olds he'd probably have got hurt as, despite him being big and heavy, he wouldn't have the muscle mass or the aggression.

DURDERS – I just can't see the benefit in children who aren't fully developed yet being potentially battered by children who are much bigger, heavier and stronger. Some people would probably say it's character-building, but I would say, knowing we know what we know, the junior game at the very least must err on the side of caution.

FLATS – There's a club local to me called Trowbridge that a mate of mine plays for and last week I watched a video of them playing against a team that featured the Samoan centre Alafoti Fa'osiliva. Alafoti played the full 80 minutes and scored five tries while absolutely battering a load of 18-year-olds. He was whooping and hollering after every try and I remember thinking to myself, *What on earth can a recently retired professional Samoan monster be getting out of obliterating a load of kids? What a prick.* I actually left a voicemail for somebody at that club voicing my displeasure, although I'm not expecting a reply. It's ridiculous, though. And, it's obviously dangerous.

DURDERS – Is there something else that rugby could be doing, apart from ruling out tackles above shoulder height, that would help to safeguard the players and ultimately the future of the game? I keep on hearing more and more people saying things like 'My son's had three concussions. He was in the first team but won't play rugby ever again.' Claiming that it's a threat to the sport's future might be a bit sensationalist, I suppose, but at grassroots level it's a very real threat. The powers that be are obviously on the case, but accelerating the process of making the sport safer has to be a priority or I suppose rugby could turn into a dwindling minority sport.

FLATS – I agree with you. As much as we both love BT Sport, who do a great job, I think the two things that threaten rugby union most are pay-to-view TV and head injuries.

DURDERS – And what's the worst-case scenario regarding the latter?

FLATS – The worst-case scenario is that somebody like the rugby journalist Sam Peters, who is driven, balanced, incredibly bright and appropriately relentless, uncovers some information that proves once and for all that the powers that be knew about the dangers but pushed them to one side. That's the absolute worst thing that could happen.

DURDERS – And what would be the result of that? What would rugby look like?

FLATS – Reputationally, anybody can recover from anything these days. Take our government, for instance. I'm not saying that any other party would have been more competent or transparent, but they have been entirely full of shit and lies yet haven't been held to account. At all. They might do it charismatically at times, but they do it all the same and get off scot-free. Reputationally, then, I think rugby would recover, but not necessarily financially.

Unlike football, rugby isn't awash with billionaires, and what would trigger the worst-case scenario is the guys mounting a case effectively winning it by proving that there was a level of negligence. Winning pay-outs, basically. If that happens, you'll get to a point where schools and clubs either won't be able to get insurance or will be terrified about being sued and in that situation they'd simply cease to be. As long as it remains inconclusive that there's a high chance that full-contact rugby can give you brain damage, then the game will tick along just fine. Even if you prove that there's a certain amount of risk, it'll survive that, as people don't mind taking risks.

DURDERS – So what do you think is the intention of Steve Thompson and the others bringing the case? Surely it's not rugby's extinction?

FLATS – I'm not sure what their intention is exactly but I think they probably feel very embittered, scared and let down. There has been some speculation, however — that's privately by the way, not publicly — that money is a motivation for some parties. I stay well away from those conversations, but they happen, nonetheless. If some people can't empathise with a cause or a situation, they have to stick a label on it, regardless of whether that's fair or not. In this case it happens to be greed and/or profiteering, which is unfortunate and potentially quite damning. I'm trying to find a production company at the moment who will help me make a documentary about the situation as I feel aggressively balanced about it and I want to hear both sides. That's my point of view. The point of view of some others is that some of these guys just want a pay-out and it's all bollocks. One person whose motives you should not be sceptical of, if I may, is Steve Thompson. I've known Steve a very, very long time and as well as being a lovely fella and a great rugby player, I honestly don't think he has the capacity to lie. What's happening to him is heartbreaking and one can only hope that, in addition to him getting all the help he needs and hopefully managing to keep his condition at bay for as long as possible, going public with it will ultimately be a force for good. I'm sure it will be.

Grassroots and Academies

DURDERS – I think it's fair to say that Flats, the prancing boulder, and I get misty eyed and are unapologetically nostalgic about the game of rugby, and when the publishers asked us to deliver a chapter on from whence the greats of the game – and the not-so-great – emerge, we thought we'd use it as an excuse to take another quick trip down memory lane.

Strangely for a man who was born and bred in north London, whose mother was 50 per cent Scottish, 50 per cent English, and whose father was a genealogical mess of English, Irish and French, my grassroots and the clippings all have a Welsh hue. Those grassroots Welshified as a result of the aforementioned Huw Thomas, resident of Belsize Park, and his father, Hywel. (The Welsh have great imaginations when it comes to birthnames – stick to what you know, or pretty close to it, and you won't go too far wrong, seems to be the theory.) My father was a great sports enthusiast and pretty talented too. He played cricket for the Combined Services and at Minor Counties level, as well as for Northwood CC for many years. He also played top-flight hockey for Surbiton. Needless to say, on a sporting level – and many other levels, when you come to think about it – his son has been a crushing disappointment. The point I'm trying to make in a typically round-about way is that rugby wasn't perhaps my father's number one area of expertise. So we needed the Welsh. A bit like the Battle of Buttington in 893.

FLATS – Excuse me?!

DURDERS – You've never heard of the famous Battle of Buttington? In 893? When the Anglo-Saxons joined forces with the Welsh to stick it to the Vikings? I'm embarrassed for you.

Anyway, back to grassroots. My children will have been traumatised by their first memories of grassroots rugby. I was desperate for them to get into rugby. I remember taking my twins sons, Archie and Freddie, to Battersea Ironsides on a Sunday morning, where the pitches were frozen and the temperature was minus three. It was the proverbial baptism of ice. I watched them standing there with their tags on, shivering like a Floridian in Siberia. Their initial enthusiasm gradually evaporated as the hypothermia set in. Because I worked a lot of weekends, it would have been up to my wife, Rachel, to continue the sub-zero torture, but with our younger daughter, Rosie, also demanding her time and attention it would have been a tall order. After two weeks, they swapped the frozen pitches at Battersea Ironsides for watching *Fireman Sam* on a sofa in our toasty sitting room in Wandsworth. (Unusually for a Welsh-born, Rachel was also more into Fireman Sam than rugby.) Despite this inauspicious start, the boys, Archie and Freddie, now love their rugby and my daughter dreamed of playing for England. That dream lasted precisely the two hours we spent watching an England open training session at Twickenham and hasn't been mentioned since.

FLATS – Back on point please, bumbler-in-chief. How come you ended up playing for London Welsh? Was that through your special rugby friend?

DURDERS – It was indeed. I was an honorary Welsh person for a few years of my life. In fact, I should have changed my name to Dafydd or Gruffydd. Missed a trick there. The winter Sundays had a magical rhythm to them. We'd head down to Kew, in one car or two, and while the dads were having their bacon butties, we'd be pinging around with Gareths, Reeses and Huws and the occasional Jeremy. Why is it always bacon butties, or sausage sandwiches, by the way? Was that 1970s and '80s fare? Is there a vegan option at any grassroots rugby club these days?

FLATS – There's a vegan equivalent to a bacon butty at every grassroots rugby club. It's called a roll with ketchup in it. And no butter, obviously.

DURDERS – Sounds delicious. Now a grassroots big picture, simple question for you: do you think Covid will have any long-term negative impact on participation numbers in grassroots rugby?

FLATS – I'm obviously hoping not. In 2019 a global study by Nielsen recorded 877 million followers and 405 million fans of rugby union worldwide, which was up 11 per cent and 18 per cent on the 2018 figures respectively. Of course, this would have been influenced by the World Cup, but providing enough people stick two fingers up to Covid and don't let that cloud their thinking, it should be in a good place.

DURDERS – Hear hear to that. What was your childhood team again? Maidstone?

FLATS – That is correct. Although I did something there that very few people had done before me.

DURDERS – You ate the mascot?

FLATS – Not even close. I left Maidstone Rugby Club. I know you're looking at me like I'm a tit, but you have no idea how big a deal that was. Seriously, leaving Maidstone Rugby Club in those days was considered a heinous crime.

And the reason I left my childhood club was because games were constantly being cancelled because they couldn't get the numbers and I was desperate to play rugby. My dad asked me where I wanted to play, expecting me to say Old Elthamians, which is where Andy Sheridan played. 'No, I want to beat them,' I said. 'I don't want to play for them.' I ended up migrating to Sevenoaks Rugby Club, where a few of my mates played. They had a great set-up there and were never short of players.

DURDERS – Did you prevail against the mighty Old Elthamians?

FLATS – We did indeed. Beat them 3-0 in the Kent Cup. Like you, though, my early days at Maidstone, which was my first rugby club, were some of the best days of my life. I was never the best player in the team (at any age) but what I lacked in natural talent I definitely made up for in enthusiasm. I had such a relish for it. Changing clubs at 13 was basically confirmation of that, as the sole reason for me leaving was because I wanted to play rugby. I don't want to paint myself as the most driven 13-year-old ever. I wasn't. But I also wasn't content to just turn up, do a few handling drills in the mud and then go home. I wanted to compete, and I was more than ready to do that.

DURDERS — What about school?

FLATS — I went to a school in Maidstone from the age of 11 to 16 and I hated it, and the reason I hated it was because the rugby was crap. It was meant to be a rugby school, but there were never any games and never any training. It was rubbish. All I could do was try and keep myself in shape, which is why I went to the gym every day after school. One day yet another game was cancelled at the school and I said to my dad, 'I don't want to go in. There's just no point.' It was such a shame as the rugby coach was great and I was surrounded by good players. The trouble is, like Maidstone, there were never really enough of them. It was a football school that also played rugby, basically. My dad said to me, 'Okay, what do you want to do about it?' and I said that I wanted to change schools. 'Where do you want to go?' he asked. 'Dulwich College, please,' I replied.

DURDERS — As in *the* famous Dulwich College? The education establishment that began life as the College of God's Gift (true story) and boasts an alumni including Sir Ernest Shackleton, P. G. Wodehouse, Bob Monkhouse and, wait for it, Nigel Farage?

FLATS — The very same. Its rugby alumni, which includes

Andy Sheridan and Nick Easter, boasts more than 200 inter-national caps, don't you know. Eight of which belong to *moi*.

DURDERS — I seem to remember you telling me you were an Old Alleynian but I assumed you'd got confused and were referring to your cleaner, who I believe is an old Albanian?

FLATS — She's Romanian. Agripina, which means a girl who was born feet first. Anyway, I know you came from the streets, Durds, but if you came from the streets then I came from the sewers underneath the streets. We didn't have much money, so me wanting to go to Dulwich was a big ask for my parents. It was massive. I didn't know it then, but I now know that they made enormous sacrifices to send me there. There were paper rounds and everything. It was only for two years — six terms — but that completely changed my life. Not because you had to go to the right school to get picked. It was because I was in a rugby programme that had me training every day and had me playing high-intensity rugby matches every Saturday. It didn't do much for my A-Level grades, but I was in heaven.

DURDERS — What grades did you get, Flats?

FLATS — I got a B, a C and a D.

DURDERS — In my day that was probably the equivalent of getting D, E and F.

FLATS — What did you get?

DURDERS — I got a B and two Cs and an A in the General Paper, whatever that was, which in my day, compared with your era of soft marking, was the equivalent of getting seven A*s. And before you say that I would have had to work hard to get those grades, whereas you did bugger all, I also did bugger all. I lived in a climate of fear really. I left it till the last three weeks and then went into a blind panic. I literally didn't sleep in those three weeks. I need a deadline to loom very large to get my juices properly flowing. A bit like the one for completing this sure-fire bestseller in fact.

FLATS – Why didn't you do your cramming during the day and sleep at night?

DURDERS – I was round the clock. Day and night and any-thing in between.

FLATS – There isn't anything in between. Are you sure you actually got any A Levels?

DURDERS – I'll find the documents and get back to you. Let's get back to grassroots rugby. Whether it's a rugby club or school rugby, I think the most amazing gift that the sport can give to a person is that sense of belonging and combined purpose. A shot of self-esteem is also, hopefully, part of the package. Hanging out with you for nearly a decade has dec-imated my stock of self-esteem, but the sense of belonging, especially to my school and university, is still with me. That doesn't take much nurturing. Even if you see people once every 10 years, even 20 years, those bonds are deep-rooted and are still there.

FLATS – Really? Are people not trying to erase you from their lives, given half a chance? On another matter, have you ever witnessed any bad behaviour on the touchline at a grass-roots rugby club? Come on. I gave football a hammering earlier. Let's see if there are any glass houses in the vicinity.

DURDERS – I haven't really got a great deal in the dossier on that front. Although I did rebuke a good friend the other day, a rugby man through and through, who was bellowing sledges at the opposition to go with the encouragement he was giving his team. I told him sledging the oppo wasn't the done thing. I genuinely believe that and I hoped to shame him into re-evaluating his touchline protocols.

FLATS – Did he?

DURDERS – He told me I could stick my old-fashioned values 'up my arse' and let off an especially spicey volley of abuse at the away team. Anyway, do you still have any feelings for Maidstone Rugby Club or Sevenoaks?

FLATS – No. They're dead to me.

DURDERS – That's not true, surely?

FLATS – Of course it's not true. The problem I had was that in my early twenties I moved to the other side of the country from my two junior clubs. My oldest mate in the world, Matt Lary, who we called Tank in the old days, is all I really have left from that period. Sad, isn't it? I was a prop, he was hooker, and for years we were inseparable. He texted me last night during the Harry and Meghan interview on ITV. 'Awesome innit?' he said. 'Loving Oprah's glasses.' This was followed by something even more insightful: 'Good old Harry,' he said. 'Feeding the chickens while his missus hammers his family. Hell of a boy!'

Do you know, he's my only vegan friend, which is surprising really as he didn't seem to care about the fact that Harry was feeding chickens. I remember the day he went vegetarian as if it were yesterday. We were 12 and were due to go on tour to Beauvais, which is a French town that's twinned with Maidstone. Six weeks before, Matt went vegetarian in an attempt to lose weight because he was a fat bastard. It didn't work so he went vegan and has remained so ever since. You could say he was a vegan pioneer, and my word has it worked its magic. He's 5ft 4in, weighs 19 stone and looks like Sandi Toksvig pre her impressive and dramatic weight-loss regime.

DURDERS – You're joking.

FLATS – I'm not. Seriously, he looks like a cross between Eddie 'The Eagle' Edwards and Sandi Toksvig. Sandi Toksvig, by the way, is one of my all-time favourite comedian/TV personalities. Her and your mate, Clive James. The difference between her and Matt, apart from her Viking blood, is that he's nowhere near as clever as she is.

DURDERS – Did you have people at Maidstone who were kind of mainstays of the club? You know, like Ethel who used to put the urn on.

FLATS – Ethel who used to put the urn on? You are so Downton Abbey it's untrue.

DURDERS – You know what I mean. Durham University have had the amazing Ted Wood as the beating heart of the club for donkeys years. Barnes Rugby Club have Marty, a cherished, legendary sub-five foot Kiwi, who's been there for years and is as much as fixture there as the men's loos. The same goes for Kenny, Dave and Gus. They are the beating heart of the club – as is a friend called Michael Whitfield, known as Rhino. That attachment, that allegiance, that love for a club is a proper lifelong commitment. Every club must have at least one Marty or Rhino. Saying that, I can't clearly remember anybody at London Welsh, as I was a self-obsessed adolescent, but they will have been there. I do remember Neil Kinnock being one of the coaches, though. In between trying to become prime minister and not quite pulling it off, he would have a whistle in hand on a Sunday morning. He was never my coach, though. He may have sensed that I came from a family that might have been a little more blue than red.

FLATS — At Maidstone there was a barman called Bomber, and Bomber looked a bit like Giant Haystacks out of season. Big lad, he was. I used to go to the bar for a bacon bap after training and I'd always say to the lady at the bar, 'Can I have two please. Can I have two?' She'd always say, 'No, it's one each,' and then Bomber would give her a nudge and say, 'Go on, give him another. He's a growing lad!' 'Cheers, Bomber,' I'd say. 'No problem, boy. You enjoy 'em.'

DURDERS — When was the last time you went to see a grass-roots game?

FLATS — As soon as the first lockdown ended in 2020, I went to my favourite rugby club in Bath, which is called Old Sulians, with two lovely men, Mikey Rich and Jerry Quinn. Jerry's the Worcester Warriors' chef now but he used to be at Bath. Unsurprisingly, I stayed mates with Jerry and we all go biking together sometimes. That's motorbiking, by the way. I much prefer leather to Lycra.

During that first lockdown everybody had been talking

about what they were going to do once the restrictions were lifted and the vast majority of people wanted to get away for a few days, and understandably so. For me, the prospect of being able to have a couple of pints with a few of good mates was the extent of my immediate post-lockdown ambitions, and when the day finally came I was like a kid at Christmas. Unfortunately all my good mates were busy that day so I had to settle for Mikey and Jerry.

I'm not sure why we decided on Old Sulians because it has an awful clubhouse. It is walking distance from the house, though, and the beer's good. As we were sitting there, all the lads came in from training. It was absolutely as I hoped it would be. They could build them a new clubhouse. Just a suggestion.

DURDERS — Was beer an essential part of your rugby DNA, then? It was and wasn't a part of mine.

FLATS — Make your mind up. Was or wasn't it?

DURDERS — I was a cider drinker. I used to be called Apple Man. So it wasn't beer — hence the 'wasn't' bit, but I would try and keep up with everyone else, with my fermented bubbling apple juice, after a game, but invariably ended up vomiting into a gutter. I did try. I just wasn't very good at it really. I blame the bubbles. Some people absolutely love that enforced group drinking culture. I was a bit less enthusiastic than the devotees, but not a puritan. These days I think it's a lot more acceptable to be temperate and sober. But a proper club knees-up, with licence to reminisce, is hard to beat.

FLATS — I think there will be members of clubs up and down the country raising their pint glasses to that! The clubs, the

Sunday morning coaches, the makers of the butties, the people who mow the grass and paint the lines, who do the fixtures and wash the kit and all the unseen stuff all deserve a spot in heaven. They are the lifeblood of the game and we should all seek them out next time you're at your club and give them a pat on the back.

DURDERS – Couldn't agree more. I'm going to go on a pat-a-thon tour of the country. Let's now move on to the development side of things, which is the next step really if you're serious about rugby and want to become a pro. Did you attend an academy?

FLATS – No, I didn't, and the only academy I really know is Bath's academy, which is local to me. The academies now are absolutely brilliant and the only drawback to the system is the percentage of players who either don't make the grade or drop out. That's obviously not the academy's fault, and one of the reasons they do drop out is because it gets so serious. That's obviously a necessary evil as it separates those who'll really make it from those who won't. One issue, of course, is the fate of those who do stay the course but don't get the contract at the end. Being labelled a failure at the age of 18 or 19 must be a hard one to take.

DURDERS – Which is why their continuing education is so important.

FLATS – Yes, but if rugby has meant the world to you for well over half your life you're not suddenly going to go, 'Oh well. I'll go off and become an accountant or something.' People of that age often aren't used to handling life-changing rejections like that and I think it's a big issue.

DURDERS – I know you said you'd have gone to Durham to read an English book had you not become a pro, but what might you have done after that? What was the backup plan? A ballet dancer, perhaps?

FLATS – I already said I'd have gone on to become a psychologist like my dad. My sister's also a psychologist.

DURDERS – Of course, I forgot. I wonder what the collective noun is for psychologists. Actually, I've just looked it up and it might be a 'complex' of psychologists. That's got to be poor googling on my part. Anyway, back to your issue. Is there anything that can be done to soften the blow for the ones who don't make it?

FLATS – I'm not sure really. I know quite a few people who work in academies and the two main messages they try to hammer home the most are how good you have to be and how hard you have to work in order to make it and the fact that very few of you will. If any.

DURDERS – It's a tricky balancing act, stoking the fires of ambition and keeping a lid on expectations. I spoke to the chief operating officer of one of the Premier League clubs a while ago and he said that the mental health cost in these situations is huge. These teenagers are literally within touching distance of earning 50 or 100 grand a week and being heroes to millions and suddenly that dream disappears in an instant.

FLATS – They're not, though, are they? I'm obviously not playing down the gravity of the situation, but as we've said, the vast majority of teenagers at football or rugby academies are not on the brink of becoming high-earning profession-als. Some might end up playing for a semi-pro club for 12 grand a year, but the vast majority will have to give it up and find something else to fill their lives. It's all about man-aging expectations, and although I don't know the full ins and outs, I'd say the academies are probably doing what they can to do so.

DURDERS — The path into elite sport is precarious to say the least. Some of the guys I played with at 11 or 12 had Lions written all over them, or so we thought. None of them became pros. The permutations as to what can happen between then and actually making it are endless, and almost all of them will go against the player. What separates, in terms of development, the guys you knew at 13 who made it and those who didn't?

FLATS — Work rate, work ethic and a mindset that I think can't be taught. Lots of people have that mindset but not the genetics or the talent and a lot of people have the talent but not the mindset.

DURDERS — Who was the greatest wasted talent you grew up with? Somebody who could have become a legend.

FLATS — Now that is a good question. A lot of people ask me who was the greatest player I ever played with. I'm so spawny in that department. I played with Tim Horan for years and I played with Butch James, Francois Pienaar and Jonny Wilkinson. I was so lucky. The best player I ever played with, by the way, was Jason Robinson, and by a country mile. No one comes anywhere near. The second best player I ever played with — and he's a perfect example of what happens when you have the genetics and the talent but not the mindset — was a guy called Chris Brain, who I played with when I was young and am still in touch with today. Chris was an astonishingly good rugby player and from a very early age. He was always a lot bigger than the rest of us, but by the time we were all 17 or 18 we'd caught him up. Even so, he could still walk all over us. He was in a different class.

DURDERS — As the name Chris Brain isn't ringing any bells, I assume he chose a different path?

FLATS — That's correct. He didn't see rugby as a career path and wanted to go into business. Which he did and is very happy. Chris was significantly more talented than a lot of the pros I played with and I thought he was phenomenal. Had he had the mindset and the drive to continue, God only knows what might have happened. Then you look at someone like Nick Abendanon, who played for Bath for many years. If he'd been born in France, he'd have 80 caps, and if he'd been born in New Zealand he'd have 50. There were things he wasn't as good at as, say, Mike Brown. High balls, defence, last-ditch tackles, that sort of thing. But with the ball in his hands, he was an outright inspiration. What a runner.

DURDERS — What advice would you give a young person aspiring to become a pro rugby player? Give us some proper, useful nuggets of insight and wisdom that might just help the aspirers fulfil their dreams.

FLATS — Enjoy your training, practice and matches as much as possible and smile as much as possible. It has to be about enjoyment at that age, it just has to be. Why was Jason

Robinson so good? Talent and genetics? Yes, of course. But also, he decided early on that this was what he loved doing and that was always apparent. He loved to get hold of the ball and beat people. He could kick, but he hardly ever did and everyone he ever played against knew that. When the opposition know what's coming yet you can still do them over and humiliate them – wow! You must get a huge kick from that and I'm sure Jason felt it many, many times. Sure, I'd like to have been able to do that myself, but just being able to watch somebody of Jason Robinson's class play like that and have at least an inkling of how he must be feeling is still kind of special.

As important as a willingness to enjoy the sport is a willingness to learn. You need to be able to ask questions without kissing arse and you need to be able to tell people you don't agree with them without being rude. You also need to be able to take being told in public that what you are doing isn't good enough without being offended. I spoke to an old Bath team-mate of mine last week about this. He's recently retired and he said he's finding the real world fun in some ways but challenging in others. I said, 'How are you finding the honesty thing?' and he said, 'Yep, that's what I'm struggling with the most.' People think and say they want brutal honesty, but they don't, and in rugby you need to be able to give it and receive it. If you can't, you'll lose games. If you go into the real world thinking that your gift to it is honesty, you'll be in for a shock because people don't want it.

DURDERS – That is your greatest gift to our friendship. In fact, I think it's your only gift. Actually, it's more of a bauble than a fully fledged gift. What I'm referring to is you teaching me to be less worried about what everybody thinks of me and just be myself. Be honest, basically. That whole authenticity thing.

FLATS – I've never, ever told you to be yourself. Nor will I ever. That would be a mistake.

Unlikely Heroes and Villains

FLATS – This one was your idea, I think. And I take it you're referring to unlikely heroes on the field of play? Just to be awkward, I'm going to start with Tim Horan.

DURDERS – How can you shoehorn an 80-times capped Tim Horan into our unlikely hero category?

FLATS – But I haven't told you why I think he's a hero, which is where the unlikely bit comes in. Sure, Tim Horan is one of the best centres ever to play the game of rugby and was probably the best player in the world for a time, but the reason I've included him has more to do with his generosity and counsel on and off the pitch than his prowess as a rugby player. For a start, Tim Horan is without doubt one of the most approachable stars I've met.

Given his stature within the game, I found that incredible as a young player. I was so impressed. I mean, what a role model. Next up is his honesty, which I should have mentioned in the last chapter really. When he was at Saracens, Francois was our captain and our director of rugby and during a team meeting one day he pulled Tim up about something that had gone wrong during the last game. I forget the exact details but normally in this situation the player in question would have their say, Francois would have his, and they'd decide that Francois was right. On this occasion Tim thought he was in the right and after to-ing and fro-ing for about five minutes Francois actually relented. 'Okay, Timmy,' he said. 'Cool. I like that.' It didn't give everybody a licence to go toe-to-toe with Francois, of course, but I remember sitting there thinking, *Wow! I didn't realise you could be that honest without offending anyone. And without getting your arse kicked.*

Something else Tim taught me was this bizarre theory that a group of rugby players could go out and have a couple of drinks without getting shitfaced. We used to have something called the Tuesday Club at Bath, which involved us walking to the pub for a couple of pints, nattering about the issues of the day and then walking home again. I know, what a bizarre concept. The motivation behind the Tuesday Club was to promote the fact that there was more to life than training and going to the gym. Conversely, this also endorsed the notion that there was more to life than getting hammered and making a tit of yourself when you weren't training or going to the gym, so it worked both ways. Finding a sensible balance is often something that needs to be taught to young rugby players and that was a great example. That was Tim all over. He was so relaxed but so measured. You could have nights out with him and he wouldn't even talk about rugby. Not once. I wasn't used to any of that, but when you see Tim Horan doing it, you take notice.

DURDERS – If it's good enough for Tim, it's good enough for me. What a great role model to have in your life as a young rugby player.

FLATS – You're telling me. The fact that I was playing

alongside such a mercurial player was obviously a privilege, but to then learn that he's also an extremely nice and well-balanced human being who would do just about anything for anyone made the experience even more special. I absolutely loved spending time with Tim and when I left Saracens he was one of the people I missed the most.

DURDERS – It sounds like a beautiful bromance. Was it requited, this love of yours? I fear, if asked, he may respond, 'David who?'

FLATS – Well, it was love for me. How was it for you, Timmy? I know this chapter was your idea, Durds, but instead of allowing you a turn I'm going to go straight in with another one. And another Australian. This chap is a bit more in keeping with what you originally had in mind, I think. It's a man called Mark Bakewell, who was our forwards coach at Bath. Some people reading this will have heard of him. He played over 400 games in the back row for Eastern Suburbs RFU in Sydney and was also forwards coach at Bristol and Leicester after Bath. The reason Mark left such a mark on me is because he emotionally engaged with us. Today that might be the rule and not the exception, but 20 years ago it wasn't. He also recognised that we all needed different things, which again was not the norm.

I got dropped for a game, once, that I should have started. We were playing Toulouse at home in the Heineken Cup. Toulouse had a big scrum and I was a lot better at scrummaging than I was running. The player they picked ahead of me was a good friend of mine but I was livid nonetheless. The coach that didn't pick me was the head coach and not the forwards coach, so I went to Mark Bakewell and said,

'Mark, what's going on mate?' He said, 'Listen, I'm not going to shirk it but at the same time I'm not going to say anything bad about the player who's starting. What I will say is that I would like you to respond to what's happened with dignity. I want you to be able to look back in a week's time, Flats, and believe that you've done yourself justice.'

What a difference a sentence can make. I'd approached Mark full of righteous indignation and he changed my view of the situation completely, and with just a few words. Complaining about something you can't do anything about is futile and in my situation I'd have ended up making a proper arse of myself. As Mark said, the best thing to do was keep my mouth shut and see what happened.

DURDERS – How did it go? Don't tell me. The Bath scrum got butchered and you came on to save the day?

FLATS – You're like the bastard lovechild of Nostradamus and Mystic Meg. It's uncanny. Yes, the Bath scrum did get a pasting in the first half. One of the worst I've ever seen. Funnily enough, I remember sitting there thinking, *Thank God I'm on the bench!* Mark Bakewell came into the dressing room at half time and went straight up to the head coach. He said something to which the head coach nodded and then he turned to face me. His eyes were full of tears. 'I need you, mate,' he said. 'I need you to find a way back into these c**ts.'

Before coming to Bath, Mark had been the forwards coach at Brive and then Beziers and this game meant everything to him. I went on for the second half and that's the best 40 minutes I ever scrummaged in my entire life. I was completely inspired by Mark and by his predicament and we went on to draw what was a wonderful game of rugby, 3-3. That was one of the greatest days of my career. Why? Because I'd delivered for somebody who loved me and who always did their best by me. A while later I got injured and I remember Mark calling me one day while I was driving. My dad was in the car with me and when the call came in I asked him to be quiet while I took it.

DURDERS – I trust you were hands-free?

FLATS – Of course. He was just calling me to see how I was, which is something he did often, and when I hung up the call the first thing my dad said was, 'What an amazing man to have in your corner.' Mark would have done anything for me, and vice versa.

DURDERS – This is your Invictus, Flats. They'll make a movie about it. The tears, the triumphs. You don't need Pienaar or Mandela. You just need an overfed prop and a scrum coach crying his eyes out.

FLATS – As I've more than delivered on the unlikely hero front, can I include a less unlikely one? I'm going to anyway, so you don't have to answer. I'd like to nominate Mickey Skinner, who was an absolute legend in our house. I'll start off my tribute with a quick story. The night before an England match, Mickey and the rest of the team watched *Predator* with Arnie Schwarzenegger. The following day, during the game, Mickey was involved in a fracas which drew blood. 'Mick, you're bleeding,' said Will Carling. Mickey looked at him and said, 'I ain't got time to bleed.' That's a very famous line from the film, by the way, Durds. I wouldn't expect you to know that.

When I was 10, Mickey Skinner came to Maidstone

Rugby Club to do some coaching and he ended up coaching me and my mate Tank for a bit. I was a bit of a gobshite as I'm sure you can imagine and after giving Mickey a bit of backchat he cracked me one around the ear and said, 'Fuck up, you little twat!' Not 'Shut the fuck up,' but, 'Fuck up!' I sat next to Mickey at a dinner two or three years ago in London and I said, 'Look, this is unusual, but could I please have your autograph and a photo.' I think that's the first time I ever felt compelled to ask a hero of mine for their autograph. I'm usually not that bothered, but with Mickey it was different. I sent the photo to my dad and he went apeshit. He was so jealous. You should have seen Mickey's hands, though. He makes a pint glass look like a thimble. Now I'm going to talk about David Duckham.

DURDERS – David Duckham was born in 1946 and played his last game for England in 1976. How on earth do you remember him?

FLATS – I don't, in the sense that I never saw him play, nor did I ever watch him on *Rugby Special*. The reason I know about David Duckham is because of a video called *101 Great Tries* (among others), which I must have watched at least a thousand times. I said earlier that the phrase 'Never meet your heroes' was rubbish due to the fact that Frank Bruno was a top bloke. David Duckham was exactly the same. I did a couple of corporate events with him a few years ago and what a laugh. There used to be a video on YouTube of me literally dropping to my knees on the stage at one of these events because David Duckham's making me laugh so much. I had to get up very quickly, I remember, as I get really bad cramp in my stomach.

DURDERS — What did he say that made you laugh so much?

FLATS — It was silly things really. Will Carling was taking the piss out of him about something and he said, 'I don't have to be here, Will. I've got money. Okay, so it's tied up in my parents' house, but I've got money.' Trust me, when these kind of events get up and running again and you see one featuring David, get a ticket, or better still a table.

DURDERS — Is it my go now? Do you remember Andy Harriman? Played on the wing for Harlequins and once for England and won the Sevens World Cup with England. Well, he was playing in the first XV during my first year at Radley, and as well as being a lightning-quick, superb rugby player, he was also a Nigerian prince. I thought that was seriously cool. Yes, I was the King of Kentish Town, but a bona fide Nigerian prince was next-level stuff. That was proper hero worship. How could you not deify a man who, on his first day of training for Cambridge University, turned up in a gold Porsche? Aged 19, by the way. Even if that's a myth, I don't care. Did you ever play against Andy Harriman, Flats?

FLATS — No, I didn't. He did coach England A when I was playing for them alongside Ben Kay and Graham Rowntree. He was super-flash. I remember him telling us a story once about buying a new car. He said he was in a taxi one day and he got a call saying that a big deal had just gone through. 'Driver,' he said to the cabby. 'Take me to the Porsche garage.' Just as they're arriving, his phone goes again and apparently another deal had gone through. 'Driver,' he said to the cabby. 'Change of plan. Take me to the Ferrari garage.'

DURDERS — Were there ever any anti-heroes in your house? We only had one that I can remember and that was John McEnroe. My father could be considered quite conservative of mind, and he thought that John McEnroe was the devil. A very bad ambassador for tennis. He thought his behaviour was appalling.

FLATS — The 'you cannot be serious' stuff.

DURDERS — Exactly. Being at an impressionable age, an age when of course you're brainwashed into thinking your parents know best, I also thought McEnroe was a disgrace, but as soon as I developed a little independence of thought I came to love Mac. I need to revisit that debate with my father and see if his opinions have softened.

FLATS — Mike Tyson was the biggest villain in our house. Until he fought Frank Bruno I was actually a big fan of his because he was obviously a great boxer. When he beat Frank he became an enemy to me and my family. Time is a great healer, though, and after reconsidering my position I forgave him for beating Frank, and we've been lovers ever since.

DURDERS — The greatest rugby villain of all time — in my eyes at least — is David Campese. That man shattered my 1991 World Cup dreams by deliberately knocking on that pass to Rory Underwood. I've never forgiven him for that. I met him for the first time a couple of years ago and I had so much deep-seated resentment for him. I remember thinking to myself as I shook his hand, *This man stole my dreams!* I should have been shaking him by the neck really. He was also responsible for making me throw up on Platform 3 at Clapham Junction Station. I was so miserable after that game that I ended up drinking myself into oblivion. I must have cut a pathetic figure.

FLATS – What, wandering up and down the platform carrying a bottle of Pol Roger with your England top on and your collar up shouting, 'My dreams, my dreams! Campese's pinched them!'

DURDERS – Have you seen the CCTV? After subsequently chundering I was then shown up the stairs by an irate guard and then jettisoned unceremoniously from the premises. These days my balm for easing the pain is watching Campese's monumental cock-up that handed the Lions the series in 1989. It's on a loop in my mind's eye. What a nice bloke, though (said through teeth that are so gritted a trip to the dentist might be on the cards).

Our Ultimate Fifteen

FLATS – The first discussion we had about this chapter lasted about four hours and the biggest difference of opinion we had wasn't who should be in here, but how we should present our choices on the page. First we were going to have lists of players with our reasons underneath, and then we weren't. After a lot of negotiating, we decided to keep it as a discussion piece and simply go through each position and at the end decide who's chosen which player. Right then, are you sitting comfortably? Then we'll begin. You go first. Your No. 15 please.

DURDERS – I need to put in a disclaimer here, before we get going, though. I know no one on planet Earth gives a monkeys about my opinions, but I'm going to give them anyway in the hope there may be some crack-addled Martians out there who might one day find this book in a time capsule and think that I am a human of significance.

FLATS – Disclaimer noted.

DURDERS – So the player I've chosen provisionally at No. 15 is Serge Blanco. I need to have a debate, though, before I make my final choice.

FLATS — I know that Serge Blanco is a hero of yours, and he's a hero of mine. He's not Christian Cullen, though, who has to be the greatest ball-running, counter-attacking full-back of all time.

DURDERS — What about J. P. R. Williams? As a counter-attacking, hugely aggressive, big-haired full-back, he was masterly.

FLATS — There are certain players who, because of my age, I just won't have seen play before and although it would be a lovely idea to put Finlay Calder at openside, I can't because I never watched him play. I'd be submitting purely to nostalgia if I did that and I'm sorry but I won't. If I didn't see them play either live or on a TV screen, they ain't going in, at least not as one of my choices.

DURDERS — Okay, that's reasonable, I suppose, but I may end up smashing your face in if you don't at least consider the merits of some of my choices that you may not have seen in person.

FLATS — This is serious stuff, though. Along with Jason Robinson, ball in hand, Christian Cullen was the most undefendable threatening full-back I've ever seen and he was an absolute wonder to watch.

DURDERS — Actually, I think you're probably right. No human being has ever glided over a rugby field like Christian Cullen and I don't think the game has ever seen a more natural runner. He was like a Flymo in a black shirt.

FLATS — He was Iain Balshaw times five. He wasn't deceptively quick, he was just rapid, and being able to watch a player of that quality while I was growing up was a privilege.

We're both agreed, then; I've won you round with the power of my charm and the strength of my reasoning. At No. 15, we both have Christian Cullen.

DURDERS – Congratulations, Christian. I think we should send all the players we choose a medal each, or at least a little badge and a telegram. 'You in world 15 stop. Think you very good stop. Please send fiver for the badge stop.'

FLATS – Stop! If Christian Cullen is the most beautiful ball-running rugby player I've ever seen, Jason Robinson is the hardest rugby player to defend against, full stop, which is why he's my first choice on the wing. How about you, Durds? Where do you sit on Mr Robinson?

DURDERS – Love Mr Robinson. Some of my most vivid and happiest rugby-watching memories involve that man. But we must consider the merits of others. David Campese for instance. Loathed as I am to admit it, he has to be in with a shot of getting one of our coveted medals that don't actually exist?

FLATS – I'd have David Duckham over David Campese, purely because I see David Duckham on the corporate circuit quite often and it'll be awkward if I haven't picked him. Imagine if he turned up to an event, though, wearing one of our badges, looking resplendent. Campese was up there, but the truth is that given the choice I would rather have to defend against Campese than Jason Robinson. He was unplayable sometimes. Completely unplayable.

DURDERS – Just to strengthen your argument, Jason Robinson wasn't famous for making howlers like Campese was. He cost Australia matches sometimes, like the aforementioned Lions game.

FLATS – To strengthen my argument even more, yes, I do think Campese was a bit of an arse, though in person he's a nice man. My other wing, incidentally, is Jonah, obviously.

DURDERS – You can't have an ultimate 15 without Jonah Lomu. It's the law. Or at least it should be. Only people who have forgotten to include Jonah will not have Jonah in their side. Here's a question for you, and this is relevant to a lot of the players we're talking about, what kind of impact would Jonah have been making had he been in his rugby prime in the here and now, the 2020s?

FLATS – I think Jonah Lomu had a much better skill set than people remember. It wasn't any secret that he was a lot more comfortable going forwards than he was going backwards, but he did have the courage to collide when he didn't have the ball and I think he was more than just big and quick. He picked good lines and his incursions were invariably well timed, which is about more than just genetics. He also had beautiful movement, not to mention high aggression levels. His footwork could be amazing sometimes, but because he was big you often didn't see it. I played with loads of massive fast guys who dropped away because they didn't have the heart or the talent he did. One of my centres who we'll talk about in a minute had a similar gift but because he's enormous it was never mentioned. All people ever talked about was brute force. It was genetics and aggression every time.

DURDERS – I was watching a video of a game featuring Jonah the other day and I'd forgotten how dainty he was on his feet. He'd just knocked over Mike Tindall and Ben Cohen to score a try at Twickenham in 2002 and as he trotted back he looked as springy as Darcey Bussell. How can a man so big have been so light on his feet?

FLATS – Although I understand why you posed it, I do think that trying to imagine players from yesteryear playing today's game is pointless, as you're never comparing like with like. You can obviously only guess how they might have fared, although given how rugby players have evolved over the past 20 years I'd guess that Jonah Lomu circa 2021 would probably be similarly freaky given he'd be on an advanced strength and conditioning programme.

DURDERS – I'm by no means trying to have either Jason or Jonah removed from the list, but I do think there's more of a case for Mr Campese than we're giving him credit for. We kind of dismissed him because he was controversial and could be a pain in the arse, but what we've also dismissed is the fact that he was an incredibly gifted rugby player. I can't believe I'm stating the case for this man but I put it to you that the reason David Campese made quite a few mistakes is because he was willing to take risks, and that's something we see precious little of these days. He was a swashbuckler. A maverick. He had flare, he had X-Factor to burn.

FLATS – So your original back three was going to be Serge Blanco, Jonah and David Campese. I know you've swapped Blanco for Cullen, but what about Campese. Is it him or Jason?

DURDERS – When in the mood, I can be World Champion-level indecisive … and I'm very impressionable, and you got me thinking it had to be Cullen at 15, but I've still got a hankering for J. P. R. Williams at full-back. But I think my view is based on nostalgic grainy images from my childhood rather than considered assessment of what he might bring to the party. Sod it. I'm going full-on retro. J. P. R. Williams is my full-back of choice.

FLATS – Jason or Campo?

DURDERS – Despite my late charge for Campo, I'm going to go with Jason. So I have J. P. R. Williams and you have Christian Cullen at full-back and we both have Jonah and Jason on the wings. At least I was brave enough to disagree on one of the positions. I think my back three has a tiny bit more solidity than yours when the going gets tough. So there.

FLATS – Eventually! Right, then, who are your centres? I'm not bothering with inside and outside centre. They can both play left and right if they want.

DURDERS – I'm being quite presumptuous here but I think we can both agree on Brian O'Driscoll, yes? An amazing jawline, 856 caps for his country and squillions of points scored. What a player.

FLATS – Although Brian is in my 15, I very nearly dropped him in favour of Mike Gibson, another Irish centre from the old days. The reason I'm aware of Mike is because he used to turn up on lots of my dad's videos. My dad used to say, 'Quick, David, Mike Gibson's on,' and I'd run into the living room. I loved watching him play. Anyway, Brian O'Driscoll gets the nod because of his genius but I am giving a special mention to Mike Gibson. Who's your other centre, then?

DURDERS – I've got Tana Umaga written down, but then I also have – and I know this will surprise a lot of people – Will Greenwood for helping England win the World Cup.

I do have a horrible feeling that this team of mine is going to be very Englishman-light if I'm not careful, and I can't have that. Then again, I wonder if there's room in my side for players who weren't necessarily the best in their position but who produced moments of magic at the right time, like Will Greenwood. As we've said, Brian O'Driscoll is a shoo-in, not least for his performance in Brisbane. That alone requires that he's in my side as it's my fondest work-related rugby memory. My other has to be Tana Umaga. I'm sorry but I can't not have a Kiwi in the centre.

FLATS – I'm with you there, except my Kiwi is going to be Frank Bunce. I almost went for Philippe Sella, who is usually either first or second along with Brian in the all-time-great lists, but I didn't see quite enough of him, so Frank it is. He was a big, big hero of mine throughout my childhood.

DURDERS – I didn't think we were just going for our heroes.

FLATS – No, I'm not. Mike Teague was a bigger hero to me than Frank Bunce, but I didn't pick him. Brian Moore and Dean Richards are massive heroes, but I didn't pick them. I'll tell you what we'll do: at the end of this we'll also list a 15 made up solely of our heroes, and then decide which team would win. So, in conclusion for the centres, I've got O'Driscoll and Bunce and you've got O'Driscoll and Umaga. Moving on, then. I don't even have to ask who you've got at fly-half, do I? It's Dan Carter. The reason I know is because he's the best of all time, but he isn't my choice.

DURDERS – Here's a dream-team scenario for you. What would have happened if you'd had Jonathan Davies playing behind that New Zealand forward pack? Is Jonathan Davies your choice?

FLATS – That's a great shout and an amazing scenario, but no, mine's Phil Bennett. Like Mike Gibson, he was way before my time but fortunately my dad used to have loads of footage of him playing and I'd watch it all on a loop. He was just magic.

DURDERS – You're a wayward man. I thought you had to have seen them live. And despite me being a weeny bit older and wiser than you, it appears I've seen less of Phil Bennett than you, which is why I can't consider him. I'm obviously aware of his legend and reputation, but you're right in that my first choice is Dan Carter. What a sublime player he was. He did it all. He pulled all the strings, kicked the penalties, made the breaks, won the All Blacks World Cups, had great hair and perfect skin. How could he not get your nod?

FLATS – I get that, but Phil Bennett behind the forward pack would be worth the ticket price alone in my opinion.

DURDERS – But could he kick, though? What was Phil Bennett's kick rate, percentage-wise?

FLATS – It was at least 77 per cent. Actually, I just made that up. I've absolutely no idea what his percentage rate was. All I do know is that Phil Bennett is rightly regarded as one of the best players ever to play for Wales. He's my fly-half.

DURDERS – And your No. 9? As you went for Phil Bennett at fly-half I'm tempted to assume that Gareth Edwards might be your man. Am I right?

FLATS – You're rubbish at reading my very complex mind. Nope. My No. 9 is the late and extremely great Joost van der Westhuizen. I grew up watching Joost van der Westhuizen thinking he was a freak. Then I played against him and had this confirmed. I got to late tackle him once. My dad said to me before the game, 'If you do anything in this match, get that little bastard!' Then I realised that he wasn't a little bastard at all. He was a big bastard. I did get him, though, but then André Venter punched me in the head for it. That hurt.

DURDERS – Given he's no longer with us, I'm not sure I should give you my honest opinion of Joost van der Westhuizen. Actually, I probably should, shouldn't I? After all, I doubt he'd be either bothered or upset. The truth is, as a fan, I cannot think of a player I disliked more than Joost van der Westhuizen. Even David Campese sits in a favourable light to him, which is saying something. I don't hate easily, Flats, as well you know, but Joost was up there for me. I'm still surprised that you haven't gone with Gareth Edwards. All that wonderful Lions and Barbarians footage from the '70s. And *that* try, of course.

FLATS – Gareth Edwards probably is the best of all time, but for some reason I haven't seen as much footage of him as I have of Phil Bennett. I've only seen the highlights and the tries and that isn't enough for me. I also think you're letting your sporting hatred of Joost van der Westhuizen cloud your judgement slightly, not to mention your veneration of Sir Gareth. I, too, couldn't stand the sight of Joost van der Westhuizen, but part of the reason I couldn't stand him was because he was a great player. Same as Campo. Sure, he used to wind us all up, which is why my dad wanted me to get him during that match. But as much as we all hated the likes of Joost and Campo, or said we did, we'd have loved them on our team.

DURDERS – I was watching the Lions series against South Africa the other day, which Joost ended up losing for them. I have to say he had a very laboured pass. Was he famous for having the quickest pass in the game? I don't think he was, was he?

FLATS – Joost really did get to you, didn't he?

DURDERS – Speaking purely as a fan, yes. When I did get to meet him on the one occasion, what a nice and humble bloke. Years of loathing from afar, evaporated in an instant!

FLATS – So I'm going for him and you're going for Gareth Edwards. I think you're probably right, but I'm going to stick with Joost, as when I think of great scrum-halves his name enters my head first.

DURDERS – At the start of this chapter I was quite prepared to defer to your experience and better judgement, but not now. You choosing Joost to my Gareth has given me the confidence to stand up and be heard. And, for the sake of the chapter, the confidence that my team might actually beat yours.

FLATS – Who've you got at No. 8, then? Kieran Read, Imanol Harinordoquy? Mervyn Davies? Lawrence?!

DURDERS – No, no, no, no and no. I'm going with Sergio Parisse. A lovely bit of finesse with a hint of brawn. What a ball player. Why are you shaking your head? What's wrong with Parisse?

FLATS – He wasn't even in my top 10, mate.

DURDERS – I bet it's Kieran Read.

FLATS – Well, my choice is a bit left field, but I'm absolutely adamant that for a period of time this man was the greatest No. 8 on the planet, and that man is Henry Tuilagi. I can see you're looking a bit incredulous, but all I'd say is go and have a word with some of the people who played either with or against him. Ask Martin Johnson what he thinks of Henry Tuilagi. Ask Jonny Wilkinson. Listen to the greats of the game. He was so big, so enormous, yet he still had the best power-to-weight ratio of anyone I ever played against. He was just astonishingly explosive.

DURDERS – How about Buck Shelford?

FLATS – That's a funny one for me. I was always a really big fan of Buck's as a player but then he came and coached me at Saracens. A year later, I felt sufficiently underwhelmed to want to leave the club, which I did. Rightly or wrongly, that's clouded my view of him really, so he'd never be more than an honourable mention for me.

DURDERS – I can't say for sure, of course, but I'd hazard a guess that the majority of people reading this hugely stimulating tome of ours would probably go for Zinzan Brooke at No. 8.

FLATS – Of course they would, but I'd still rather play against Zinzan Brooke than I would Henry Tuilagi. Every day of the week. When he signed for Perpignan in 2007 – honestly, the ripple that went around the Premiership was funny and telling. There were lads texting each other for days saying, 'Thank fuck for that!' Shortly after it was announced that he was going to Perpignan, Bath were playing against Leicester. Henry was playing but I was out injured. It was a terrible game – mud everywhere – but Henry was making breaks and smashing people all over the place. No one could run in the deep mud in that game except him and he was by far the heaviest guy. He was in a different class to everyone else. After the game I walked into our dressing room and said, 'How was Henry?' 'Off to France he fucks,' said one of the players. 'And good riddance!' He was just otherworldly. I know you like that word, so I thought I'd slip it in again.

DURDERS – I've just looked him up on YouTube and the first five clips of Henry are all entitled, 'A Tribute to The Butcher'. So why did Kieran Read not get a look-in? You've made a very good case for Henry Tuilagi, but surely Kieran Read was more of a complete package? Handling, line-outs, attacking threat, leadership. There were no weak links in his game. None whatsoever.

FLATS – Why doesn't Eddie Jones pick Sam Simmonds then? No, it's my team and I'll pick who I want, and I want Henry.

DURDERS – Okay, keep your ill-fitting shirt on. My man Sergio's barely been given a sentence, which is a bit unfair. Anyway, we have to move on. We're not going to argue about No. 7, are we? That's a foregone conclusion.

FLATS – It isn't, and I think we probably are. I know you fancied yourself as being the maverick in this conversation, but you've failed miserably. You're nothing but a weak conformist really. A puppet of the establishment. The disgusting bourgeoisie!

DURDERS – Well if I'm the bourgeoisie that makes you the proletariat. Actually, shall we leave Marxist philosophy out of this? Neither of us own the means of production and our labours as a means to survive aren't worth a light. My choice, by the way, which I fear will do nothing to dispel your accusations of conformity, is Richie McCaw.

FLATS – No! Really? Richie McCaw? Are you sure?

DURDERS – I also wanted to put Jean-Pierre Rives in there purely for the amount of blood spilled for France. Surely no player spilled more blood for their country than Jean-Pierre Rives. Richie McCaw, though. He's the one. Two World Cups, one of the greatest athletes of all time and an all-round good bloke. The man who just kept on coming. The engine on that man was even better than the brand-new Autograph Range Rover you have outside. Seriously, though, how many games did you watch featuring Richie McCaw that he did not influence? I bet it's none at all.

FLATS – You think that giving a blood-soaked Frenchman an honourable mention makes you sound interesting? Well you're wrong, *mon brave*. That said, any argument not to include Richie McCaw in an all-time XV is a weak one. And I have not put Richie McCaw in my all-time XV.

DURDERS – Don't tell me. You've gone with another player like Henry Tuilagi who was less consistent and less of an all-round package than the obvious choice but was astonishing on their day. Am I correct?

FLATS – You are indeed. How very astute. My No. 7 is going to be Olivier Magne. I know he only got the wood on McCaw once or twice in those New Zealand v. France Test matches. I know that. Richie McCaw's magic was his attitude and perseverance, whereas Olivier Magne's magic was a kind of mercurial gift. An attitude is more impressive and effective than a gift, but a gift is more interesting. Does that make sense?

DURDERS – Not a lot.

FLATS – Look, I know that Richie McCaw is the greatest openside of all time and I know that he should be in my team and captain, but I just cannot leave out Olivier Magne. This is the archetypal 'My heart says this but my head says something else' situation, and this time I'm going with my heart. I remember my dad taking me on the Eurostar to watch France versus New Zealand and Olivier was just magnificent. What I wouldn't give to have played a game with Olivier Magne.

DURDERS – I'm just looking at Magne's stats and he won four Grand Slams and one other Six Nations title. Not bad. Okay, for No. 6 I have a blank at the moment. I want to get Richard Hill in there somewhere. The Silent Assassin. He could play at six, couldn't he? Anyway, you go first on this one. Give me your top three sixes.

FLATS – I'll give you my top two. My hero No. 6 is Mickey Skinner and my all-time No. 6 is Richard Hill. All day long.

DURDERS – You'll have been expecting us to disagree on this position, but I'm afraid that where chaos usually reigns, there is harmony at No. 6. As far as I'm concerned, if you had Richie McCaw and Richard Hill in your back row, you would not lose a game of rugby. And you certainly wouldn't sub them. Don't you think we're perhaps missing a few Celtic wonders in our teams? I don't want to receive any complaints from the Welsh, Irish and Scottish contingent.

FLATS – You mean apart from Phil Bennett, Sir Gareth Edwards and Brian O'Driscoll? Three isn't too bad. Anyway, let's get on to the second row. I take it you've got Johnno in there?

DURDERS – I have indeed. Martin Johnson, CBE, and Brodie Retallick.

FLATS – That's exactly what I've got! That's three players we've agreed on. What's happening?

DURDERS – I could easily stick Paul O'Connell in there instead of Johnson or Retallick.

FLATS – I think what you've got to do is take the greatest rugby teams that they didn't play for – the Welsh in the '80s or the World Cup-winning New Zealand or Springbok teams – and ask, would our second-rows get into those teams ahead of the guys who are already in them? Would you pick Johnno or Brodie Retallick over Eben Etzebeth? Yes, you would. Would you pick them over John Eales? Yes, you would. Would you pick Johnno or Retallick in their prime over Alun Wyn Jones? Yes, you would. If you're Welsh you wouldn't, but if you're not, you would.

DURDERS – Playing devil's advocate for a moment, if I had Richie McCaw and Martin Johnson in my team but Richie McCaw was captain, why should I pick Martin Johnson?

FLATS – He was a brilliant defender, very good line-out operator, very good scrummager (which not all good second-rows are), incredibly fit (which meant he rarely missed a minute), not prone to injury and he obviously thinks you're a bit of a knob. That's just for starters. Johnno was also a very underrated attacking player. I remember during my brief period playing for England that they would regularly give out an award for attacking player of the week and Johnno would regularly win it. The press reports after a game would always talk about someone he'd chinned or stamped on and would rarely mention his prowess as a tactician or communicator. He had everything as a captain and as a player. He wasn't just a hard bloke.

As for Retallick, he's just the Lebron James of rugby. He does everything as well as anyone else. He's the best ball-carrying lock, he's a brilliant defender, he's perfect in a line-out because he's about 8ft tall and has arms like an orangutan, he's bright, he's abrasive, he knuckles down, he's good in heavy traffic, he's good in open space – he has got everything. He's the best lock on the planet when he's fit.

DURDERS – He shouldn't be anywhere near as athletic as he is, don't you think? He's another one of those giants who shouldn't be able to do what he can do. You shouldn't be that coordinated when you're that enormous.

FLATS – He's Peter Crouch on a protein shake, basically.

DURDERS – What number did you wear on your back? Was it three or one? I'm just working out whether I can get you into my team.

FLATS – I was No. 1, and in every sense of the word. I bet you any money we don't agree on any of the front row. You'll be expecting me to have an Argentinian or two in there, I know you will. You'll be disappointed, though. There's plenty in my hero team, but not here.

DURDERS – I should care a lot more about my props really, because they're the cornerstone of a good XV.

FLATS – You just want your fly-halves to have a nice day, don't you? You just want a couple of bookends. I've got Sean Fitzpatrick at hooker.

DURDERS — I'm in a similar situation to the one you were in with Richie McCaw and Olivier Magne, in that my head is saying Sean Fitzpatrick but my heart is saying Keith Wood. Apart from all of the other stuff he could do, it's his attitude and spirit that makes me want to have Keith Wood in my team.

FLATS — The reason I've gone with Sean is basically because of the number of games he didn't lose. Keith Wood, though, is as good as anyone else who has ever played in that position.

DURDERS — So you're not going to admonish me for putting Keith Wood in there? I thought you'd say his line-out throwing wasn't good enough, or something like that.

FLATS — People regard Keith Wood in the same way they regard Johnno, except that instead of him being considered a hard nut who just muscled his way through games, he's supposed to have been this 'personality' who could lift a team just by being there, which is probably why you picked him. That's all well and good but once again you and everyone else are ignoring the fact that Keith Wood was both a talented and effective rugby player. He was quick, powerful, aggressive, fit. A great scrummager. I'm sure Keith would be chuffed to bits about being included in anyone's all-time XV, but to have him there just for his 'spirit' is doing him a massive disservice. Do you want me to give you my props? It might give you some inspiration.

DURDERS — You can't be swayed, then? Sean, not Keith, still your man?

FLATS — Yup — this man ain't for swaying.

DURDERS – The juices are flowing now. So, for my No. 1 I'm going with David Flatman. I'm certainly not putting you in my all-time-heroes 15, as you're anything but, but I do have to include you somewhere, if not out of a sense of loyalty then out of a sense of sheer stupidity. I sort of wanted Os du Randt in there, but then remembered what Scott Gibbs did to him during the Lions tour. That's just too embarrassing really. Jason Leonard's another who could go in. Crikey, horns of a dilemma. Okay, stand by. Here's my front row: David Flatman at one, just for the hell of it, Keith Wood at two, and I'd better have a bit of solidity in there, so maybe I will go with Os du Randt at three. Yes, I will. Flatman, Wood and du Randt. I know Keith and Os would lose the plot with me if I was their coach for making them play with you, but this is the only World XV you're ever going to make. So congratulations.

FLATS – I'm touched, but Du Randt's a loosehead like me, you idiot. He can't play that side. We're doing this properly. Well, kind of. While you're scratching your head, I'll give you my tighthead. Carl Hayman, whose nickname happens to be Zarg. No idea why. Carl Hayman was enormous, incredibly strong, tackled like a demon, never broke his shape, collided brilliantly, and had real integrity as a prop. He never cheated. It was all about strength and technique with him. He was also very humble and very generous, which are qualities you don't always find in the front row. At least on the field of play.

I played against him a few times and if you had a good scrum he'd be the first one to say well done. 'Great scrum, brother,' he used to say. You definitely raise your game when you're playing against somebody of that quality. He was probably one of the first of that new breed of prop who guys like Kyle Sinckler have now taken to the next level. In his time, though, Carl Hayman was unbeatable. In fact, he was the world's best tighthead by quite a long way, and in an era when the world was full of great props. I did consider going for Jeff Probyn or Omar Hasan – both wonderful players – but for me, all roads lead to Carl Hayman. He had the lot.

DURDERS – So is there no room at all for Tom Smith in your front row? Purely because he just shouldn't have been able to hold up a scrum.

FLATS – That's a great shout but no. There are guys who were better in my opinion. Christian Califano and Os du Randt being two. I got to play with and against Christian Califano, with when he was at Saracens and against when he was at Gloucester. He was coming to the end of his career by then, but he was still rock hard. I remember Andy Beattie, who was playing for Bath at the time, chinning Califano once at the side of a ruck. Andy only hit him once, but Califano hit him back 13 times – it was hilarious. I remember watching a video of this and I sent Andy a text saying, 'He hit you 15 times, Beast.' He said, 'Thirteen, see the video.' I was trying to sneak a couple in. Califano was crazy, hilarious, explosive. The sort of guy who, if he smelt blood, would just wipe you out. Together with Carl Hayman, he changed the way that props play rugby. He was that effective and that important.

DURDERS – Despite what you've just said, I'm keeping you in my XV – you'll just have to learn to play tighthead. Your time has come, I think. You've been overlooked way too long and I think you'd thrive in that environment.

FLATS — I don't wish to appear conceited, but I think you're right to select me. Are we choosing head coaches, by the way? I think we should. I'm going for Warren Gatland.

DURDERS — Really? Is he going to get the best out of our teams, the way he plays the game?

FLATS — Think about how few players there are in Wales. Now think about all the Grand Slams and Six Nations titles. Just think about those results. Considering hardly anyone lives there, let alone plays rugby, he did a magnificent job. Sporting alchemy, that's what I'd call it. He's King Wazza Midas in my eyes.

DURDERS — Even after the latest underwhelming and uninspiring Lions defeat in South Africa in the summer of 2021?

FLATS — Think about how few players there are in Wales. Now think about all the Grand Slams and Six Nations titles. Just think about those results. Considering hardly anyone lives there, let alone plays rugby, he did a magnificent job. Sporting alchemy, that's what I'd call it. While I think I'd rather like an attacking coach with licence to thrill alongside Warren G, I like Gatland's ability to mix often-winning rugby with good times between matches. That's what I like in a coach so yep, he's the chap for me.

DURDERS — I considered Sir Clive Ronald for obvious reasons — and some less obvious, namely that I love the man and his wife, Lady Jane — but I'm going for Jim Telfer. I like my head coaches to be gifted man-motivators. I would love to have Sir Ian McGeechan alongside him, but I know you're a dullard stickler for the rules so won't allow it.

FLATS — No, I certainly will not.

DURDERS – Okay, Telfer it is. Has there ever been a coach better at pressing the players' buttons? Getting their combative and competitive juices flowing? His honest-player speech during the 1997 Lions tour, which I've watched countless times on the outstanding *Living with the Lions* documentary, would have surely got even the most mild-mannered punching holes in walls. Churchill himself would have been proud of that speech, as would Shakespeare. It's rugby's version of the St Crispin's Day speech. In tribute to Mr Telfer, I'm going to include a transcript of the speech and insist that for the audiobook Mr Flatman reads it out in his best Jim Telfer impression. Those of you who haven't bought the audiobook will have to just imagine this as you're reading.

There are two types of rugby players, boys. There's honest ones, and there's the rest. The honest player gets up in the morning and looks himself in the fucking mirror, and sets his standard. Sets his stall out, and says 'I'm going to get better. I'm going to get better. I'm going to get better.' He doesn't complain about the food, or the beds, or the referees, or all these sorts of things. These are just peripheral things that weak players have always complained about. The dishonest player. If I tell a player he's too high, or he's not tight enough, he's too fucking high, he's not tight enough. And that's it. And I'm the judge, and not the player. And we accept that, and we do something about it.

I've coached Lions teams before, and we've complained and carped about that and the next thing. And I liken it a bit to the British and the Irish going abroad on holiday. The first thing they look for is a fucking English pub, the second thing they look for is a pint of Guinness, and the third thing they look for is a fish-and-chip shop. The only thing they accept is the sun. They don't take on anything that's good or decent or different abroad. If we do that, we're sunk. We don't go back bitchin'. We don't go back carpin', 'Oh we've done it this way at Twickenham or Cardiff Arms Park or Lansdowne Road or Murrayfield!' No, no. These days are past. What's accepted over there is not accepted over here. It's not accepted by us – me and you.

So from now on the page is turned. We're in a new book, different attitudes. We're honest with ourselves. And in many respects in the forward play – and let's be fuckin' honest – we've been second best. We can match them, but only if we get it right here [points to his head] and right here [points to his heart]. Two weeks. There's battles all along the way. There's a battle on Wednesday. There's a battle on Saturday. There's a battle next Wednesday. Then there's a battle the following Saturday. There's battle the following Tuesday – until we're fuckin' into the big arena. The one we'll be on Saturday. And by that time the fuckin' Lions have to make them fuckin' roar for us. Because they'll be baying for blood. Let's hope it's fucking Springbok blood. We're focused. From now on, kid gloves are off. It's bare-knuckle fuckin' stuff. And only at the end of the day will the man that's standing on his feet win the fuckin' battle.

DURDERS – Stirring stuff. Who wants a fight? Those are our ultimate XVs. We know the bench is a key part of the modern game, but that will get way too complicated if we go down that route and we only have single digit brain cells between us. Our final XVs are listed at the end of the chapters and I'm sure you'll all agree that mine is a superior team to David's.

FLATS – I've got better things to do with my time than respond to that.

DURDERS – Like what?

FLATS – Order my Durders' World XV badge for starters.

Ultimate XV

Flats		Durders
Os du Randt	1	David Flatman
Sean Fitzpatrick	2	Keith Wood
Carl Hayman	3	Os du Randt
Brodie Retallick	4	Brodie Retallick
Martin Johnson	5	Martin Johnson
Richard Hill	6	Richard Hill
Olivier Magne	7	Richie McCaw
Henry Tuilagi	8	Sergio Parisse
Joost van der Westhuizen	9	Gareth Edwards
Phil Bennett	10	Dan Carter
Jonah Lomu	11	Tana Umaga
Frank Bunce	12	Brian O'Driscoll
Brian O'Driscoll	13	Jason Robinson
Jason Robinson	14	Jonah Lomu
Christian Cullen	15	J. P. R. Williams
Warren Gatland	Head coach	Jim Telfer

Hero Fifteen

DURDERS – Shall we run through our hero teams, then? Our XVs selected purely using the heart and not the head. Those players who, for whatever reason, worked their ways into our affections and have stayed there, embedded for eternity.

FLATS – As always, you're being unnecessarily flowery but that is the gist – albeit an elongated gist, but a gist nonetheless.

DURDERS – You're not exactly the King of Succinct yourself, you know? Anyway, being far more spiritually in touch with the game than you are, I think my Hero XV, like my Ultimate XV, will trump yours. And I'm definitely going first. One thing you will be pleased about is that two of my early choices are people who went bald prematurely, just like your good self. One of whom is Dusty Hare, who, in addition to playing almost 400 times for Leicester and 25 times for England, also played cricket for Nottinghamshire. When I was just a wee slip of a lad – actually 'wee' and 'slip' were never words used to describe my childhood self – I used to go and watch Dusty play for Leicester against the Barbarians every year the day after Boxing Day. They're such vivid memories. He may not be all-time-XV material but he's certainly hero material. My two other contenders for this position were J. P. R. Williams again and Andy Irvine, but Dusty just pipped it. Actually, couldn't I just put J. P. R. and Andy on the wing?

FLATS – Do what you like, it's your XV. Andy Irvine's a friend of my parents. He's a lovely man.

DURDERS – Let me have a think about it. Who's your No. 15, then? I bet it's Matt Perry. And I bet it's because he's one of your best mates.

FLATS – It *is* Matt Perry, but it's not because he's my mate. It's because of how he cuts his hair. Do you know what he does? He gets a Bic razor, holds it like a drumstick, with a firm but relaxed grip, and then just runs it over his full head of hair. It looks like he's done it with a knife and fork in the bath. I also love the fact that he once went out to pick up a takeaway at 6 p.m. in the evening and arrived back the next day at four o'clock in the morning – with the takeaway! His now ex-wife (they're still friends) said to him, 'Where the hell have you been?' 'I've got your bloody takeaway,' he slurred. 'What's the problem?' 'It's four o'clock in the morning,' she said. 'Where?' asked Matt.

DURDERS – That can't be your reason for picking him, surely?

FLATS – What do you take me for? Some kind of oik? I played with some pretty tough blokes during my career but he was probably the toughest. I don't mean 'tough' as in he'd punch your lights out. Not at all. I mean tough as in brave and fearless. People often talk about Lewis Moody in that vein, but Moodos was a big man. Matt Perry wasn't. He can't have weighed more than about 13 stone, but it made absolutely no difference. He was fearless on a Tuesday morning at training, he was fearless on a Saturday afternoon at the Rec, and he was fearless for England and the Lions. You almost forgot how brilliant he was because he was just so hard. There's something to be said about the ball getting booted over your head, which it does a lot in rugby union, and never for a second thinking that it won't be caught and returned. That's how much confidence Matt instilled in us all. He was like Andre Agassi. He'd get anything back. He was just inspirational.

DURDERS — What a great choice. And if you're not careful you'll be in danger of refuting my accusation that you're less spiritually in touch with the game than I am. Anyway, I'm definitely going to put J. P. R. Williams out on the wing. He did play on the wing sometimes, didn't he, Flats?

FLATS — Just say he did. No one'll know.

DURDERS — He was also a doctor, you see, so if anybody got hurt he'd be able to fix them.

FLATS — Who, the butcher of Bridgend? My first winger, by the way, is going to be Chris Oti. Together with Dean Richards, he was the reason I fell in love with rugby and he is still one of the most exciting players I ever had the good fortune to watch. That said, I have to admit that Chris's and Dean's status may have been elevated somewhat by my dad's commentary while we watched them play. The opposition No. 9 or 10 would kick the ball, Dean Richards would catch it and my dad would say, 'He always knows exactly where to be. What a player!' I now know that it's a completely standard role for a No. 8 to drop back and field long kicks, but back then I thought it was extraordinary.

'Look at Oti go!' he'd shout. 'He's faster than Superman!'

I'd sit there thinking, *Faster than Superman? Wow!* It's probably a form of indoctrination, so I could sue my dad, if we were American. David Duckham's my other winger. I know I've already mentioned him, and in the same context, so I won't go on. David Duckham and Chris Oti as wingers, though. Can you see me drooling?

DURDERS – Thankfully no. Duckham and Oti are worth a drool though. I'm going to settle for J. P. R. and Andy Irvine on my wings, although I fancy a bit of Duckham too, owing to his multiple features on my *101 Best Tries* VHS cassette.

FLATS – Right. Onto our hero XV centres.

DURDERS – My heroic centres are Philippe Sella, purely because of his magic feet and his joie de vivre, and Jim Renwick. I used to be obsessed by Jim Renwick when I was a child and I can't for the life of me remember why. Perhaps it was his bald pate and moustache, which made him look more like a bank clerk than an international rugby player. I guess we'll never know. He's in there, though. Okay, moving swiftly on. Who are your heroic centres?

FLATS – Mike Gibson, who I've already mentioned, and Conrad Smith. With Conrad Smith it was the power of illusion that first attracted me to him, because he looked like he should be a supply geography teacher or working in a shoe shop. He looked nothing like some of the monsters that were, and are, knocking around and because of that I used to watch him intently. As well as moving incredibly quickly, he also thought incredibly quickly, which created some distance between him and other centres. He didn't have the freakish power or size that the likes of Ma'a Nonu and Sonny Bill

Williams had, but what he lacked in those departments he more than made up for with bravery, speed and intelligence. I used to watch him defend and would think to myself, *How on earth does anyone ever make a break down that thirteen channel?*

DURDERS – A thinking person's centre? Good call. Right, then, we're on to fly-half. Did Ollie Campbell make my World XV? He didn't, did he? Okay, he's in.

FLATS – He was the one you mentioned earlier who was superstitious. I still have no idea who Ollie Campbell is, by the way.

DURDERS – He's one of the great legends of Irish rugby. He played at No. 10 when your apparent hero Mike Gibson played in the centres. I can't believe you've never heard of him. Or are you just taking the mick?

FLATS – I see what you did there.

DURDERS – Honestly, I am stunned by your ignorance. Ollie Campbell had this big tussle with the sublimely gifted Tony Ward for the Irish No. 10 shirt. Before taking kicks at goal, he used to stand on his tiptoes a bit like a prima ballerina – and then give the ball a big wallop. He was instrumental in Ireland's Triple Crown and Five Nations title in 1982. Still not ringing any bells?

FLATS – No. No bells dinging or donging here. My No. 10 is Jiffy, otherwise known as Jonathan Davies OBE. I didn't really have that many heroes as a child. If I was playing football, which all my mates did, I'd pretend to be John Barnes, and if I was playing rugby, I'd be Chris Oti. There were plenty of players I admired, of course, but hero worship just wasn't really my thing. In adulthood nothing's changed, and one of the very few players who has captured my imagination enough for me to be able to refer to him as a hero is Jiffy. If it was all about winning you'd pick Dan Carter every time, but that isn't what this is about. This is about producing moments that you'll never forget and Jonathan Davies is more likely to do that than anyone else on my team. His clips pop up on social media all the time and even though he's a mate, I still watch them and think, *Holy shit! This guy was just incredible. What a treat to have watched him when I was growing up.* A very close second would be your old friend and colleague, Stuart Barnes.

DURDERS — I couldn't possibly include him in my Hero XV as he'd remind me every time I see him from now until my dying day and we can't have that. My scrum-half is going to be Terry Holmes, who, by the look on your face, you're not familiar with either. I can't believe you don't know who Terry Holmes is. He played 25 times for Wales between 1978 and 1985 and won one Lions cap. He was a great player. Always sniping round the fringes. Always threatening. Like Jim Renwick, I'm not 100 per cent sure why I liked Terry Holmes so much. Perhaps it was the London Welsh thing, or perhaps it was my mate Huw Thomas? I can't believe you haven't heard of either of my half-backs.

FLATS — They obviously didn't appear on any of my dad's videos. I will look them up, though. Promise. My scrum-half is Grant Batty, who played for the All Blacks. Sir Gareth is the greatest, but Grant Batty was just wild. He was just 5ft 5in tall, which is obviously tiny in rugby terms, but he was fearless. The half-back Chris Laidlaw once described him as being a small man who radiated a single message to all around him, which was, 'Don't mess with me or I'll punch your lights out.' He could do all the rugby stuff but would also knock a big bloke's lights out just for looking at him the wrong way. I kind of loved that when I was growing up. He was like a Jack Russell. Fast, aggressive, tenacious. Buck Shelford wouldn't have messed with Grant Batty and Grant Batty would have fit in Shelford's pocket. Batty himself once said that he never saw his height as a disadvantage and always had the philosophy that the messages his brain sent to the rest of his body had less far to go. He only played 15 Tests for the All Blacks, but every time my dad put one of them on the video player, I was glued.

DURDERS – So you don't know about Ollie Campbell or Jim Renwick or Terry Holmes, yet you know everything about Grant Batty, who played for New Zealand between 1972 and 1977. You weren't even born! Although there's one rather fundamental thing you don't seem to know about Grant Batty – he was a winger, not a scrum half.

FLATS – Semantics, Markie. You'll have to take this up with my dad, I'm afraid. He was the archivist and projectionist in our house, and I can only assume my mistake was caused by his inability to produce a clear picture. He and mum used to have some friends who lived in Brisbane and they would tape games involving Australia or New Zealand for Dad back in the 1980s and then post them to him. When they first started arriving he didn't have a video player so went to Currys or wherever to buy one. The shop assistant asked him whether it was VHS or Betamax and apparently he said, 'I dunno. It's just a massive bloody tape.' Instead of going back and bringing the tape back in, he ended up buying a Betamax machine and the tapes were VHS. He was sitting there for ages apparently going, 'Why won't this bloody thing fit? Hilary!' He took it back and swapped it for a VHS machine, which is obviously when the fun started.

DURDERS — As fascinating as the technical issues in the Flatman household are, we ought to gloss over the fact that you've got an All Black winger playing at No. 9 in your hero XV and move on to our hero No. 8s, and I think we might have an agreement here. Does the name Dean Richards mean anything to you? My father, a former naval officer, was never his biggest fan for the simple reason that he used to play with his socks around his ankles. 'What a shambles of a man,' he used to say. But what an effective shambles. Now that Newcastle Falcons are back in the Premiership, we've interviewed him quite a lot. I hope he doesn't feel uncomfortable with his interviewers looking at him with barely concealed adoration in their eyes.

FLATS — Yep, he's my choice too. When you describe somebody as having no frills, it can make them sound dull, but in his case it's the opposite as it's the absence of frilliness that makes Dean Richards so incredibly charismatic. There's also a very high rugby IQ there.

DURDERS — Where are you on the frilly front?

FLATS — Nowhere near you, that's for sure. You're like a human doily in suede dune boots. Something else I love about Dean Richards is that he doesn't need anyone else's approval or validation. He's very comfortable being exactly who he is and operating exactly how he sees fit. He's the sort of person you could imagine reading a very critical piece about him and his club in the newspapers and then completely disregarding it. Other people's opinions just don't matter.

DURDERS — We're obviously at the business end now and next up I'm choosing Mr Blood-and-Guts himself, Jean-Pierre Rives. It should be a legal requirement to growl after saying his name. After Giant Haystacks and Big Daddy, he was the man I wanted to be the most when I was a child and was the epitome of what a hero should be. Do you know what his Twitter biog says? It says, 'I left everything on the pitch including teeth, blood, sweat and a lot of tears.'

FLATS — My other back rows are Peter Winterbottom and Mike Teague. Straight, hard players who were relentlessly combative and an inspiration to young forwards like me. The player who most reminded me of Mike Teague during my playing career was Martin Corry. The game cleaned up a bit towards the end of his career so he couldn't be as aggressive but he, too, was just relentless. We used to play against Leicester and they'd have at least 25 internationals in their starting XV as well as Josh Kronfeld and Franck Tournaire on the bench. They had everyone playing and it was brutal but there was nobody better in that team than Martin Corry. The only difference between him and Mike Teague is that Mike Teague probably hit people a bit more readily, which I used to enjoy as a kid.

DURDERS — An all-English back row, eh? You flag-shagger! Isn't that what they call people on Twitter who use the cross of St George? Mine is actually Anglo-French, as completing my back row is Andy Ripley. Not the greatest player of all time, but he was on my second favourite show, *Superstars*, and could row really quickly and do lots and lots of squat thrusts. He was a huge hero of mine. Incidentally, Marcus Rose, who also went on *Superstars* and rocked a singlet like no other, nearly got into my hero XV because of the hairiness of his armpits. The Hanging Gardens of Babylon had nothing on the Pits of Rose. I just thought I'd throw that one in.

FLATS – And thank God you did. My first second row is the Argentinian, Patricio Albacete. He played for Toulouse for over 10 years and won a Heineken Cup with then. During the final of that tournament he got subbed late on when they knew they'd won the game, and as he was coming off the coach, Guy Novès, shook him by the hand on the sidelines and then got on his knees and did the 'We're not worthy' thing from *Wayne's World*. I played against Patricio a few times. On one occasion, as I was doing a pick-and-go, he hit me from the side. It felt like I was playing in the NFL! I saw him in the changing room after the game and he had a towel around him. He looked like he did a bit of gym but not much. I went back to our changing room and said, 'He's not even that well-built!' 'He's just a lot stronger than you are,' said my colleagues and friends. 'Get over it.'

My other second row is Wade Dooley, who was a big deal in our house. I have tried really hard not to put another Englishman from that generation in my side, but I can't resist. He was another Frank Bruno to us, but even bigger. One year during a divisional game, the North against the South East (I think I've got that right), Wade chinned Mickey Skinner across the top of a ruck. Normally Mickey Skinner would fly back in, but Wade hit him so hard with a jab that he just stood there wobbling a bit. Mickey had been treading on somebody and Wade had given him a warning. He'd obviously taken no notice and so Wade put a stop to it. I remember rewinding that bit about 50 times.

DURDERS – Wasn't he a policeman in Blackpool for a few years?

FLATS – He was, and because he was 6ft 8in they used to call him the Blackpool Tower. Imagine getting nicked by Wade Dooley? It'd be terrifying. He broke Phil Davies's jaw back in 1987 and the match had only been going about two minutes.

DURDERS – My own favourite Wade Dooley story is one I heard Will Carling tell. During a team meeting prior to an Australia game once, the forwards coach asked Wade if he knew who he'd be playing against. You're going to have to assume a deadpan Lancastrian accent for this. 'Somebody called John Eales,' said Wade, referring to a piece of paper he'd written it down on. 'Okay, Wade,' continued the forwards coach. 'So what do you know about him?' 'He is an art student,' replied Wade, referring again to the piece of paper. 'Anything else, Wade?' said the coach. 'That', said Wade, 'is all I need to know.'

FLATS – Apparently he ran a tea room with his wife until quite recently. Try getting your head around that.

DURDERS – Can I have Steve Austin in my team?

FLATS – Stone Cold Steve Austin the wrestler or the Six Million Dollar Man?

DURDERS – The latter. He was a massive hero of mine, as was Black Beauty. They could be my second row.

FLATS – If you're doing that, I want Steve Redgrave in there and Herbie from *The Love Bug*. These could be wildcards? Nobody said anything about us only choosing rugby players. By the way, putting a horse in the second row is just ridiculous. You'd have to have it out on the wing, surely? Or wherever the grass was longest?

DURDERS – No, I want Black Beauty in my engine room with the Six Million Dollar Man. I concede they may have a few issues binding, but once they've got that sorted, Steve Austin could slip her a sugar lump before the engage and then I'd sit back and watch the scrum penalties flow. The No. 1 in my team, Jason Leonard, would love it. He's the governor. He's also somebody who is even better for knowing. Who's your No. 1, Flats?

FLATS – Os du Randt. He was probably one of the very first freakishly large props, yet he was also explosively powerful. Yep. No. 1's got to be The Ox. I agree with you re. Jason, though. He is a flat-out hero. It was Os du Randt's extremeness that tipped it for me.

DURDERS – I think those select few who've made both our ultimate and Hero XVs will feel a similar glow to those who get named on the Queen's New Year Honours list, but let's press on. My No. 2 is Ciaran Fitzgerald. Ever heard of him?

FLATS – Nope. Don't tell me. Another Irish legend from the 1970s?

DURDERS – Wrong. He was 1980s really. He captained Ireland to the Triple Crown in 1982 and 1985 and the Five Nations in 1983. He also captained the British and Irish Lions on their 1983 tour and then after retirement became head coach of Ireland. And you've never heard of him? Are you a fraud? A rugby imposter who's only in it for the moola? Who's your hooker, then?

FLATS – Shota Horie is my heroic hooker. After the last World Cup, he could have been a World XV player. More than that, I just love watching him play. Skill, vision, intelligence and bravery. There was nothing he wouldn't try and there was no one he wouldn't smash into. He barely made a mistake in that World Cup and I wouldn't change a single aspect of his game. He does everything. He also advertises really weird little drinks in Japan and looks cool on the bill-board because he's got dreads. Who's your tighthead prop?

DURDERS – Giant Haystacks. David Sole almost got in there, though.

FLATS – He's a loosehead.

DURDERS – Is he? Okay, then, I'll stick with Giant Haystacks. You see, if I was going to do a talent identification pro-gramme like *Britain's Got Talent* or *Pop Idol* for front-row rugby players and he came along, I'd be like Simon Cowell and sign him up to a long-term contract immediately.

FLATS – Like 'Prop Idol', you mean? I'm going for Omar Hasan, who I've already mentioned several times. He was literally designed by the DNA gods to be a tighthead prop and it's impossible for him to move backwards. But he also sings opera, for heaven's sake, and is great company. Are you really going with a 685lb wrestler who stood at almost seven feet tall as your tighthead? You are, aren't you. Okay then: manager? I'm going for Geech.

DURDERS – I think we're in danger of ending this chap-ter with an agreement, as I too was thinking of Sir Ian McGeechan. The regs didn't allow him to be joint head coach of my Ultimate XV so he's in the mix for this one.

FLATS – Many years ago I was going through a bit of con-tractual argy-bargy with the people at Bath and Geech fought my corner. He never mentioned it. Never said a word. In fact, I only found out after he'd left the club. He just did it. Brilliant man.

DURDERS — I've actually changed my mind. Couldn't we have Claudia Winkleman as manager? She'd certainly get the best out of my team. No doubt about it. Managed by a low-hanging fringe.

FLATS — I would likely die for that fringe, and I've never even met her. Yep. Sod Geech and his altruism — Claudia's in.

DURDERS —This Heroes XV has taken a wrong turn somewhere, but I think my lot are simply unbeatable.

FLATS — I wouldn't be so sure. My sugar-lump dealer sells some good shit.

Hero XV

Flats		Durders
Os du Randt	1	Jason Leonard
Shota Horie	2	Ciaran Fitzgerald
Omar Hasan	3	Giant Haystacks
Patricio Albacete	4	Steve Austin
Wade Dooley	5	Black Beauty
Mike Teague	6	Andy Ripley
Peter Winterbottom	7	Jean-Pierre Rives
Dean Richards	8	Dean Richards
Grant Batty	9	Terry Holmes
Jonathan Davies	10	Ollie Campbell
David Duckham	11	Jim Renwick
Mike Gibson	12	Philippe Sella
Conrad Smith	13	Andy Irvine
Chris Oti	14	J. P. R. Williams
Matt Perry	15	Dusty Hare
Claudia Winkleman	Head coach	Claudia Winkleman

World Cup

DURDERS – This chapter actually means something to me on a personal level. Not only because I am a proud and fanatical England supporter who has experienced more than a few ups and downs since the Webb Ellis Cup was first handed to New Zealand's David Kirk in 1987, but also because the man who sired me – actually I'm feeling queasy about putting it that way so I'm just going to go with 'my father' – my father had a go at getting a Rugby World Cup off the ground five years before it finally did in 1987. He went on a world tour, trying to get all the relevant governing bodies to sign up. The countries were all game, but unfortunately the IRB (now World Rugby), who had already scuppered several attempts at starting a World Cup before then, put the mockers on it. Bit short-sighted if you ask me.

FLATS – You mean your dad – the enigmatic and legendary Neil Durden-Smith – very nearly became the Bernie Ecclestone of rugby?

DURDERS – He did indeed. I kept a scrapbook of his adventures and there's even an article written by Ian Wooldridge in there with the headline, 'The Six Million Pound Man

They Can't Refuse'. Unfortunately they did refuse him. Or to be more precise a few unions were reluctant to sign up and scuppered the plan.

FLATS – Do you remember much about that first World Cup?

DURDERS – Very little really, apart from the odd grainy memory of John Kirwan running through everybody. My first vivid memories are of the 1991 World Cup, which is when the pain started. This obviously brings us back to the Dark Lord of Australian rugby, David Campese. Have you ever actually seen that footage, Flats, of David Campese's knock-on during the 1991 World Cup final?

FLATS – I honestly don't think I have. I've obviously listened to you talk about it – a lot – but I don't think I've ever seen it.

DURDERS – You're going to make me relive it again. It's a three-on-one, and if Winterbottom gets the ball out to Rory Underwood, England have won the World Cup, on home soil, at Twickenham, and in front of 80,000 people. David Campese then deliberately knocks the ball on, England get a penalty, the penalty isn't enough, and it's game over. The Australian fans will probably have a different view of what might have happened had Campese not had his own 'hand of God' moment, but an Englishman's view is that we would have won the World Cup. That is probably the most painful thing I have ever watched on a rugby field. Apart from having a bird's-eye view of my own disasters.

FLATS – I have seen Campo interviewed about this a couple of times and he always comes out with the line, 'What would you have done?' Out of interest, Durds, what would you have done?

DURDERS – I'd have smashed his bloody face in! I can't believe that you don't know the historical context of this. England had played boring rugby throughout the entire tournament, to the point where the Australia coach, Bob Dwyer, had come out and said that we'd put the game back 20 years. I wouldn't have gone that far personally but I would concede England hadn't been the most entertaining to watch. Anyway, that was a recurring problem throughout that period. You're lucky you don't remember much. By the way, you remember I told you that I had expunged some of my innards on Platform 3 at Clapham Junction Station?

FLATS – Vomited. Yes, I remember. How on earth could I possibly forget?

DURDERS – Well, I've just remembered it wasn't on Platform 3. That's incorrect. I vomited over a bridge and onto the railway tracks just above Clapham Junction Station. I was unceremoniously removed from there, however, just like I said.

FLATS – Because the tracks are electrified, I'd have been worried that one continuous stream of vomit might have acted as a liquid electrical conductor, which undoubtedly would have resulted in your premature and rigid death.

DURDERS – The bridge was at least 20 feet from the tracks and it wasn't a continuous stream. Thanks for your concern, though. Okay, let's move on. You'd have been 15 in 1995, right? You must remember this one, surely? The highlight for me was undoubtedly watching Rob Andrew score a drop goal in the 82nd minute of the quarter-final against Australia with the score poised at 22-22. He followed it up by performing a kind of Macarena-based celebration, which was a little geeky but utterly joyous. I also remember Brian Moore going absolutely ballistic at the final whistle. We lost in the semi-final, of course, against New Zealand, when we got Lomu-ed. I was at a friend's house down in Malvern for that quarter-final and when Rob Andrew scored the drop goal I ended up at the bottom of a pile-on that must have been at least 12 people deep. Have you got a World Cup version of this? Surely you have.

FLATS – I'm afraid I'm in danger of spoiling this chapter, or at least giving it a slightly different angle. I don't have much of a memory at the best of times, but I'm afraid I don't have many World Cup recollections to share. At least not the kind I think you're referring to, such as watching last-minute drop goals and then ending up at the bottom of a pile-on or vomiting onto a train track before being removed from the station. I have recollections of my dad taking me to Twickenham to watch England, such as the game where Rory Underwood scored against Ireland in the Five Nations, but the Bank of World Cups is a bit scant, I'm afraid. Or at least it is at the moment. Perhaps a chat like this might uncover something.

Around the time of the 1995 World Cup, I have to admit that my favourite international players were Tim Horan and Michael Lynagh. I appreciate that may sound slightly controversial, but that's the truth. I was so obsessed by the game itself that I didn't care about where the players came from or which country they played for. It was all about how good they were. The reason I mention Tim Horan and Michael Lynagh is because two years after the 1995 World Cup, in the summer of 1997, I had the honour of being invited to join Saracens for pre-season training. I was supposed to have been going to Gran Canaria with the lads for a couple of weeks but ended up at Saracens for six.

DURDERS – Quick question. Had you gone to the Canaries with your pals, would you have been lead Casanova? Would heads have turned as you walked into the local discotheque?

FLATS – Discotheque? This was 1997. What are you talking about? In answer to your question: no, I wasn't. I always had to give girls a bit of time to realise I wasn't quite so physically repulsive as they first declared and that they might like me if they gave me a chance. The fact that my ears were usually bleeding and I looked like I'd been in a fight didn't help. Anyway, now we've cleared that important matter up, I'll continue.

DURDERS – Please do.

FLATS – When I received the invitation to join Saracens for training, I'd just passed my driving test, so I drove around from Maidstone on the M25 to Saracens and back every day. I'd get home and the first thing my dad would do is take my car to the petrol station and fill it up for me. Then, when he got back, he'd make me clean my boots for the following day. It was summer, so they didn't need cleaning, but he didn't care. He and my mum were as invested in this as I was.

On the first day, I got there at eight o'clock in the morning and the first person I saw was the fitness coach, Mike Yates. Before I carry on, I've got a great story about Yatesy. He later moved from Saracens to Bath. I think he's about 200 now but I'm sure he's still alive. In fact, if there's ever a nuclear war, the only things that will survive will be rats, cockroaches and Yatesy.

When I moved to Bath he was already a legend there and the prop, David Barnes, had made a living out of winding him up. One day Barnesy said that he'd come up with the ultimate wind-up for Yatesy, and if everything went to plan it would result in him having a heart attack. 'I'm going to kill the bastard,' he said. 'It's going to be hilarious.' What Barnesy intended on doing was letting himself into the training centre before Yatesy arrived, locking up again, hiding in the toilets, and then jumping out at Yatesy when he came in for his morning wee. It wasn't exactly a complex plan, but he was confident about the outcome. 'Wouldn't it be funny if he died of a heart attack,' he said. 'Or shat himself.'

When Yatesy finally came in for said wee, Barnesy jumped out and went, 'WAAAAAA!' So far so good. Yatesy then went, 'WAAAAAA!', after which he punched Barnesy full-on in the face, who then fell against a urinal and dropped to the ground unconscious. We like to add to the story that Barnesy then pissed himself, even if that's not quite true. The reason he always got away with winding Yatesy up was because he was a good trainer, but that day he got chinned and it was great.

DURDERS – I've noticed that every time you get excited by a story you start to rub or pick your left nostril. (We're on

Zoom, FYI.) That one was a four-rub/pick story, which equates to a rating of good to very good.

FLATS – It just popped into my head. Anyway, on my first day at Saracens, Yatesy said, 'Okay, fella. You're going to lift some weights today. Do you know where the gym is?' 'Afraid not,' I said. 'Don't worry,' said Yatesy. 'Mike will show you. He needs a lift. Hey, Michael. This lad's going to give you a lift to the gym.' When I got home that evening I said to my dad, 'You'll never guess who I drove to the gym earlier.' He said, 'It better not be Michael Lynagh?' I said, 'It is. I'm doing it again tomorrow.' 'Hilary!' he shouted, calling to my mum. 'Hilary! David's become Michael Lynagh's driver!' 'Who's Michael Lynagh?' 'Oh for God's sake!' He then went outside, had a look inside my car and told me off for not having cleared it of sandwich wrappers and flapjack crumbs.

DURDERS – You were actually Michael Lynagh's gym bitch? That's amazing.

FLATS – Guilty as charged. I remember finishing a weight session once and I said to Yatesy, 'Mike, is there any more I can do?' Francois Pienaar was in the gym at the time and he said, 'Hey, boys. Did you hear that? This young guy, he's asking for extras. That's the sort of attitude that'll get you to the top, boy.' Michael Lynagh then shook his head and said, 'Don't be a brown-nose, mate. It's a long career. You don't wanna to lose any friends this early.'

DURDERS – As much as I'm enjoying your tales of Sarceonian gym bitchery, is there any chance of something World Cup-related?

FLATS – I'll try. This has kind of warmed me up a bit so there's a chance of something materialising. I'll just talk and see what happens. Well, despite the eventual result, the 1995 World Cup was all about Jonah Lomu. To me, at least. I'm afraid I missed the political significance regarding Nelson Mandela and Francois at the time. I don't think there's anyone who has done as much for rugby union just by being themselves as Jonah Lomu. There'd never been anyone so physically dominant in that position before and there hasn't been anyone since. He is what I remember about that World Cup. I got to play against Jonah at Twickenham a few years later and I absolutely smashed him. He's no longer with us so he can't disprove that.

DURDERS – You mean it's not true.

FLATS – No, it's not. Somebody else tackled him and I piled in at the end. My dad had been on at me before the game to tackle him and this was my chance. Somebody else got him by the legs and I just piled into the upper body and knocked him over. They all count.

DURDERS – So I take it you wanted the All Blacks to win the 1995 World Cup?

FLATS – Hell, yeah! I was gutted when they didn't. It's one of the few times I have been gutted when an international team has lost a game of rugby.

DURDERS – Are you saying that you've never cared whether England win a game or not? The country of your birth? The country you represented?

FLATS – Since I retired, no. It's something to do with being a little bit bitter that I didn't achieve what I thought I would, internationally. Or what I hoped I'd achieve. And I don't have any resentment to England Rugby.

DURDERS – Just Clive Woodward. Come on, admit you have an effigy of Clive somewhere in your home that you occasionally stick pins into?

FLATS – Nah. I lent it to Eddie Jones and he's never given it back. The World Cups have more appeal to me as a broadcaster than they ever did as a player, or even as a fan, come to think of it. I've been lucky enough to work on two as a broadcaster so far and I've loved every moment. This is going to upset you, Durds, but in 1991 and 1995 I preferred watching New Zealand and Australia than I did England, for the simple reason they had much better players and were a lot more entertaining to watch.

DURDERS – Is that Tower in London still open to incarcerate treasonable ruffians? Call yourself an Englishman? I'm afraid I didn't have the emotional intelligence to be able to appreciate the opposition when England were involved and was also far too invested in one side. I can't believe you didn't feel the pain of defeat.

FLATS – The most excited I ever got watching a game of rugby on TV at home was in 1993 when England won the Sevens World Cup. They beat Australia at Murrayfield and the chaps I remember playing were Adedayo Adebayo, Nick Beal, Justyn Cassell, Lawrence Dallaglio, Matt Dawson, Andy Harriman and Chris Sheasby. I was with my cousin Ben, who also played, and we were just in heaven.

DURDERS – How do you prefer watching a game of rugby – on your own or with other people?

FLATS – People can be with me, but I'm easily distracted, so if I'm honest I'd rather watch a game of rugby on my own.

DURDERS – I'm glad you've told me this after 10 years. We watch a lot of rugby together and that's personally quite insulting.

FLATS – If we're watching it in the stands that's different. I'm talking about watching a game at home. I know that as a teenager you liked having pile-ons in Malvern with your chums when you were watching rugger, but when I was watching rugby at that age I was sitting at home on my own thinking, *I could have him. I could do that.* It was a very different experience.

By the way, at the final of the 2015 World Cup I wasn't commentating but had some great tickets. Even so, after the anthems and everything I decided to go and watch it from the media room, which I knew would be a lot quieter. I think you were with me that day and you remained in the stand. I had no interest whatsoever in the atmosphere. All I wanted to do was watch a very important and potentially entertaining game of rugby undisturbed. When I got to the media room, which, compared to the stands, is completely soulless and silent, there must have been at least 25 ex-internationals in there who, like me, all had excellent tickets. They, too, were obviously numb to the atmosphere and just wanted to watch the game.

DURDERS – You remember the quarter-final of that World Cup when Scotland were on the wrong end of that dodgy

Craig Joubert decision against Australia that we mentioned many moons and pages ago, which basically ruined their chances of progressing? Mark Bennett's interception try with seven minutes to go seemed to have sealed it for them, but then a couple of minutes after that Joubert called a deliberate offside when replays seemed to indicate the ball had come off an Australian. Bernard Foley then stroked the ball between the posts and the game was theirs. My point here is that, sitting in the stands, I felt the emotion of the crowd and the significance of the moment, but missed the technical, forensic assessment of the controversy. We had to re-record bits for the World Cup highlights show that night, having reviewed the footage. The ideal, and the norm actually, is to be pitchside with a monitor so you get the best of both worlds.

FLATS – Funnily enough, I commentated on that game for ITV, and when Craig Joubert awarded Australia the penalty, Scott Hastings said he'd made the wrong decision. I then chuckled and accused him of clutching at straws but was eventually proved wrong, and Scott right, after the game. I remember going on social media afterwards and the Scotland rugby fans were hammering the guys in the studio for not spotting it. I was the one who'd been commentating and as well as missing it I'd even accused Scott of clutching at straws. I didn't get a single comment, though. Not one. I saw Scott Hastings about six months later at a game we were covering and he said, 'I've just got to remind you of something. That decision during the ...' 'We don't talk about that, Scotty,' I said, interrupting him. 'We all make mistakes.'

DURDERS – How about 2003? Had it not been for injuries,

you could have been at that World Cup, could you not? I always wonder how those guys who could have won a World Cup, which would obviously have been life-transforming, feel about missing out. Are you able to watch it without thinking, *That could have been me?*

FLATS – No, you're not, is the short answer. It's a weird contradiction of feelings. Pretty much everyone in that 2003 World Cup-winning team was a mate of mine and I thought all of them were lovely, including Clive. I had this very odd feeling, though, of wanting them to win but wanting England to lose. I obviously couldn't admit that to anybody, but that's exactly how I felt. How could I not want England to win the World Cup yet want all my mates to win – who were playing for England? It was so contradictory.

I watched the game in my flat in Bath with Martin Wood, who was the player that England flew out as injury cover before Austin Healey. Woody got flown out for 24 hours, though. That was it. I think it was Matt Dawson who was injured and when it broke it was all over the news. Woody ended up having to borrow my kit bag when he flew out there and he sent me a photo of it at the airport with the message, 'This is the closest you'll ever get to a World Cup, mate.' Him and I were sharing a flat with Paul Sampson at the time and as Woody left the flat he said, 'I'll bring the cup home for you, lads.' When he got out there, he wasn't allowed to make contact with the squad unless he was being registered, so he got put in a hotel. After then going out for something to eat (at McDonald's!), he came back, went to sleep, and when he woke up there was a voicemail waiting for him saying, 'We don't need you now. You're going straight home.' When I found out, all I could think about was him saying to me and Paul Sampson, 'I'll bring the cup home for you, lads.' It was brilliant.

DURDERS – So he got home in time for the final then.

FLATS – What? He had days to spare! As I said, he was in Australia for less than 24 hours. We were actually told not to watch the final as we had a game against Harlequins the following day. We did, though, and I remember feeling a bit numb after England won. They'd just won the biggest game the sport has to offer and we were off, a bit bleary-eyed, to play Harlequins in an untelevised Premiership match. We beat them, though, with 14 men.

DURDERS – Did missing out on that World Cup not ramp up your motivation to make the next one in 2007?

FLATS – It did, and had it not been for the foot injuries I mentioned earlier that kept me out for so long, perhaps I might have made it to France in 2007. Who knows, eh? And who ruddy cares?!

DURDERS – While we're on the subject of World Cups, can I apologise for something I did directly after the 2003 World Cup final? Something I'm very ashamed of and that made me the enemy of around 80 very angry intoxicated rugby fans.

FLATS – This actually sounds quite promising.

DURDERS – As you know, I managed to get to the 2003 final, and afterwards I ended up in a nightclub. After getting suitably refreshed, I then joined what I assumed was the queue at a taxi rank. Just two minutes later a taxi appeared, in I jumped and told the driver where I needed to go. My instructions were drowned out by a cacophony of boos and loud shouts of 'Wanker!' I recall vaguely registering the booing and shouting but I couldn't work out what had prompted them, so on I went, on my significantly merry little way. According to a friend, who happened to be waiting patiently in the middle of this whopping queue, I had gone straight to the front of the queue, not the back, and I was the 'wanker' in question. So I would like to take this opportunity to humbly apologise to all of the angry Australians and Anglo-Saxons concerned.

FLATS – Seriously, though, is that it? You pinched somebody's taxi. I thought you were going to say you'd shat in somebody's handbag or goosed the cloakroom attendant. So where was your seat in the stadium? I bet you had corporate hospitality. Daddy pull a few strings, did he?

DURDERS – Not at all. Being a man of the people, I roughed it and cruised down the river to the stadium on a motor yacht, and then took my seat in the stands with my best man, Biggs, face painted with the George Cross and hair sprayed white. We had a great view of Ben Kay's agonising drop right in front of us and, more importantly, as we were behind the far-end goal posts, we could see Jonny's drop goal was going over from the moment he connected with the ball. The sweetest of memories.

FLATS – Man of the people, my arse. My most vivid World Cup memories (a few more are coming back to me now) are from 2019, which probably won't surprise you. The most vivid of the lot is the super-typhoon called Hagibis that wreaked havoc throughout the country while the tournament was taking place. I was on the 37th floor of the Hilton Hotel in central Tokyo when the shit started hitting the fan and at one point the entire place started swaying. Not by very much, but enough to make my little tummy feel a bit funny.

DURDERS – I like a typhoon-themed World Cup memory as much as the next man, but do you have any in your locker that relates to something that happened on a rugby pitch in Japan?

FLATS – That's just as easy. It's the Japan v. Scotland game which I got to commentate on. I'm as emotional as the next guy, in that I'm neither overtly emotional nor unemotional. The atmosphere was just so incredible and there were times during the game when I couldn't speak. On your headphones you have a switch that can turn the ambient atmosphere noise up or down. I remember turning it all the way down, which you should never do really, as if you then speak you have no idea what you're talking over. Even after doing that, it was still so loud. I've never experienced anything like it either before or after. There was a moment when the Korean-born Japanese tighthead prop injured his ribs but he tried to battle on. Having been a prop myself, I spotted it and I said to my co-commentator that we needed to keep an eye on him. He hit a few more scrums but it wasn't working and when he went off he was devastated. Even his opposite number for Scotland gave him a pat as he was going off. When he got to the touchline he turned around and bowed to his team. That was the most emotional I've ever been during a game of rugby.

DURDERS – Japan won, didn't they?

FLATS – Yes, and deservedly so: 28-21 was the final score. Some people said afterwards that they won with passion and enthusiasm, but they didn't. They won it by playing brilliant rugby. We also hoped that the way Japan played rugby was maybe going to be a blueprint for how to overcome the power game that's taken over the world. That hasn't changed, really.

DURDERS – Talking of opportunities that arose at the last World Cup . . . Back in England, I was hoping that a second outright England victory might help to lure my sons away from the cult of Welsh rugby. The vision I had was that, on England lifting the World Cup, my boys – remember my daughter, Rosie, was already in my Red Rose club of two – would then summon their mother and their maternal grandparents and hand over their Wales shirts, put on a couple of crisp, white England shirts and then sing to the gang of rabid Welsh cultists a chorus or 12 of 'Swing Low Sweet Chariot'. I still play the scene out in my head sometimes. You know, seven or eight times a day.

FLATS – What actually unfolded, then?

DURDERS – I'd rather not go into any detail if that's okay. Suffice to say that it involved a lot of noise and gallons of salty tears. The final left me feeling more deflated than any other game I've watched – the Lions' third and deciding Test of the 2021 series in South Africa running it a very close second. After that performance against New Zealand in the semi-final, expectations couldn't have been higher, could they? My god-daughter, also a Rosie, was the only one watching with us who wasn't hurting acutely as she spent the final doing her dissertation on her laptop. Lucky her. Having said all that, the sight of Siya Kolisi lifting the Webb Ellis Cup, with all the significance that had, was pretty special and helped soothe the pain of defeat.

I know you don't feel passion of the rugby variety unless you're either sitting in a media box with fellow ex-players or watching Japan, but while you were over there having a lovely time, I was over here hurting like I'd been hit by a frenzied bullock in Pamplona. Anyway, let's go back a game and try to put a positive spin on the proceedings. Come on, get me out of the doldrums by answering me this: Was England's performance against New Zealand in the semi-final of the 2019 World Cup the best England performance you've ever seen in a World Cup, including the 2003 World Cup final?

FLATS – Yes, I believe that was the best performance I've ever seen by an England side at a World Cup.

DURDERS – Including the 2003 final?

FLATS – Including the 2003 final. Happy? The semi-final against New Zealand and the final against South Africa were obviously two very different games. That said, as somebody who was working on the sidelines at both, they also had a lot in common. Let me explain. Imagine if you've got a 15- or 16-year-old son or daughter and they're playing rugby against a school or club and they've got two massive kids who are crunching everybody. The kids all get up and are fine, but you think to yourself, *They've got 80 minutes of this!* It was like that for New Zealand in the semi-final. England just crushed them physically. There was intensity, there was ambition, there was accuracy, there was great prep and great coaching.

Physically, though, England were on a different level. When you're that close to the pitch you can just feel it.

The final was exactly the same, except this time England were on the receiving end. The rugby wasn't as thrilling and there probably weren't as many phases, but South Africa dominated England right from the very start. Anyone who's played in the front row for any amount of time would have said exactly the same thing. I just happened to be there. I was on the touchline for the final doing analysis with Paul O'Connell. During each half they'd come to us for some words of wisdom and if there was something you wanted to say you had to press a button that would get you through to the director and you'd say, 'It's Flats here. I've got something for you.' You'd then tell them what you'd got and they'd either say, 'Okay, we'll come to you now,' or just leave it.

About 20 or 25 minutes in, I pressed the button and said that I wanted to go on and say that Mako Vunipola needs to be substituted now and that Joe Marler needs to take his place. 'That's great,' said the director. 'You definitely think you're right, yeah?' 'I definitely think I'm right.'

A few minutes later the director came on and said, 'The moment's gone now. We're going to leave it,' which is what happens to at least 50 per cent of what you suggest. I asked if I could say something at half time, but they said no as they'd be going straight to Jonny Wilkinson and Clive Woodward. I always regret that not happening, as I could have saved the day and England might have won their second World Cup. Also, everybody would have thought, *Wow! This guy may have been a distinctly average rugby player, but he really knows the game.* The reality is that my dad was texting me saying, 'Mako off, Marler on.'

DURDERS – You're counting on the fact that your words of wisdom would eventually have made their way to Eddie Jones. Not only that, but him then saying to himself, *My God, Flats is right! Why didn't I think of that? Somebody tell Joe Marler to warm up.* When did he eventually make the swap? I think it was about five minutes into the second half, wasn't it?

FLATS – Everybody seemed to blame Dan Cole for that game. 'Oh, if only Dan Cole hadn't come on for so long,' they all said. Of the two – Sinckler and Cole – Cole, at that point, was seen as the superior scrummager so, in scrummaging terms, to get him on early in place of Sinckler wasn't going to weaken England. Sure, Dan Cole had a bad day against Tendai Mtawarira. That was brutal.

What about the last 25 minutes of the game, when Joe Marler came on? Did England continue to get hammered in the scrum? No. They achieved parity and then dominance towards the end. They actually shoved the South African scrum backwards. And who was at tighthead when England began to dominate? Dan Cole. The guy who can't play for 80 minutes, apparently, because he's too old. That doesn't make any sense. Dan Cole was on there when they were getting smashed and he was also on there when they weren't getting smashed and were scrummaging really well. The difference was Joe Marler. Mako was unable to keep the South African tighthead engaged on him so he just steamed past him and across onto Jamie George. That made it three on two, with all the weight going onto Dan Cole and Mako being effectively spat out to the side.

DURDERS – I swear this isn't a flippant question, but if Eddie Jones had been walking past you 20 minutes into that game, after your dad had just told you what to think and say, might you have said to him, "'Ere, Eddie. My dad says get Mako off now and get Marler on.'

FLATS – No, I would not have done that. It's a bit like being a wildlife documentary cameraman who sees a leopard stalking an impala. What does he do? Start shouting at the impala to run like frig or let nature take its course? I was in no mood to play God that day.

DURDERS – Neil Hatley was the scrum coach. Why did he not see it?

FLATS – Maybe he did see it. You won't find many people on this earth who know as much about arranging a scrum as Neil Hatley. He doesn't pick the team, though, does he? All joking aside, I went on a podcast a few days before the final and suggested that Joe Marler should start the game and I was slated for it. 'You can't drop Mako,' everyone said. 'He was amazing in the semi-final.' My reasoning was that Frans Malherbe is a 140kg tighthead prop and he was going to be on that field for one reason and one reason only.

You don't get many one-trick ponies in the World game any more. Everybody does a bit of everything. Frans Malherbe is a scrummaging machine, pure and simple. He can whack the odd ruck here and there, but he was put on this earth to guarantee good set-piece ball and to disrupt opposition set-piece ball. Sometimes you need to respect the opposition *before* you take to the field of play, and in my humble opinion England failed to do that. Joe Marler would not have struggled against Frans Malherbe.

DURDERS – It's not an exact science, is it? You and I can be watching a game together and the following day we'll read a report which will mention something significant that neither of us spotted.

FLATS – That happens a lot when I'm commentating with either Austin Healey or Paul Grayson. We'll be sitting there talking about the same game and suddenly they'll start talking about something I missed. So you're right, it's not an exact science, but in terms of a World Cup final it should be as near as damn it.

DURDERS – Can that kind of call ever come from a player? As in, if they're struggling, if they know they can't do what they've been asked to do, even though they're willing, would they ever suggest they should be replaced for the good of the team?

FLATS – Of course. I remember playing in a Premiership semi-final against Leicester Tigers away. I was loosehead for Bath and they started with Martin Castrogiovanni and had Dan Cole on the bench. All coaches say before a match that if you're rooted, put your hand up and we'll get you off. Just give it everything. After about 50 minutes they brought on Dan Cole and after 55 I was dead on my feet. Not because of the scrummaging, but because of the defensive work I'd had to do. It was also really hot. I was, indeed, rooted. I remember the physio coming on to see to another player and I said, 'Mate, I'm done. I'm toast.' When I eventually came off, after about 70 minutes, I'd lost 8.1 kilos in bodyweight. They said that before I had a beer, I had to drink 8 litres of water with electrolytes in it.

DURDERS – 8.1 kilos. You lost the equivalent of a

white-bellied spider monkey in weight? You're exaggerating for effect. That's impossible!

FLATS – No, it's not. I was put on a saline drip straight after the game and had to drink gallons and gallons of water. By the time I went to bed I was the same weight as I had been before the game as it was all liquid. The following day I was pissing like a racehorse. The reason I've mentioned this is because not long after Dan Cole came on I was asking to come off, but they kept on saying, 'Just give it another five minutes.' Because I was so exhausted, I ended up conceding a penalty or two and because they kicked the points, they won the game. When I finally came off, I looked over to the coaches as if to say, 'Why the hell didn't you listen to me?' But they were actually looking at me as if I'd lost us the game.

DURDERS – The lesson to take away from this chapter, is listen to the Lesser Spotted Flatypus at all times. He knows his onions.

The Gallagher Premiership and the Future of the Game

DURDERS – I think it's only right and proper for us to conclude our deliberations and pontifications by discussing the Gallagher Premiership and the future of the game. Two pretty vast subjects, I think you'll agree, about which my trusted and learned friend here will no doubt harbour various opinions thereon.

FLATS – Honestly, it's like talking to somebody from the 1920s sometimes. Because I also work for BT Sport, I end up watching all of the games in the Gallagher Premiership and I'm a huge fan of the league, which is lucky really. I do get a big buzz doing the international games, but that's not where my heart is. I obviously played in the league for a number of years, and there are some real attachments there. The feelings of arriving at Franklin's Gardens or Kingston Park or Kingsholm for a game, even now, are both familiar and very dear to me.

As a rule I think the league is sufficiently progressive. It's embraced technology really well and the same goes for player safety. I also think that in some ways it does its best to maximise the appeal of its product. The RFU did the league a massive favour by not centrally contracting its top players quickly enough when the game turned pro, which means there are at least some limits on how often the star players can be rested or removed. But it has created an ongoing wrangle between club and country. Could you imagine going to see Liverpool or Man City 25 times in a season and for 12 of those games not seeing seven or eight of the top players? It's unthinkable. Equally, you can't just stick an England game on a Wednesday night. So how do you solve the wrangle? Do you reduce the number of games? It ain't easy, but, in pure sporting terms, the jeopardy of relegation is one that I believe should not be forfeited.

DURDERS — And what about the domestic cup? The Premiership Rugby Cup as it's now called – although Covid caused its cancellation in the 2020/21 season.

FLATS — Bin it. We don't need a cup. Everyone loves the FA Cup, but you don't see the first teams play these days until the fifth round. I think you're much better off having a second-team league instead, which they used to call the A League. Even more controversially, I would reduce the salary cap, as I think players are being paid too much. I love the fact that lads are earning loads of money, but at the same time it's just not sustainable. I would reduce it and I would also put in, if it's possible, a minimum squad size, and then push for a second-team league.

DURDERS — These are pretty bold and contentious suggestions you're making.

FLATS – I don't follow fashion, Markie. I just think some of the potential answers to some of rugby's problems are relatively simple. Mind you, implementing them might be a touch more complex a mission.

DURDERS – But who would this new second-team league appeal to?

FLATS – I think your club fans would love it, and that's a good place to start. Providing you schedule the games for the same time every week. Our highlights show on Channel 5 gets moved around sometimes, and that effects viewing figures, whereas *Top Gear*, for instance, is 8 p.m. on a Sunday evening whatever happens. I expect that means less and less in television terms these days, because of catch-up, but in terms of live sport, if you as a Premiership rugby fan knew that every other Monday or Tuesday night at 7.30 p.m. there'd be a second-team game at your ground that wouldn't cost you more than, say, a fiver to get in, you'd go, wouldn't you? I'd certainly take my kids to it. I think the students would love it too.

DURDERS – Why not take your kids on a Saturday?

FLATS – I don't want to spend 50, 60 or 70 quid on rugby tickets for my kids. They don't care enough. I would take them down to watch something like this, and if they're bored at half time they can leave. Conversely, if they go mad for it, we can think about going to a first-team game. I really do think there's something in that.

DURDERS – What about play-offs?

FLATS – As a rule I like the play-offs, although I also played for a team that got done over by the initial play-off format. It was 2004 and I was at Bath. After finishing top of the league by some distance, we then had three weeks off while the other teams battled it out for the right to play us in the final. By the time the final arrived, the team that had prevailed, Wasps, were obviously match-fit, whereas we'd played just one friendly against Newbury. The boys were hanging, we lost the final, and after that the powers that be changed the format.

DURDERS – I like the format now. Some of the best moments we've had watching Premiership rugby have been in those Twickenham finals. The 2021 final between eventual winners Harlequins and Exeter is right up there as one of the best – actually the best in my opinion (that no one cares about before you chime in). As a sport, I think it needs those moments. You compare rugby to football, but rugby doesn't get 2 million viewers for a Premiership game. It probably gets 250,000 on an average day, up to 700,000 on a terrestrial platform. So it needs those showcase moments. Remind me, are you for or against the play-offs now?

FLATS – I'm for them now that the format's changed. But I also believe in having jeopardy at both ends of the league and so ring-fencing is an idea I'm against. I'm open to being proven wrong, of course. If you did bring four clubs up from the Championship, I'd be fine with giving them a couple of years' grace, but the key element to that would be the funding. I think you need relegation and promotion and even the Six Nations suffers from not having it.

DURDERS – I'm very much with you on that. Can you give us a bit more detail on the World According to Flats salary-cap plans? You've said you'd lower the salary cap, but what about the rules on marquee player signings that are outside the salary-cap rules? They allow some of the best players on the planet to play in an English club rugby. Would you leave those rules as they are?

FLATS – This one annoys me a little bit because the idea behind the initiative was to bring players like Faf de Klerk to the Premiership. What some clubs have done is nominate their top earner as their marquee player, take him off the salary cap, and then spend another three or four hundred thousand on signing seven or eight teenagers. I love the marquee-player idea initiative, but the fact that not every club uses it to sign a rock-star player from another country, which is why it was introduced, rankles with me.

Take Marcus Smith at Harlequins, for instance, who is their registered marquee player. If he was from any other country on the planet, he'd have had 20 or 30 caps by now, but he's from England so he hasn't. He had a big offer a while ago to move from Harlequins to Bath and had he gone to Bath they wouldn't have been able to make him their marquee player because they'd be signing him from another Premiership club. Even if he'd wanted to go, Harlequins would have been able to offer him whatever they liked because his salary doesn't count towards the cap.

DURDERS – So the reason clubs make players like Marcus Smith, who was not signed from overseas and is home-grown, their marquee player is basically to stop other Premiership clubs from signing them.

FLATS – I think that's correct. It's not an exact science, of course, but it minimises the risk and at the same time frees up cash for other players. All of these initiatives are flawed, unfortunately. Or should I say the rules of the initiatives are too often open to interpretation. Look at the salary cap. Every club has the same amount of money to spend, yet one club will have 35 pros and another club will have 52. It's like *Championship Manager*. Even so, you could argue that that's a flaw in the system, which is one of the reasons I think second-team rugby is such a good idea.

DURDERS – What about the north of the country? At the moment we have just two teams above Leicester and in the 2020/21 season it was only one. There's a perception – maybe it's a reality – that the north of England is basically too consumed by football and rugby league to have room for rugby union to thrive. The irony is that grassroots rugby union is huge in the north of England, with vibrant local clubs at the heart of many local communities, but for some reason that doesn't translate to the professional game. How do you change that?

FLATS – You said it. One of the main reasons rugby is so popular in the south of England, yet struggles in the north, is football. Think about it. The north-west of England is strewn with massive football clubs, as is the north-east. In West Yorkshire and Lancashire you also have rugby league to contend with, and North Yorkshire, Cumbria and Northumberland have a combined population of about 10. Another problem Newcastle Falcons have is location. Years ago, when I was waiting to see if Bath were going to offer me a new contract, somebody asked me – purely hypothetically – if I'd be interested in moving to Newcastle. I loved the lads at Newcastle, loved a night out on the Toon, but there was no way I could ever move that far away. Every game is an absolute ball-ache to get to, whereas if you live in Bath you can cruise to pretty much everywhere. Even Salford's only about three hours from Bath on a good day. Newcastle always used to spend well under the salary cap, which made it even more difficult for them to tempt players north.

DURDERS – So Newcastle wanted you, and as you said earlier, Leicester were also up for a bit of Flatman in the East Midlands?

FLATS – Yup. Amazingly the Tigers came in for me and offered me the same amount of money plus a bit more for relocating. I turned them down. They signed Marcos Ayerza and he became one of the most successful looseheads in the history of the Premiership. They did okay out of that.

DURDERS – So how do you attract the casual non-committed sports lover to rugby? We know the World Cup and the Six Nations will get 6, 7 or 8 million viewers, but domestic rugby just doesn't. The gap between the two is huge, but the fact that so many people are watching the Six Nations does seem to present a massive opportunity.

FLATS – I don't know about these days, but when I worked at Bath, all the emphasis, and all the money, went on signing players. More probably needed spending on the matchday experience. There was endless talk of making The Rec a great day out for the family, then someone told me that buggies were banned because they took up too much room! I suggested we create a giant crèche so that parents could actually dump their kids somewhere safe and watch the game, but nope. Money.

We hired The Wurzels once and they were brilliant. They had a rider that had cheese and pickle sandwiches with no crusts on and a few gallons of Scrumpy Jack cider. I loved that. They weren't mucking about. That's genuinely all they wanted. That was a great day. The thing is, in order for these things to work, you have to do them consistently. It's no good just waiting for a good forecast and then hiring The Wurzels. Make your club the best family day out there is for every single game.

DURDERS – I've been involved with rugby professionally since 1997, on and off, and I still think it's an amazing product. The quality of the sport and the standard of the sportspeople who play it is off the charts. I appreciate the fact that there were obviously great players in the amateur era, but the skill levels these days are just phenomenal. I think the main challenge for rugby is to get the rules right. Having said that, I defy any sports fan, in fact any fan of high-quality drama, sports fan or not, to watch the Gallagher Premiership semi-final between Bristol and Harlequins or that final between Exeter and Quins a week later, and not think that was entertainment of the very highest order.

FLATS – I agree. They were otherworldly. But on the rules question, they could start by shortening the length of time it takes to bind up for a scrummage. I don't find resetting boring. That just happens; it's physics. What I find boring is the time it takes from the ref blowing their whistle to the ball getting put in. It's infuriating. I genuinely believe that this and the 300 box kicks we sometimes see in matches are the two biggest visual hindrances at the moment, and although rugby is quite complex, I don't believe that it stops casual observers from watching. In fact, I know it doesn't because of the amount of people who watch the Six Nations. What I do believe, however, is that the rules that lead to such gaps between explosive moments is one of the things that stops these people from wanting to watch rugby on a regular basis.

DURDERS – I don't entirely agree with that. Sometimes when there's a break in play the commentators will add texture by explaining what's going on, which brings it all to life. I used to find scrummaging really boring, but having now listened to commentators such as yourself explaining why it's so important in the context of the game and what makes a successful scrummage, and what to look out for, I no longer feel that way. It's like when Shirley Ballas or Bruno Tonioli get technical on *Strictly Come Dancing*, you almost certainly won't have a clue what they're talking about, but your viewing experience is being enriched.

FLATS – As I said, it's the time it takes to get a scrummage underway that bothers me. Also, most games won't have ex-professional props commentating, so the technical analysis you're talking about will be the exception and not the rule. If commentators started trying to explain the reasoning behind every occurrence during a game of rugby, not only would they have to talk at a thousand miles an hour in order to keep up, but they'd lose their core audience.

DURDERS – So what should be the law on kicking, for instance? Should you only be allowed one kick each before you pass the ball? Or a variant on that theme that encourages more ball in hand and less boot to ball?

FLATS – I'd want to spend an hour with Paul Grayson before I declared my hand on that, and I'd just copy what he said. The thing is, if you know that the opposition can't kick then you don't have to drop your wingers and your full-back back to cover, so your defensive line becomes impregnable. The result of that is that you cut down space on the field, so if teams weren't allowed to kick the ball at any point it would become far too easy to defend.

DURDERS – Taking into account everything you've said, then, how optimistic are you that in 10 years' time the stands at Premiership matches will be even fuller and the TV audiences higher? How rosy is the future of Premiership rugby?

FLATS – I think it will plod along very nicely regardless, as it's an excellent product. CVC arriving offers financial security, but I think it's erroneous to suggest that the only way the game can grow is by pumping in more cash. I think that if you reduce the salary cap, which will probably happen anyway, and have a minimum squad size, which will help with player welfare as they'll be less likely to be over-played, that will give you a shiny new product that would be equally, if not more, exciting and more sustainable. And let's not forget that, even after reducing the salary cap, plenty of players would still be earning big cash, so they won't be struggling. What do you think?

DURDERS – I think you're right with regards to the finances. A more realistic attitude is needed and I think is being embraced. The only thing that worries me with the salary-cap reduction is that it might become a less attractive career option.

FLATS – I think that if you offered even 100 grand to somebody who had the wherewithal to become a pro and 200 grand to go and work for a bank in the City, for instance, which is what I could have done at one point, 99 per cent of them would choose to play rugby, because they love it.

DURDERS – Before we take our leave and are ushered unceremoniously into our publisher's legal department, never to be seen again, we have been asked to issue a clarion call to the game of rugby to move on to ever greater success. So grab your clarion and call away.

FLATS – There will always be cries to sanitise and make safer things that are dangerous. Some things are obvious and should be changed, but others aren't. My main worry is that, in an effort to appease certain parties, an unnecessary amount of sanitising will take place and make the game less appealing. Within a lot of human beings there is a need to either watch or participate in something combative, and in my opinion rugby is a relatively safe way to satisfy and potentially exhaust that need. I'm not particularly alpha, despite looking it, but the reason I got offered lots of rugby contracts was because I had combat in me. I had less than Martin Johnson, as did Thor, but I had more than my mum, and despite the fact that I no longer play the game, it continues to satisfy that need. Controlled, honourable aggression, you could call it. The biggest drawback to the game is obviously safety, and despite the fact that there's a code of behaviour and an ever-changing set of laws, there will always be a danger that you might get hurt, and so there should be. Without that risk you have no combat, no honour, no aggression, and no sense of achievement at the end. You have no game, basically.

We've already touched on this, but what rugby gives all of my mates down here in the West Country are friendships for life and a sense of community. And I'm not talking about the pros. Forget about them. They're fine. I'm talking about the lifeblood of the game. The not-very-silent majority. It doesn't matter what you need doing, there'll always be somebody within your circle of rugby mates who can help you out, and they *will* help you out. There's also something very unique about the bond that being physically reliant on somebody creates. You're not always going to win together, but when somebody comes through for you on a rugby field, you feel beholden to them, protective towards them, and you love them.

For rugby to disappear or be sanitised to a point where people abandoned it would be a genuine tragedy. People who aren't involved in the game probably wouldn't empathise with that, but it's not about them. It's about the people who know it and love it and I think rugby has every chance of thriving over the next 10 or 20 years.

DURDERS – I'm with you every step of the way. And, of course, one of the many joys of rugby is that when it comes to participation, you need all shapes and sizes, and to me that has and always will be one of the game's biggest strengths.

FLATS – The thing is, and I'm finally getting back to my clarion call here, in order to keep the beasts like me interested, you cannot over-sanitise it. If you do, all of a sudden we won't want to play any more, and you need blokes like me, just like you need blokes like you. Sometimes.

In conclusion, if rugby is continually tweaked, which it will be, with the emphasis being put on safety around the head – and I'm not talking about a token effort here; I'm talking time, money and effort going forward indefinitely – then I think rugby has a chance of becoming even more appealing by the year. Hallelujah, praise the Lord!

DURDERS – Hallelujah – praise be! Do you know what a clarion is, by the way? It's a shrill, narrow-tubed war trumpet, you in XS basically. Anyway, I think there are so many people for whom rugby is that thing that sustains them, decade after decade, and I sincerely hope that this game of ours, in its weird and quirky way, continues to grow and thrive and provide amazing entertainment. I don't even mind the fact that people are constantly trying to change it. In fact, that's part of its appeal. The aim of rugby, when all's said and done, is to find ways of getting a ball across a line within a set of confoundingly intricate laws, and the fact that the game and these laws are constantly changing and evolving means that it's very much alive.

You have left us all feeling warm and tingly, David Luke, Marquis of Maidstone. So on that uplifting note, ladies and gentlemen, we really will take our leave. Any final message for our reader, Flats?

FLATS – Always go to bed when you're told to, never agree to a shared takeaway meal, don't talk to strange men, and don't whistle indoors because you'll summon the devil.

DURDERS – Here endeth the lesson.

Acknowledgements

DURDERS – As I'm sure a Megan-and-Harry-level book deal will follow this first book of ours, I don't think this ode of thanks needs to be too extensive, I'll save that for Volume IV, but just for the hell of it, I am going to thank a few people, in print, for their love and support.

Topping the list, the Welsh pygmy love of my life, The Tat, and our three sprung-offs Archie, Freddie and Rosie. (Listed in alphabetical order to avoid an almighty screaming match at supper time.) In turn, my mighty parental double act, Neil the Deal and Jude the Dude, and my big sister Em – the least-favoured child – and all her lot definitely merit a mention they'd probably rather not have. Tough. My wondrous Welsh family, who've welcomed me into the cult without any especially uncomfortable initiation ceremonies, and who are also probably denying any association with me, must also get a hefty waft of gratitude whether they like it or not.

James Hogg, our co-author-in-chief, merits huge thanks and praise for helping make sense of the ramblings of two epic windbags. No mean feat. All the team at Simon & Schuster, led by Ian and Fran, and Michelle of MLB

Management must also feel the cool mist of our gratitude for leading two lost literary sheep into the light.

And finally to Flats – the least flat person I know – for being a constant source of friendship, fun and meat-marinating tips. You are a one off – for which we must all be eternally grateful.

FLATS – My children Peanut and Buddha (not their actual names) are my inspiration, my heart, and my soul. I've no idea if they will ever read this book, but if they do it will almost certainly be under duress and will involve both bribes and the forced removal of all Apple products. To them, to my heavenly girlfriend, and to all of my amazing mates I dedicate this rival-to-the-Bible classic.

Oh, and I'd also like to mention my agent, Michelle. Because she's completely wonderful and I'd be lost without her. And also because she asked me to. Repeatedly.

Allez.